Diocese of Orange

Learning, Loving, Living our Faith

REV.
WILLIAM
KREKELBERG

SHIRL
GIACOMI

To my bishop;
with the admiration and respect
of his archivist for the great
example of hope in adversity
and grace under pressure.
Bless you in your continuing
role in this history.
William Krekelberg

ÉDITIONS DU SIGNE

● *Pope Benedict XVI*

Publisher :

ÉDITIONS
DU SIGNE

Éditions du Signe

B.P. 94 F

67038 Strasbourg Cedex 2

Email : info@editionsdusigne.fr

Phone : 011 333 88 78 91 91

Fax : 011 333 88 78 91 99

Publishing Director : Christian Riehl

Director of publication : Joëlle Bernhard

Publishing assistant : Marc de Jong

Layout : Atelier du Signe

Photography : John Glover

© Copyright text : Diocese of Orange

Photo engraving : Atelier du Signe

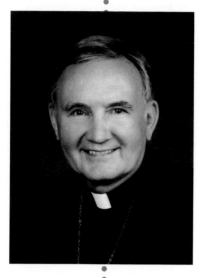

DIOCESE OF ORANGE

Office of the Bishop
Marywood Center
P.O Box 14195
2811 E. Villa Real Drive
Orange, California 92863-1595
Phone (714) 282-3112
FAX (714) 282-3029

■ You have in your hands an excellent account of our extraordinary diocese at thirty years of age. In the words and pictures that follow, you will see how three hundred thousand Catholics in forty-four Catholic parishes quickly joined together to become a united, vibrant and fervent people of faith. You will learn how, in these last thirty years, we have grown by 243% to more than a million Catholics. To match our growth we have added nineteen new parishes and pastoral centers and have built eighteen new churches and one new high school. In each of our diverse parishes, pastoral centers and schools, many, many dedicated Catholics—clergy, religious and laity—work together to do all those things Jesus asked us to do.

This is a chronicle of our discipleship, an expression of our faith.

Orange County is no longer just a place of orange groves and suburban homes in the shadow of Los Angeles. (In fact, I'm not sure I've seen an orange grove in years!) We have become our own major center of arts, entertainment and industry and I am proud of the part that so many of you have had in these staggering and impressive developments. But we are also those who have joined with others to make Orange County a place where neighbors can become friends, where those in need are served and where God is the center of so many families. I am sure you will see on the pages of this book so many ways we are and have been blessed.

I want to express my gratitude to Fr. Bill Krekelberg, our archivist, who put many hours into this remarkable labor, and to Shirl Giacomi who organized the effort to gather all the needed materials together. I want too to thank those in our parishes who took the time to tell us their story and share with us their pictures.

And now, on to the next thirty years!

In Christ our Savior,

Tod David Brown

Bishop of Orange

Table of Contents

1 1769 First Encounter .... p. 7

2 Mission San Juan Capistrano .... p. 13

3 Years of Transition .... p. 17
   1840's   p. 17
   1850's   p. 18

4 Expansion Beginnings .... p. 21
   1860's   p. 21
   1870's   p. 24

5 Orange County .... p. 27
   1880's   p. 27
   1890's   p. 29

6 A new Century .... p. 33
   1900's   p. 33
   1910's   p. 36
   1920's   p. 37
   1930's   p. 40
   1940's   p. 41

7 Major Growth and Expansion .... p. 43
   1950's   p. 43
   1960's   p. 45
   1970's   p. 47

8 The Diocese of Orange in California .... p. 49
   1980's   p. 58
   1990's   p. 71

9 The Millenium and Beyond .... p. 81
   2000-2007   p. 81

10 Demographics .... p. 103

11 Parishes .... p. 128

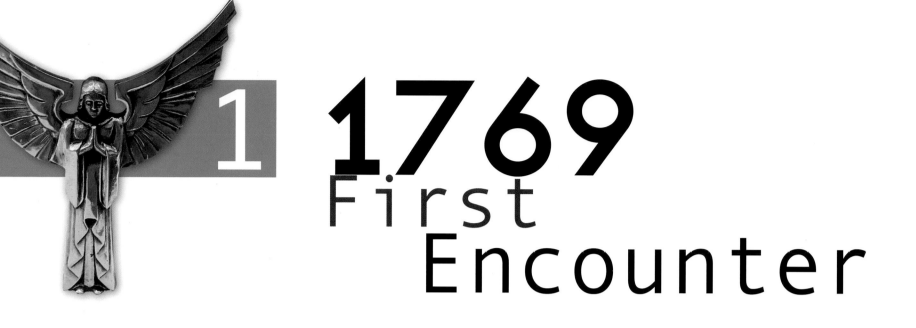

1 1769 First Encounter

In July of 1769, the first Spanish land expedition was making its way north through uncharted territory in Alta California. Spanish soldiers and missionaries had just established a settlement in San Diego, and they wanted to make another one at Monterey Bay. This expedition, under Governor Don Gaspar de Portolá with sixty-two men and one hundred pack mules, was headed overland to try and locate the bay. San Diego and Monterey were to be Spain's first foothold in Alta California.

FIRST BAPTISM IN THE STATE OF CALIFORNIA, JULY 22, 1769.

Las Cristianitas

The southernmost city in Orange County is San Clemente. Nearby is the site of California's first baptisms. On Saturday, July 22, the Portolá Expedition arrived at a canyon where they discovered two very sick little girls. One was an infant and the other about two-and-a-half years old, a burn victim, whose health was rapidly deteriorating.

Two Franciscan Missionaries were accompanying the expedition: Father Juan Crespi and Father Francisco Gomez. They gently convinced the Indians to allow them to help the sick girls with a little ritual. Father Gomez baptized the infant and gave her the Christian name, Maria Magdalena. It was the Feast Day of Saint Mary Magdalen. Father Juan Crespi baptized the older girl and gave her the name Margarita. The feast day of Saint Margaret had recently been observed on the 20 of July.

Normally, baptism would not be administered without religious instruction and parental consent, but these children were in danger of death. The missionaries took quite literally the New Testament scripture: "I solemnly assure you, no one can enter into God's Kingdom, without being begotten of water and Spirit" (Mt. 3:5).

Father Crespi, who kept a diary, wrote, "I have no doubt she (Margarita) will die and we have come just in time that this soul may go to heaven."

Father Crespi named the valley, where they made their camp, San Apolinario whose feast day was the following day. The soldiers came to call it Valle de los Bautismos, (Valley of the Baptisms) or Valle de los Cristianos (Valley of the Christians). Today it is known as Cristianitos (Little Christians) Canyon. However, the proper Spanish female form is Cristianitas.

Today a historical marker in San Clemente commemorates California's first baptisms. A pageant has also been produced there to celebrate this spiritually significant event.

Santa Maria Magdalena

On Sunday, July 23, 1769, the Portolá Expedition left Cristianitos Canyon and trekked through valleys and over hills for about four hours. They made camp on a hill on the north side of the San Juan Canyon and the San Juan Creek. This is about four-and-a-half miles north of Mission San Juan Capistrano. Of course, at that time, the Mission was not yet there. They named the valley and creek Santa Maria Magdalena. Her feast day was the day before and it was her name that was given to the baptized infant. Later on, after the Mission was founded in 1776, the valley and creek became known as San Juan. This title remains to the present day.

San Francisco Solano

On Monday, July 24, the Portolá Expedition journeyed north then northwest over fairly rough terrain. After about three hours they arrived at the south end of a mesa that was approximately three miles long and a mile wide. They made camp there and called the place San Francisco Solano whose feast day was celebrated that day. The expedition had encountered many friendly Indians along the way. Father Crespi noted that the opportunities for missionary work among them were very favorable. This location was particularly good: "The place and docility of the heathens invite it." As he dedicated this location to the Franciscan "Apostle to the Americas," San Francisco Solano, he prayed, "With his intercession the conversion of these docile heathens may be accomplished." [It may be noted that at this time the Indians did not yet know that they were heathens, even though they may have felt something was wrong.]

The mesa where they camped also came to be known as the Plano Trabuco (Trabuco Plane). The nearby creek became the Trabuco Creek and its canyon became the Trabuco Canyon. A trabuco is a Spanish blunderbuss, an army issue weapon. One of the soldiers of the expedition lost his trabuco here and so the name has been associated with the area ever since.

Years later, the Plano Trabuco became one of the important grazing areas for cattle belonging to Mission San Juan Capistrano. It remained so during the Rancho Period through modern times. When the Rancho Mission Viejo Company developed it in the 1980's, it was given the name Rancho Santa Margarita.

Santa Margarita was the name given by the Portolá encampment on July 22, 1769, the feast day of Saint Margaret. That area later became the great Rancho Santa Margarita y Las Flores. In 1923, it had become part of the still greater land holdings of Jerome O'Neill and James Flood. They incorporated it all as the Santa Margarita Company. During World War II, the original ranch site in San Diego County was acquired by the U.S. Government and became the Camp Pendleton Marine Base. The remainder of the land in south Orange County belonged to the O'Neill Family and became the Rancho Mission Viejo Company. When they later developed their property on the Trabuco Mesa, they called it Rancho Santa Margarita in honor of these historic origins.

On April 18, 1986, Bishop William Johnson, first Bishop of the Diocese of Orange, presided at groundbreaking ceremonies for a high school in the new community. It was aptly named Santa Margarita Catholic High School.

The second Bishop of Orange, Bishop Norman McFarland, established a parish for Rancho Santa Margarita on July 3, 1989. He gave it the name Father Juan Crespi had given the area 220 years earlier: San Francisco Solano.

Santiago

Tuesday, July 25, 1769, was the feast day of Santiago, St. James the Greater, Apostle and Patron of Spain. Father Crespi and Father Gomez celebrated Mass at their camp on the mesa, and Governor Portolá decided to give the expedition a day of rest.

210 years later, on July 1, 1979, Bishop William Johnson founded a parish in Lake Forest about five miles west of this encampment. He gave it the name of the great shrine to Saint James in Spain, Santiago de Compostela.

Santa Ana

On Wednesday, July 26, the feast day of Saint Anne, mother of Mary, Father Crespi and Father Gomez celebrated Mass with all in attendance. Although it was not recorded, it may be conjectured that this was the occasion when the nearby mountains were referred to as the Santa Anas – La Sierra de Santa Ana.

The expedition left their San Francisco Solano encampment about three in the afternoon of the same day. They headed northwest over hot dry land through what is now northern Mission Viejo and Lake Forest. After two-and-a-half hours they made their camp at a place Father Crespi called San Panteleon, whose feast was the following day. Father Gomez discovered a springs nearby. The thirsty and grateful soldiers called the place, rather unimaginatively, the "Springs of Father Gomez". Much later on it would appear on maps as Tomato Springs. Today it is near the Lambert Reservoir not far from the north end of the north runway of the decommissioned El Toro Marine Air Station.

• *Indian Basket*

• *Indian Dwelling*

Santiago Creek

At six in the morning on Thursday, July 27, the feast of San Panteleon, Governor Portolá and his expedition left their camp and again headed northwest. They traveled through what is now Northwood in Irvine, then passed between Red Hill and Lemon Heights above Tustin and on into what is now the City of Orange. Here about a half-mile above the present day Chapman Avenue Bridge, they happily discovered a fairly large creek, which they named Santiago in honor of Saint James. This creek has its source near the summit of Santiago Peak, the highest point in the Santa Ana Mountains.

Santa Ana River

If they liked the Santiago Creek, they were sure to like what was just ahead of them. On Friday morning, July 28, they broke camp early at seven a.m. and headed north to an area later known as Olive, which now is the northernmost section of the City of Orange. Here, after just a three-mile march, they encountered a great river flowing from the northeast to the southwest across a vast plane. Just on the other side of the river was a large Indian village. About 50 astonished Indians crossed over to visit them. In their excitement they begged them to stay.

They may have withdrawn their invitation if they knew what was about to happen. Warm enthusiasm turned to cold fear in the early afternoon. About one p.m. a violent earthquake shook the whole area. Lest they forget, which was highly unlikely, the quake was followed by four aftershocks. An Indian Medicine Man's wild and noisy incantations did nothing to calm their nerves. No doubt everyone's thoughts turned to the Almighty. Father Crespi named this river El Rio del Dulcissimo Nombre de Jesus, the River of the Most Holy Name of Jesus. It is not known whether he gave it this name before, during, or after the earthquakes. It does sound something like a sudden, prayerful exclamation. Whatever the case may be, "de los Temblores" (of the Earthquakes) was added to the title. No latter day real estate agents or developers have acknowledged this title in their housing promotions.

Perhaps the title was chosen more out of piety than panic. It is worth noting that devotion to the Holy Name of Jesus was popular and zealously preached by the fifteenth century Franciscan Saint Bernardine of Siena. It was especially regarded as a spiritual weapon against blasphemy.

El Rio del Dulcissimo Nombre de Jesus de los Temblores was a long name for a long river. The practical, if not always so pious, soldiers simply called it the Santa Ana River. It appeared to them, albeit erroneously, that it flowed from the nearby Santa Ana Mountains. Wrong! Nevertheless, the name stuck.

One of the soldiers of the expedition, José Antonio Yorba, would one day return to this area. In 1810, some 41 years after this first visit, he and Juan Pablo Peralta would receive the use of this land as a great rancho. It was the first Spanish grant entirely within what is now Orange County. They called their 62,000 plus acreage the Rancho Santiago de Santa Ana (Saint James of Saint Anne).

Later on, settlements in this area north and south along the Santa Ana River would be called Santa Ana Arriba and Santa Ana Abajo (Upper and Lower Santa Ana). Still later, in 1868, the great rancho was partitioned to satisfy heirs. In 1869, William Spurgeon bought a portion of it from Jacob Ross who had acquired it from one of the heirs, Zenobia Yorba de Rowland. The enterprising Spurgeon laid out plans for a future town on this property that he called Santa Ana. At long last, in 1923, one of Santa Ana's Catholic Churches was very appropriately named Saint Anne's.

Santa Marta

On Saturday, July 29, the Portolá Expedition left their shaky Santa Ana River camp at two in the afternoon. They crossed the river and headed northwest through what is now East Anaheim, Placentia, and on into Fullerton. After this two-hour march they camped on a hill above a rather large Indian Village in the lower Brea Canyon. They called this place Santa Marta (Saint Martha) whose feast day it was. In modern times this site is very

near Saint Jude Medical Center. The Santa Marta encampment is about a half-mile away on one of the East Coyote Hills just northwest of Hillcrest Park.

Santa Marta was their last encampment in Orange County. The following day, July 30, was a Sunday, and so Father Crespi and Father Gomez celebrated Mass for the expedition. Afterwards, at seven in the morning, they traveled through the center of what is now La Habra. They exited Orange County as they continued north through a pass (Hacienda Boulevard) in the La Habra Heights of the Puente Hills.

It took six years following the Portolá Expedition before the Franciscans were able to return to the area and promote their missionary work. Alta California was a big area and there was much to be done, most of it difficult, some of it contentious, and all of it time-consuming. They hadn't forgotten the area. They had their eyes on it. They passed through it from time to time as they made use of the humble trail to which they gave the grand title, El Camino Real, the King's Highway.

2 Mission
San Juan Capistrano

The founding of Mission San Juan Capistrano took place in a very pleasant valley at the location then described as "between the Missions of San Diego and San Gabriel of the Earthquakes, about 20 leagues from both and two from the coastline of the South Sea." Here at a makeshift arbor near a rather large cross, Father Junipero Serra implored all that was holy to insure the success of this new Mission. It was All Saints Day, November 1, 1776.

• *Fray Junipero Serra*

The cross was a reminder that this was not the first but a fresh start. In 1775, Father Fermin Lasuen had blessed and placed the cross there and celebrated Mass. He and Father Gregorio Amurrio, at Father Serra's direction, had come there to establish a new mission. But it was a mission that was not yet meant to be.

Work at the new site had been underway for only a week when a courier arrived from San Diego with unsettling news. Hostile Indians had attacked the Mission and killed one of its missionaries. The Capistrano project had to be abandoned. Its heavy mission bells were buried, and the would-be founders hurried back to the Presidio of San Diego.

A year had elapsed since the unsuccessful attempt. Now Father Serra, the President of the Missions, was himself to preside at a new beginning. He had arrived there with Father Gregorio Amurrio, Father Pablo Mugartegui, and an escort of 11 soldiers. They unearthed the mission bells and summoned local Indians to witness the initial rites. Undoubtedly, they prayed that this double founding would bring the new mission double blessing and prosperity.

Shortly thereafter, Father Serra made a brief trip to Mission San Gabriel to obtain Indian workers and supplies for Capistrano. It was a trip that nearly proved to be his undoing. On his way back he encountered hostile Indians who threatened him with their weapons. His own Indian companion managed to persuade them that any harm done to the padre would only bring disaster on them. Father Serra distributed gifts of beads to them as a sign of his friendship. He blessed them and proceeded on his way.

Upon his return, Father Serra supervised the work of the mission through the end of November. He carefully prepared the various registry books. He held conference with Father Mugartegui and Father Amurrio. And, confident that all was in order, he placed them in charge and returned to his headquarters at Carmel.

Providence had indeed wrought a double blessing on Mission San Juan Capistrano. Both the nature of the area and the character of the Indians who occupied it would insure its rapid growth and prosperity.

The mission lands were not only beautiful, but enjoyed a rich fertility and a moderate climate. Grapes grew wild here.

• *Sacred Garden (San Juan Capistrano)*

• *1876 View*

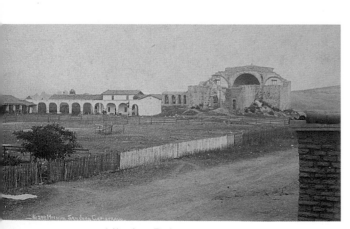

• *Mission Ruins*

Fruits and vegetables thrived in its soil and sunshine. In one year alone, it would produce over 14,000 bushels of foodstuffs – a tremendous crop that included wheat, barley, corn, peas, and garbanzos.

The hills and valleys would prove an excellent host for the mission's cattle, horses, mules, sheep, goats, and pigs. By 1818, the Mission would record a massive herd of livestock that numbered over 30,000.

The Indians who lived here proved to be rich soil for the "seeds of Faith." Their friendliness and docility made them receptive to Christian instruction. Father Francisco Palou wrote about them, "Unlike the Indians at other Missions, as the Father wrote to me in the beginning, who would molest the missionaries by begging eatables and other presents, these of San Juan Capistrano molested the missionaries with petitions for Baptism, because the period of instruction was too long for them."

Less than two months after the Mission's founding, on December 19, 1776, Father Amurrio baptized a six-year-old Indian child named Nanojibar. He gave him the appropriate Christian name of Juan Bautista. It was the first of four baptisms that year.

Within ten years, the Mission could attest to over 700 baptisms. By the turn of the century it would be over 2,000. And in another 25 years, it would be over 4,000, and still increasing.

In 1778, the Mission was relocated a short distance to its present site where there were better resources. It was here in its chapel that Father Serra is known to have celebrated Mass, and administered the sacraments of Baptism and Confirmation. The chapel survives today and has the distinction of being the oldest surviving building in California. Today it is known as the "Serra Chapel."

Many other buildings were constructed to meet the Mission's growing needs. There were living-quarters for the priests, soldiers, and Indians. There were kitchens, a hospital, storehouses, various trade shops, tallow vats, and even a smelter. They comprised quite a complex – a visible testimony to the Mission's increased prosperity.

A larger more appropriate church was needed to grace such a place. The Serra Church had been enlarged, but before long it had become inadequate. Something had to be done, and so plans were drawn up for a new church.

In 1797, the first stone was set in place for what would one day be a spacious and beautiful, great stone church. Mission Indians brought the stone from a quarry six miles northeast of the Mission. A master stonemason was brought up from Culiacan, Mexico to supervise the project.

The church would have a cruciform shape. It would measure 180 feet long and 40 feet wide. Its ceiling would be vaulted and surmounted by seven domes. The entrance would be crowned with 120-foot bell tower, containing the Mission's four bells. It would take nine years to complete, but when it was finished, it was the most magnificent church in California.

The ceremonies that marked its completion went on for three days. On September

7, 1806, Father Esteven Tapis, then President of the Missions, blessed the new church in the presence of Governor Jose Joaquin de Arrillaga and church and civil officials from all over California. On September 8, Father Marcos Victoria celebrated Solemn High Mass there, and Father Jose Antonio de Uresti of Mission San Gabriel preached the sermon. And on the following day, September 9, a Solemn Requiem Mass was offered and the remains of the Mission's Father Vicente Fuster who died in 1800 were translated from the old church to the new.

This splendid new church was the pride of the Capistrano Mission. But however elegantly it stood, it was destined to serve only a short time. Six years after its opening, the building was the victim of a disaster.

During the early morning Mass on December 8, 1812, a violent earthquake rolled through the area. The tower swayed back and forth and crashed into a heap of rubble. The vaulted ceiling split open and collapsed to the floor, killing 40 people in the congregation. In sorrow, the people of Capistrano buried their dead. In a few short minutes, the Great Stone Church had become a dangerous and useless mass of ruins. Hereafter, religious services would return to the humble, but noble Serra Church.

The mission community endured that trial with resignation. It had suffered a great tragedy, but it would go on with its work. It would still see two more decades of prosperity. There would still be large harvests, the great herds, and a vigorous trade with the Boston ships. But after that, it would have to endure its darkest days.

The Mission's severest trial came in 1833 in the form of a man-made catastrophe known as "secularization." Idealistically, it seemed like a social good. It sought to divide the Mission and its lands in such a way that there would be a town, the property needed to support it, and individual parcels of land for each Indian family. This was presented as the emancipation of the Indians. In reality, premature secularization destroyed a successful mission system and dispersed the Indians in poverty. Administrators disposed of the property as they saw fit. The Indians, who didn't understand their new social advantage, often lost their property to speculators who cared little for their welfare. In ten years, only a handful of Indians were left at the Mission.

The Mission itself was nearly destroyed. Portions of its buildings were rented out for various, sometimes-questionable purposes. The buildings began to decay rapidly. Tiles and timber were sold, given away, or just plain plundered. The adobe walls without their former protection began to wash away. The only thing that spared Father Serra's Church was that it became a hay barn and its roof was left alone.

By the end of 1842, there was no longer a resident priest at the Mission. And on December 4, 1845, Governor Pio Pico sold this once proud and beautiful mission at public auction to his brother-in-law, John Forster, and James McKinley.

The Mission had suffered its darkest hour, but Providence would not let it be destroyed. It was destined to be restored and serve a new period of history. California became part of the United States in 1848. And in 1865, President Abraham Lincoln signed the patent of title, which restored the Mission and its immediate property to the Church. From then on its restoration was just a matter of time and abundant grace.

• *1776 coin*

• *North Wing*

3 Years of Transition

1840's

1845 Pueblo of Los Angeles
Population: 1,250

California

In California, the 1840's were marked by major upheaval. Political turmoil in Mexico led to consequent unrest in its California Province, which at times was in rebellion. The missions deteriorated and former Indian lands became large Mexican land grants. Tensions between the United States and Mexico led to a full-scale war. As a result of that war, California became a part of the United States in 1848. The following year the discovery of gold in Northern California created a gold rush that brought thousands of people into the area. The Hispanic character of California transformed into a multicultural population. The change was rapid, radical, and at times chaotic. It seemed that just about everything that could change, did.

The Church

Major changes also took place in California's ecclesiastical structure. The "Mission Period", for all practical purposes, had come to an end. On April 27, 1840, Pope Gregory XVI established the Diocese of the Californias, with Fray Francisco Garcia Diego y Moreno, O.F.M. as its bishop. His jurisdiction included Baja and Alta California, as well as considerable portions of what is now Nevada and Utah.

Bishop Garcia Diego's enthusiasm was soon tempered by harsh reality. His experiences were troubled and his efforts frustrated. The Mexican Government held back supposedly guaranteed financial support. The designated ecclesiastical seat of the diocese, San Diego, proved to be a poor choice. He transferred his residence to Santa Barbara in 1842. There an enthusiastic welcome was followed by much less enthusiastic support. A merciful Lord delivered him from his earthly woes when, on April 30, 1846, God called his beleaguered bishop from his unhappy Santa Barbara residence to his eternal home.

To say that the departed bishop would be in good company doesn't refer to the obvious encounter with the Heavenly Host. In just a month, on June 1, Pope Gregory XVI, who had appointed Garcia Diego to the Californias, joined him in the Communion of Saints.

Pope Pius IX was elected on June 16, 1846 and would wear the "shoes of the fisherman" for the next 32 years. No doubt, he had more than one pair.

San Juan Capistrano

Hard times continued in San Juan Capistrano. In 1841, the lands in the immediate vicinity of the Mission were offered as lots in a not very successful effort to create a town, the Pueblo of San Juan de Arguello (Santiago Arguello had been a secular administrator of the Mission). Father Jose Maria Zalvidea, failing in health, departed for San Luis Rey in 1842. This left San Juan Capistrano without a resident priest for the first time in its 72 years. In 1845, the mission buildings, except for the church and the vacant priest's quarters, were sold off to private parties. Father Vicente Pascual de Oliva, O.F.M. took over priestly duties at San Juan Capistrano in September of 1846. He was there during the war years between Mexico and the United States. He passed away on January 2, 1848, and was interred in the sanctuary of the Serra Church. The Mission then came under the care of Mission San Gabriel.

1850's

1850 Orange County Area
Population: c.500

Los Angeles County
Population: 8,329
California
Population: 92,597

California

On September 9, 1850, California became the 31st State of the United States. Only two years before it had been a part of Mexico. The sudden ascension from territory to statehood was accelerated both by the gold in the Golden State and by the desire to create a balance between Free and Slave States. Although California joined the Union as a Free State, Indian, Chinese, and Mexican laborers would question the accuracy of that claim for years to come.

Campo Aleman

In 1850, a colony of German immigrants purchased over a thousand acres from Juan Pacifico Ontiveros who owned the Rancho San Juan Cajon de Santa Ana. Their "Los Angeles Vineyard Society" laid out a town with lots for residences and farmland for growing grapes: their intended primary product and means of support. The new town was to be called Anaheim. The "Ana" stood for the Santa Ana River where it got its water and the "heim" was German for town. Locals would refer to it as the Campo Aleman, the German Camp.

Anaheim was located right on the El Camino Real, which provided a convenient roadway for its comings and goings. In 1858, the actual work of preparing the property and bringing water to it was carried out. In the fall of 1859, the first colonists arrived and began to take up residence.

California Catholics were expecting some changes and they were about to get them. California had been without a bishop for four years. In the interim, Father Jose Gonzales Rubio, O.F.M. of Santa Barbara had served as diocesan administrator. One of his greatest concerns was how to serve the multitude of English-speaking people who had descended upon California during the gold rush. With some success, he appealed for help from Church authorities in Oregon and the Sandwich (Hawaiian) Islands.

On May 31, 1850, Pope Pius IX appointed a Dominican, Reverend Joseph Sadoc Alemany, O.P., as the new bishop. Monterey was to be his official residence and the new name of the diocese reflected that: the Diocese of Monterey. Bishop Alemany was a Spaniard who had become an American citizen. He arrived to take possession of his diocese on December 6, 1850. The Mexican Government did not want an American bishop to rule in their territory, so the Holy See removed Baja California from Alemany's jurisdiction in 1851.

On July 29, 1853, the pope again divided the Diocese of Monterey. In the populous North, he created the Archdiocese of San Francisco and appointed Alemany as its Archbishop. Central and Southern California remained as the Diocese of Monterey. Pope Pius IX appointed Vincentian Father Thaddeus Amat, C.M. as Bishop of Monterey.

Bishop Amat decided Los Angeles was a better place for him to conduct his ministry and so he moved there in 1856. When he visited Rome in 1859, he asked to have the diocese renamed as the Diocese of Monterey-Los Angeles. It was and it remained so for the next 63 years.

San Juan Capistrano

By 1850, San Juan Capistrano had been under the care of Mission San Gabriel for two years. On February 20, Father Jose Maria Rosales became its first resident diocesan priest. He first served there as a delegate from San Gabriel. Bishop Alemany, newly arrived, appointed him pastor in December of 1850. Father Rosales ministered at Capistrano for about three-and-a-half years. Then, in November of 1853, he returned to his native Mexico. Newly ordained, Father Peter Bagaria came to take his place. He served for four years, after which he received permission to leave the diocese. On October 3, 1856, Bishop Amat appointed Father Jaime Vila to the Mission and also charged him with the care of San Luis Rey and San Diego. This was a far-ranging assignment, but was remedied somewhat at the end of the year. Bishop Amat then transferred Father Vila to San Diego and sent Father John Molinier to Capistrano. Both of them were asked to look after San Luis Rey. Father Molinier served at the Mission for the next two years. Father Vicente Llover then replaced him in April of 1859.

• *Fr. Vicente Llover*

San Antonio de Padua

According to Yorba family tradition, there was a private chapel in a second floor room of the hacienda of Don Bernardo Yorba, owner of the Rancho Cañon de Santa Ana, sometimes also known as the Rancho de San Antonio. Don Bernardo was one of the sons of Jose Antonio Yorba, a member of the Portolá Expedition and a grantee of the original Rancho Santiago de Santa Ana. On November 6, 1858, as Don Bernardo was nearing the end of his life, he and his wife, Andrea, deeded to the diocese a portion of his land to be used for a church, a priest's house, a garden, and a cemetery. In fact, building was already underway. The expenses were to be shared by various residents of the upper Santa Ana ranch community. To make sure the work would be completed, Don Bernardo made a provision in his will to pay for the completion of the chapel. Not long after these arrangements, he passed away on November 20, 1858.

• *Serra Church, San Juan Capistrano*

• *San Antonio Chapel*

• Fr. Joseph Mut

• Pope Pius IX

On March 18, 1865, President Abraham Lincoln signed the patent of title, which returned the San Juan Capistrano Mission to the Catholic Church. Ownership had been an issue since Mexican Governor Pio Pico ordered it auctioned in 1845.

In 1866, Father Duran requested a transfer to the Plaza Church in Los Angeles. Bishop Amat accommodated him and replaced him at Capistrano with Father Joseph Mut on August 7. With Father Mut came much needed stability. He spent the next 20 years serving the people there and in the vast outlying districts.

In 1867, Father Mut oversaw major repair work on the Serra Church. The roof above the sanctuary had collapsed. A new adobe wall was erected to meet the part of the roof that remained intact. This had the effect of shortening the church, leaving the old sanctuary outside along with the remains of three mission padres who had been buried beneath its floor. It appears that Father Mut was practical, if not always sentimental.

San Antonio de Padua

In the absence of the bishop, the Very Reverend Blas Raho, C.M., Vicar General, blessed the San Antonio Church at Rancho Cañon de Santa Ana on April 29, 1860. Father Llover from Capistrano came north for the occasion. Father Domingo Serrano, C.P. of San Gabriel celebrated the Mass, offering it up for the repose of the soul of Don Bernardo Yorba. Afterwards, members of the rancho community pledged themselves to provide $200 a year and a horse so that a priest from San Gabriel could travel down twice a month to celebrate Mass in the chapel.

In 1862, Father Jaime Borgatta of San Bernardino moved to the Yorba Ranch and took up residence at the San Antonio Chapel. He provided services there until 1868 when he returned to his native Italy. Oversight of the church then reverted to San Gabriel. It is known from an entry in the baptismal register that on June 4, 1868, the year of Father Borgatta's departure, Bishop Amat himself visited the San Antonio Chapel.

Anaheim

Cultural diversity is not a new social challenge. Imagine what it was like for generations of Spanish-speaking residents to suddenly have a whole town of Germans settling among them. Then as now assimilation required openness to change. Some made it easier, embracing the challenge through intermarriage. Such was the case for Herr Theodore Rimpau and Señorita Francisca Avila.

Theodore Rimpau was a German immigrant who came to San Francisco in 1848. In 1849, he moved to Los Angeles where on Christmas Day in 1850, he married Francisca Avila in the old Plaza Church. She was Catholic. He was not.

The Rimpaus divided their time between Los Angeles and the Avila Rancho. In 1860, they moved with their family to the Rancho San Joaquin where he engaged in the livestock business. In 1865, they joined the German colony at Anaheim where he cultivated grapes, raised sheep, and ran a mercantile store.

It is said that Father Peter Verdaguer celebrated the first Mass in Anaheim in the Rimpau home. In 1867, he was assigned to San Gabriel Mission, which oversaw this area. So it may well have been that year that Anaheim had its first Mass.

Anaheim did not have a resident priest until 1875. Priests from San Gabriel and Los Angeles would come down from time to time to provide services there. A day or two before the arrival of the priest, Mrs. Rimpau, a devout Catholic, would send her sons as messengers on horseback to ride through the town and surrounding area. They rang a hand bell and shouted the news of the priest's intended visit. Everyone interested was invited to the Rimpau home where Mass would be celebrated and instructions provided for the children. Various priests, including Bishop Amat, were honored guests at their home.

When the Rimpau house became too small to accommodate local Catholics, arrangements were made to use the small adobe Escuela Publica (Public School). When that too became unsuitable, Theodore Rimpau petitioned the Anaheim Water Company for a town lot where a church could be built. The request was granted and in 1869, Anaheim had its first, albeit ever so humble, Catholic Church.

1870's

1870 Los Angeles County
Population: 15,309
California
Population 560,247

Centennials

Although the country was still trying to recover from the catastrophe of the Civil War, it pulled itself together enough to celebrate its centennial, July 4, 1876 – Two hundred years of independence.

November 1, 1876 was also the centennial of Mission San Juan Capistrano. No record remains of how, or even if it was celebrated. The Mission was still in the early stages of its own recovery from the sad aftermath of secularization.

Railroad Connections

It is remarkable that in 1875, just six years after the completion of the Transcontinental Railroad, the Southern Pacific steamed its way into Anaheim. And by 1878, it made its way down to Santa Ana. People were pleased and proud to share in such high technology. The modern advantages of this railroad made the already promising area even more promising.

Our Towns

Come and live in our town! The welcome mat was out and smiling promoters enthusiastically extolled the advantages of being among the first to get in on the deal. Planning new towns was becoming a real estate sport.

By 1870, Columbus Tustin (Tustin City) and William Spurgeon (Santa Ana) were in competition. Alfred Chapman and Andrew Glassell entered the game in 1872. As lawyers, they had been involved in the partitioning of Rancho Santiago de Santa Ana. To no one's surprise, they wound up with a large portion of the land themselves. They laid out a town and called in Richland – a not too subtle enticement to farmers. However, there already was a town by that name in California, so the Post Office Department required a different name. The enterprising attorneys changed the name to Orange.

Tea, anyone? In 1872, the Reverend Lemuel F. Webber, a Presbyterian minister, purchased nearly 7,000 acres and founded the City of Westminster as a temperance colony. By October 22, 1874, the quiet and sober community had its first post office.

In 1876, Alonzo Cook, an attorney, and Converse Howe, a schoolteacher, got into the development game. They helped form a town site in an area where farmers had been gradually settling since 1870. On March 16,1877, a post office opened there bearing the name Garden Grove.

Church

Vatican Council I (1869-1870) solemnly declared the pope doctrinally infallible. Nevertheless, he was still mortal. On February 7,1878, Pope Pius IX passed away after 32 years – the longest papacy ever. Less than two weeks later, Cardinal Vincenzo Pecci, Bishop of Perugia, was elected pope. He took the name Leo XIII.

Bishop Thaddeus Amat, C.M., who had participated in the Vatican Council, passed away on May 12, a little more than three months after the death of Pius IX. His coadjutor, Bishop Francis Mora, immediately succeeded him.

San Juan Capistrano

In December of 1878, Father Joseph Mut – with the bishop's permission, of course – gave himself a well-deserved Christmas gift. He added second-story living quarters to the Mission's south wing where he had been living in the original padre's rooms. By this act his personal living situation soared from deplorable to slightly miserable.

Anaheim

In 1878, Bishop Amat gave parish status to the Catholic community of Anaheim and its surroundings. He placed it under the patronage of Saint Boniface, Apostle of Germany. He named Father Victor Foran its first resident priest, as pastor and charged him also with the care of San Antonio de Padua Church at the Yorba Rancho.

• *Fr. Victor Foran*

• *Pope Leo XIII*

ANAHEIM CHURCH

• *St. Boniface Church*

5 Orange County

1880's

1880 Los Angeles County
Population: 33,381

California
Population 864,694

Santa Fe

Railroads greatly improved transportation and brought opportunities for population growth and commercial prosperity. Of course it helped when there was competition. Southlanders welcomed the Southern Pacific in the late 1870s. They took back some of that welcome when they discovered how high-handed and demanding a monopoly could be. However, prices dropped significantly in 1887 when the California Central (Santa Fe) Railroad built a line through the Santa Ana Canyon from San Bernardino to Orange. It then extended to Santa Ana and on down through El Toro and San Juan Capistrano. In 1888, another line ran from Los Angeles through Buena Park, Fullerton, Anaheim,

and down to Orange. Steel rails connected communities to each other, the outside world, and the future.

Railroad competition meant lower fares and lower freight rates. The railroads themselves boasted of the increased affordability. Of course, it was in their own interest to encourage people to take advantage of this situation since they also had extensive land holdings. And the more people lured into Southern California, the more customers they would have for both their land and their railroad services. They advertised widely and the interest they created brought about the economic spike known as the "Boom of the Eighties."

New Communities

The "Boom of the Eighties" was a boom in the development and promotion of new towns and want-to-be towns. In 1886, a colony of Quakers from Indiana settled in a place east of Orange called Earlham. This later became El Modena. That same year, James Whitaker purchased land near the Southern Pacific tracks and the proposed Santa Fe line. He called his town site Buena Park. Also in 1886, Santa Ana honored

its own progress and potential by incorporating as a city. In 1887, George and Edward Amerige laid out the town site of Fullerton at a promising location near the new Santa Fe tracks. The town of Aliso City was also laid out near the Santa Fe tracks in El Toro. It didn't prosper, but what did develop there retained the name of El Toro for many years. In 1888, the ever-enterprising McFadden brothers, James and Robert, built a wharf on the ocean side of what is now the Balboa Peninsula. A town began to develop around this scenic commercial area and gradually expanded into what eventually became Balboa and Newport Beach.

Orange County

The growing communities in the southern portion of Los Angeles County felt ready to stand on their own. The inconvenience of conducting government business in Los Angeles and the perception that the area wasn't getting its fair share of tax revenue brought community leaders to Sacramento to lobby for independence. These efforts eventually paid off (an expression familiar in politics) and won legislative approval. On March

11, 1889, Governor Robert W. Waterman signed a bill creating the County of Orange. Local voters endorsed this bill by giving their overwhelming assent, favoring Santa Ana as the seat of their county government.

The Church
San Juan Capistrano

In San Juan Capistrano, Father Joseph Mut was transferred to San Miguel Mission on May 20, 1886. He had served at Capistrano for twenty years. In his place Bishop Mora sent Father Miguel Duran. Father Duran had served at the Mission from 1863 to 1866. That fact made him both Father Mut's predecessor as well as his successor. However, Father Duran was in very poor health and his assignment would be short. In 1889, on October 15, Bishop Mora sent Father Hugh Curran to take over duties at Capistrano. Two weeks later, on October 29, Father Duran passed away.

San Antonio de Padua

By 1880, the deteriorating, adobe church in Yorba, San Antonio de Padua, had to be replaced. A modern, New England style wooden structure took its place. This church and its community remained as a mission under the care of Saint Boniface Parish.

Anaheim

Saint Boniface Parish enjoyed notable progress during this period. In 1885, Father Patrick Hawe, the parish's second pastor, improved his situation by building a house. It was the first rectory at Saint Boniface. He was also responsible for making the church more audible and obvious.

He added to it a bell tower and, of course, a bell. The Church in Anaheim was noticeably rising in importance.

• *St Catherine's Convent, Anaheim*

In 1888, Father Peter Stoters, the third pastor, made an effort to further Catholic Education. He invited the Dominican Sisters of San Jose to open a school in Anaheim. Their superior, Mother Pia, visited Anaheim that year with Sister Hyacinth and purchased three acres of land. Soon after, construction began on a very impressive, three-story, brick building. On March 19, 1889, just eight days after the creation of the County of Orange, Saint Catherine's School was dedicated in Anaheim. It was a boarding and day school with a complete curriculum. On March 14 it opened for its first term. There was much fanfare and enthusiasm, but the first years were wrought with financial struggle.

Santa Ana

Santa Ana was sixteen years old when it incorporated in 1886. Its Catholics traveled to Anaheim to attend services at Saint Boniface. In 1887, they built their own church. Bishop Francis Mora came down to bless and dedicate it on October 2, 1887. The church was named Our Lady of the Rosary whose feast day was approaching on October 7. The bishop designated it as a mission under the care of Father Stoters, the pastor of Saint Boniface.

> **DOMINICAN SISTERS OF SAN JOSE**
> The Dominican Sisters of San Jose are the first religious community of women in Orange County. Their faithful ministry has continued to the present day.

1880 Los Angeles County
Population Increase: 68,093
California
Population Increase : 348,704

• *St Catherine's School*

Orange and Santa Ana Motor, Cal.

1890's

1890 Orange County
Population: 13,589
Los Angeles
Population: 101,459
California
Population 1,213,398

Orange County

The first decade of Orange County was the last decade of the nineteenth century. During this time, new communities began to emerge, strengthening the county's beginnings and assuring its successful entry into the 20th century. By 1891, enough people had settled along Laguna Beach's cool and scenic shores to warrant the opening of a post office, initially called Lagona. In 1895, the Cypress School District was formed at Waterville, a farming area with abundant artesian wells. In 1896, some people acquired a sweet taste for the company town forming around the new Los Alamitos Sugar Company. In 1899, a post office opened for the people of Talbert, a farming village that would later be reborn as Fountain Valley. Agriculture fed the county's growth and was the promise of even better things to come.

The Church

On April 8, 1894, the Very Reverend George Montgomery, Chancellor of the Archdiocese of San Francisco, was consecrated as the Coadjutor Bishop of Monterey-Los Angeles. He later succeeded Bishop Francis Mora who resigned in 1896 because of failing health.

San Juan Capistrano

On October 16, 1890, Father Hugh Curran transferred from San Juan Capistrano to Saint Joseph's in Madera. This was the beginning of a 19- year period – the longest in its history – during which the Old Mission no longer had a resident pastor. With Father Curran's departure, care of the Mission fell to Our Lady of the Rosary in Santa Ana, which had just become a parish.

Anaheim

Opportunities were opening up in Anaheim. In 1891, Father Peter Stoters broke ground for a parish cemetery (East Center and Coffman Streets). Although occupants were reluctant, there were no complaints.

In 1894, the Dominican Sisters were asked to take in orphan boys. They accepted and received 30 in their first group, including a three-month-old child.

Santa Ana

On October 16, 1890, Bishop Mora gave parish status to Our Lady of the Rosary in Santa Ana. He placed Father Patrick Grogan in charge as pastor and also entrusted to him the care of Mission San Juan Capistrano. The boundaries of the parish included the Pacific Ocean and everything south of the Santa Ana River up to the county lines of San Bernardino and San Diego.

In 1893, Father Alois Reidhaar replaced Father Grogan as pastor of Our Lady of the Rosary (sometime simply referred to as Holy Rosary).

Disaster struck in 1896 when the church burned to the ground. Local Catholics were stunned, but they rebounded with the encouragement of the new bishop, Bishop George Montgomery. That same year they built a new church, which the bishop dedicated and placed under the patronage of Saint Joseph. (It was felt that Our Lady would not be upset). The new church, however, was returned to its old status and became a mission under the care of Saint Boniface Parish.

1890 Orange County
Population Increase: 6,107
Los Angeles
Population Increase : 68,844
California
Population Increase : 270,656

• *St. Joseph Church, Santa Ana*

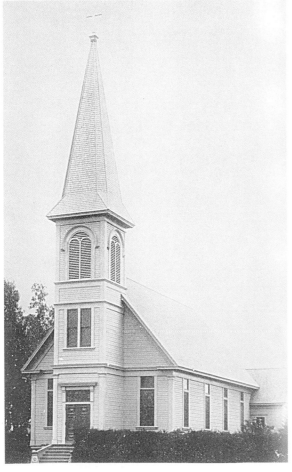

CORONA-DEL-MAR
Where the Bay and Ocean Me[e]
BALBOA, CALIFORNIA

1644

6 A New Century

1900's

1900 Orange County
Population: 19,696

Los Angeles
County Population: 170,298

California
Population 1,485,054

The County

The basis of Orange County growth became increasingly evident during this decade. Farming could be prosperous enough, but subdividing and laying out whole new communities did even better. Fledgling entrepreneurs began to pop out like oranges and their blossoms, although often neither as savory nor as fragrant. Sometimes they partnered with railroad men, knowing that somehow steel rails made the land financially more fertile wherever they were planted. Even with the mere anticipation of their arrival, new communities sprang up in welcome.

• Railroad Station, Fullerton

Fullerton, the fruit of the Santa Fe Railroad, ripened and incorporated as a city in 1904. The community of Bay City, now known as Seal Beach, formed as the Pacific Electric Railway extended through it from Long Beach to Huntington Beach. In 1905 the community of Benedict (now Stanton) formed as the Pacific Electric stretched through it from what is now Cypress to Garden Grove and Santa Ana. Along the coast the rails continued from Huntington Beach to Newport. In 1906, they tracked into East Newport and Balboa. That same year, just to the north, the community of Harper began to form in what would later become Costa Mesa.

Still farther to the north, in 1908, as the Pacific Electric arrived in La Habra new communities grew at Randolph (Brea) and Yorba Linda. The next year they too were connected to the system.

Also in 1909, the Pacific Electric ran a new line from Santa Ana to Huntington Beach, which incorporated that year.

Where the railways went the people went and where the people went the Church followed. The growth of the Church in Orange County paralleled the county's growth in general, although the pace was seldom, if ever, equal.

The Church

Having steered the Church into the twentieth century, Pope Leo XIII passed away on July 20, 1903. On August 4, 1903 the College of Cardinals elected Cardinal Giuseppe Sarto, Patriarch of Venice, as the new pope. He took the name Pius X. The Church now remembers and honors him as Saint Pius X.

In 1902, Bishop George Montgomery became the Coadjutor Archbishop of San Francisco. The following year Bishop Thomas J. Conaty succeeded him as the Bishop of Monterey-Los Angeles. In his first year, he doubled the

• *St. Boniface Church under construction*

• *Balboa*

number of parishes in Orange County – now there were two! The new parish of Saint Joseph in the bustling county seat of Santa Ana joined Saint Boniface in spiritual co-responsibility for the people of Orange County. There is no record of complaint from Saint Boniface Parish. Everything indicates that they were ready, willing, and only too happy to share.

This was not the only ministry boom during this decade. In 1909, Father Alfred Quetu, a semi-retired French priest, purchased with some of his relatives, a ranch in San Juan Capistrano. The Old Mission had been without a resident priest for years. He offered to provide a Mass there on a regular basis if the bishop so approved. The bishop saw that it was good, and so it came to be.

Also in 1909, the Joseph Yoch family, devout members of Saint Joseph Parish in Santa Ana, provided a building to be used as a Catholic Chapel in the small village of Laguna Beach, where they had a vacation home. Saint Joseph Chapel, named after Mr. Yoch's patron saint, was under the care of the Santa Ana parish. It was only occasionally served by various priests, usually on vacation themselves.

• *Pope St. Pius X*

1900-1910 Orange County
Population Increase: 14,740
Los Angeles
Population Increase : 333,833
California
Population Increase : 892,495

• *Orange County Court House, Santa Ana*

• *Anaheim*

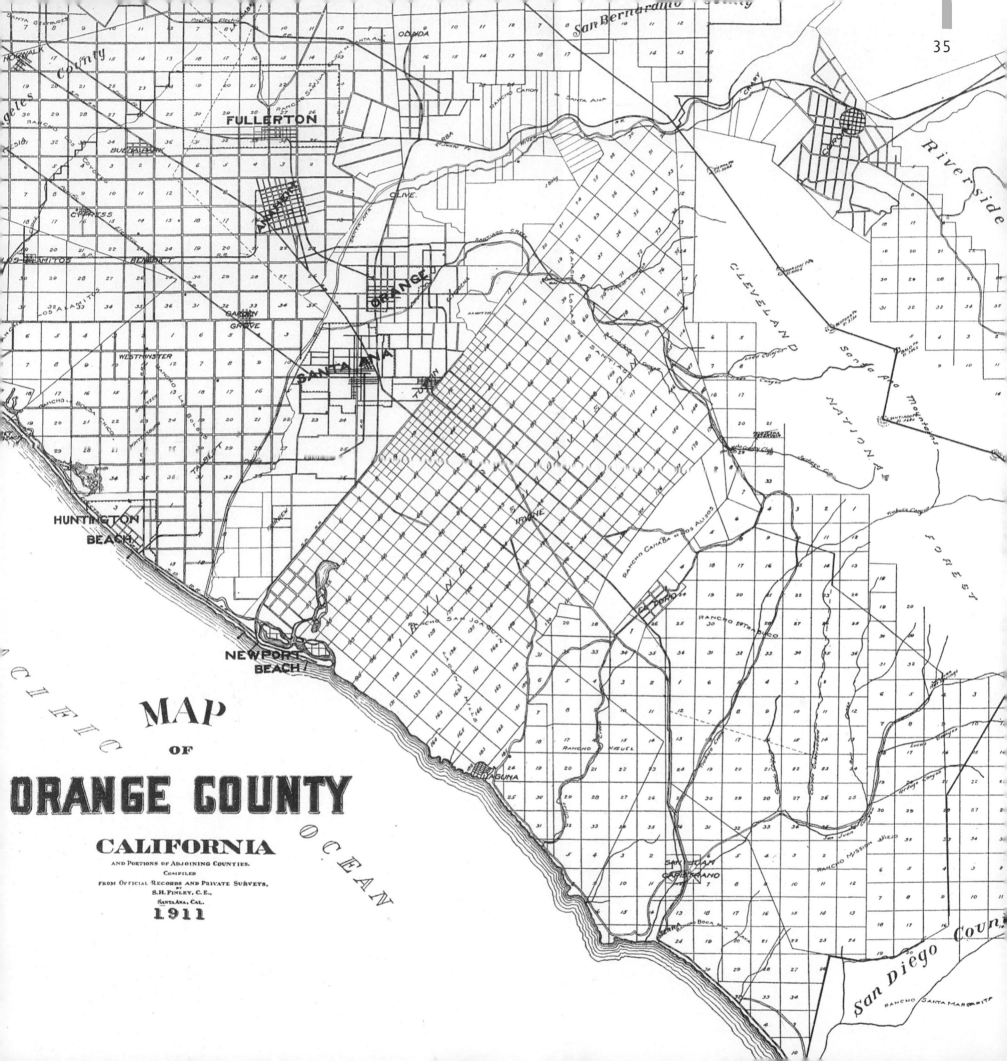

MAP
OF
ORANGE COUNTY
CALIFORNIA
AND PORTIONS OF ADJOINING COUNTIES.
COMPILED
FROM OFFICIAL RECORDS AND PRIVATE SURVEYS,
BY
S. H. FINLEY, C. E.,
SANTA ANA, CAL.
1911

1910's

The County

Once again the railways were the catalyst for growth in Orange County. In 1910, the Pacific Electric opened for service in Yorba Linda. The community of Placentia formed along the way. In 1914, the "Red Cars" brought greater mobility to the good citizens of Orange – good meaning anyone who would pay the fare. The railways promised progress seemed to be confirmed when its beneficiaries incorporated as cities: Seal Beach in 1915 and Brea in 1917.

The Church

Major changes took place in Church leadership during this decade. Following the death of Pope Saint Pius X, who passed away on August 20, 1914, the College of Cardinals elected Pope Benedict XV on September 3, 1914.

In 1915, Bishop Thomas Conaty died in Coronado and transferred to Eternal Life, generally recognized as a promotion. In 1917, after considerable reflection, Pope Benedict XV appointed San Francisco's Vicar General, the Very Reverend and the very Irish John J. Cantwell, to succeed Conaty as the Bishop of Monterey-Los Angles. This too was considered a promotion by some, but not as many.

On the local scene there were several significant Church occurrences during this time period. In 1910, Father Alfred Quetu invited Father St.John O'Sullivan to come and help out at Mission San Juan Capistrano. O'Sullivan was a priest from Kentucky with serious lung problems who had come west for his health. Capistrano agreed with him and his health improved. He took a great interest in the Old Mission and its community. He learned Spanish, quickly befriended the locals, and worked to renovate the aging mission. His personality was such that others were infected by his enthusiasm and joined his campaign of repairs and restoration. Father Quetu was happy to let him have at it and soon yielded the Mission entirely to his care.

Besides their devotion to the sun and the sand, Catholics in Huntington Beach established a building as a place for worship in 1911. Their Saint Mary's Chapel was initially a mission cared for by the priest's of Long Beach, who came down via the Red Car to celebrate Mass for the local, laid back flock.

In 1912, Bishop Conaty established Saint Mary's Parish in Fullerton and appointed Father John Gallagher as its pastor. In 1919, the care of Saint Anthony's in Yorba also came under its jurisdiction.

Catholic Education

Formal Catholic education in the county took two steps forward in the 1910's. Saint Joseph's Academy opened in Anaheim in 1912. And another Saint Joseph's, Saint Joseph Parish School, opened in Santa Ana in 1914. Sharing the same name and the same patron saint must have discouraged any temptation to an unseemly rivalry.

• *Orphanage, Anaheim*

• *Santa Ana Valley*

• *Bishop Conaty in Anaheim*

1920's

• *Pope Benedict XV*

• *Pope Pius XI*

1920 Orange County
Population: 61,375

Los Angeles
County Population: 936,455

California
Population 3,426,861

The County

The county did reasonably well following the dark days of World War I. There was a spirit of victory and confidence. People were on the move especially since automobiles were becoming more available and roads were added and improved. Population in the county more than doubled. In 1924 a new community formed in Dana Point and another at San Clemente the following year. Some older communities took the next step and incorporated as cities: La Habra in 1925, Placentia in 1926, and Laguna Beach and Tustin in 1927. Although the "Twenties" did not exactly "roar" in conservative Orange County, the county clearly did its best to live up to its share of the nation's enthusiastic reach for prosperity.

The Church

Pope Benedict XV passed away on January 22, 1922. On February 6, 1922, the Cardinals elected as his successor, Cardinal Ambrogio Damiano Achille Ratti, the Archbishop of Venice. He took the name Pius XI.

That same year the newly elected pope took notice of California's growth and increasing spiritual need. He divided the Diocese of Monterey-Los Angeles. Central California became the separate Diocese of Monterey-Fresno. The Southland, growing with no end in sight, became the Diocese of Los Angeles-San Diego. Bishop Cantwell continued to shepherd this southern jurisdiction.

• *Saints Simon and Jude, Huntington Beach*

For Catholics in Orange County this was a time of unprecedented Church expansion and development. In 1921, Saints Simon and Jude was established in Huntington Beach. A major oil discovery in the area brought with it a flood of workers and speculators. Little Saint Mary's Chapel was quickly outgrown. No amount of oil could help squeeze all the newcomers between its humble walls.

Still other churches made their appearance in 1921. In Seal Beach, Saint Anne's opened its doors – not to the seals, but to a grateful flock. And in Orange, Holy Family Church, neither aware of nor appearing like the cathedral it was to become, humbly opened its doors to eager parishioners happy to have their own church. 1922 became the year of the three Guadalupes. Our Lady of Guadalupe Church opened in Santa Ana. South of the city, Our Lady of Guadalupe Gloryetta opened as a mission in the Delhi area where many Catholics worked at its sugar beet plant. The third Guadalupe Church was a mission established in Stanton to serve its Spanish-

38

• Saint Anne's, Seal Beach

• Holy Family, Orange

• Fr. O'Sullivan and the Mission School

speaking workers and their families.

1923 marked the beginning of Our Lady of Mount Carmel Church on the sands of the Balboa Peninsula. It also witnessed the opening of Saint Anne's Church on Main Street in the city that bears her name. And in the artistic community of Laguna Beach, Saint Catherine of Siena Church enjoyed a resident priest to tend to the spiritual needs of its sun-kissed Catholics. Their quaint Saint Joseph Church was becoming too small to serve the communities year rounders and summer seasoners.

Bishop Cantwell saw the growing number of the Spanish-speaking Catholics and did a lot to provide for them. Besides Saint Isidore's and the Three Guadalupes he also oversaw the establishment of a series of Hispanic Missions: Our Lady of Lourdes in the Colonia Manzanillo of Santa Ana/Garden Grove (1924); La Purisima in El Modena (1925); another Our Lady of Guadalupe in the La Jolla District in East Anaheim (1925); and the Sacred Heart Mission at Independencia in West Anaheim (1926). During this decade, there had been a sharp increase in immigration from Mexico. Not only were immigrants looking for work; many were fleeing for their lives because of a violent persecution of the Church by the Mexican Government.

Catholic Education

Catholic education continued to progress in the '20s with the opening of Saint Mary's School in Fullerton (1923) and the Mission School in San Juan Capistrano (1928).

The Serra Church

Father St. John O'Sullivan completely restored the Serra Church. He decorated it with original mission art and an antique, hand-carved, gold altar (retablo) from Spain. The old once again became the new parish church of San Juan Capistrano. It opened for eager parishioners and admiring visitors in 1924.

Sisters of Saint Joseph Healthcare

In 1922, the Sisters of Saint Joseph established their Motherhouse in Orange. Their presence in the county would prove to be an abiding blessing. In 1929, they opened Saint Joseph Hospital, the first facility of what was to become a much needed and welcome healthcare system.

• St. Joseph Hospital

1929

The end of the decade brought an abrupt halt to what had been an amazing time of prosperity. The bubble burst. The Stock Market Crash of 1929 ushered in the calamity known as the Great Depression – a harsh reminder that the "almighty dollar" of Wall Street was an unreliable and unworthy object of worship.

1920 Orange County
Population Increase: 57,299
Los Angeles
Population Increase : 1,272,037
California
Population Increase : 2,250,390

ORANGE COUNTY *California*

Nature's Prolific Wonderland—

The land of the orange blossom,
With its mountains, vales and hills,
Its wealth of olive, fruit and oil,
And sunny, singing rills;
The home of the palm and
poppy, the blue Pacific too,
Orange County, Nature's
wonderland, is calling,
calling you.

Spring Eternal

1930's

1930 Orange County
Population: 118,674
Los Angeles
County Population: 2,208,492
California
Population 5,677,251

The County

Although at a much- reduced rate, the population continued to grow in California in spite of the Great Depression and, in some cases, because of it.

The Church

Population growth in the 1930s was significant enough that in 1936, Pope Pius XI raised the status of the Church in Los Angeles to that of an Archdiocese with John J. Cantwell as the Archbishop of Los Angeles.

• Marywood High School, Anaheim

Catholic Education

There were no new parishes in Orange County during this decade, but Catholic education made some progress. In 1934, Orange County's first Catholic High School opened in Anaheim. Formerly, Saint Joseph's Academy, it addressed the need for secondary education and was transformed into Marywood High School.
Also in 1934, a small private school, Sacred Heart, was established in Laguna Beach.

Sisters of Saint Joseph

To their credit, the "Stock Market Crash" had no direct bearing on the fortunes of the Sisters of Saint Joseph of Orange. On the contrary, in 1930, they were able to build on their good work by acquiring Fullerton General Hospital.

Perpetual Care

To accommodate those for whom healthcare was no longer relevant, the diocese laid out Holy Sepulcher Cemetery in the Santiago Hills east of Orange in 1931. It remains a beautiful place of peace and dignity.

The Holy Father

The end of the decade brought a major change in Church leadership. On February 10, 1939, Pope Pius XI passed away. On March 2, 1939, the College of Cardinals elected Cardinal Eugenio Pacelli, Secretary of State, as the new pope. He took the name Pius XII.

• Celery Field

• Orange Harvest

1930 Orange County
Population Increase: 12,0869
Los Angeles
Population Increase : 577,151
California
Population Increase : 1,230,136

1940's

1940 Orange County
Population: 130,760

Los Angeles
County Population: 2,785,643

California
Population 6,907,387

A Centennial

The new Archdiocese of Los Angeles celebrated a centennial in 1940. It had been a hundred years since Pope Gregory XVI established the Diocese of the Californias. Much had changed in those hundred years. The 1940 celebration looked back with some awe as to just how much. There were successes and failures and always new challenges. There had also been good people to address the issues. There was ample room for pride in the past. The Church in California had come a long way.

World War

In 1940, the nation was emerging from the bleak ordeal of the Great Depression and headed for darker and almost unimaginable sacrifices. World War II and its aftermath would be inseparably associated with life and death in the forties.

The Church

In material terms, there was very little the Church could accomplish during the war years. Rationing and the scarcity of materials were one of the burdens of the war. Bidding farewell to men and women with clear missions and an uncertain fate were part of the triumphs and terror of the times. New churches were not built, but the existing ones were filled with devout supplicants besieging Heaven for victory and the return of loved ones in jeopardy and far from home.

In Orange County, chapels and chaplains were needed for a growing number of military facilities. Orange County Airport became the Santa Ana Army Airdrome. The government established the Army Air Base in Santa Ana, the Navy Blimp Base in Tustin, the Navy Air Station at Los Alamitos, the Marine Corps Air Station at El Toro, and the Navy Ammunition and Net Depot at Seal Beach.

In July of 1941, four months before Pearl Harbor, Archbishop Cantwell dedicated the little Chapel of Saint John Vianney on Balboa Island. That was the only church built by the Los Angeles Archdiocese in Orange County until after the war.

Some important Church-related events, other than construction, did occur during the war years. In 1942, the Columban Fathers arrived at Saint Isidore's in Los Alamitos. They began a far-ranging ministry to the many migrant farm workers at missions throughout the county. And in Santa Ana, the Franciscan Sisters opened Saint Francis Home for Aged Women – an apostolate that has continued through the years.

Post War Boom

During the war many people arrived in the Southland. Some came for military training. Others sought job opportunities in the growing war-related industries. They found the climate good and the area attractive. The chance of making a good living here was also appealing. What was not to like? Many newcomers stayed on after the war. Many who had trained here returned after military service. It was the beginning of an incredible boom. People were anxious to return to normal and then improve on it.

Church activity accelerated following the war. In 1947, Blessed Sacrament Church opened in Westminster, as did Saint Joachim's in Costa Mesa, Our Lady of Fatima in San Clemente, and Our Lady of Guadalupe in La Habra.

A Change of Shepherds

In 1947, Archbishop John J. Cantwell passed away after a fruitful and impressive ministry. The following year, Pope Pius XII appointed in his place Archbishop James Francis McIntyre from New York.

In 1948, the first year of his ministry in Los Angeles, Archbishop McIntyre established the Parish of Saint Pius V in Buena Park with former military chaplain, Father Fredrick J. Kass, as its founding pastor.

Catholic Education

The small, private Sacred Heart School closed in Laguna Beach in 1945. Aside from that, Catholic education expanded like it never had before. In that same year, Saint Anne's School opened in Santa Ana. In 1948, Blessed Sacrament School opened in Westminster. And in 1949, Catholic elementary schools also opened at Holy Family in Orange and Saint Joachim's in Costa Mesa. Catholic education was readying itself for the "war babies" and the enthusiastic post-war production of "baby boomers."

1940 Orange County
Population Increase: 85,354

Los Angeles
Population Increase : 1,366,044

California
Population Increase : 3,678,836

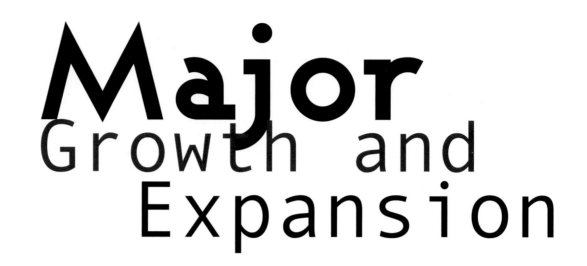

7 Major Growth and Expansion

1950's

1950 Orange County
Population: 216,114

Los Angeles
County Population: 4,151,687

California
Population 10,586,223

The County

Everything said about the post-war boom in the late 1940's boomed much louder in the 1950's. Los Angeles City and County were straining at the seams, or at least at their boundaries. Many looked with interest at the extensive farmland and charm of Orange County. Real estate agents and developers were only too happy to accommodate them. Farmers profited by selling the property at higher value. Developers profited by sub-dividing, building, and selling new homes – sometimes, whole tracts of homes. Newcomers enjoyed new homes at reasonable prices, in a quieter, less urban setting. And many of these would later profit in the re-sale of their homes at higher prices.

Orange County was called a "bedroom community" because many lived there, but worked outside the county.

Agriculture continued but had to co-exist with a rising suburban presence. In the 1950's nearly a half-million more people became Orange Countians.

During this decade, eight communities incorporated as cities: Buena Park and Costa Mesa in 1953; La Palma in 1955; Garden Grove, Stanton, and Cypress in 1956; and Fountain Valley and Westminster in 1957.

Promoters tried to out do one another with exaggerated and enticing descriptions of real estate, but no one matched the Walt Disney Company.

In 1955, "The Happiest Place on Earth" opened in Anaheim. Disneyland, which developed at the sacrifice of 160 acres of Orange Groves, was the most conspicuous example of a growing trend. This immensely popular attraction brought great attention to the area and lured many more residents and businesses to the county.

The Church

The Church valiantly struggled to keep up with the growth. In 1951, a Catholic Chapel was provided in Huntington Beach for the Mexican barrio of Colonia Juarez. In 1953, the year Pope Pius XII named Archbishop McIntyre a Cardinal, Saint Columban's Parish was established in Garden Grove and Saint Joseph's in Placentia. In 1954, Our Lady of the Pillar Parish, formerly Our Lady of Mount Carmel, opened in Santa Ana. In 1955, Saint Anthony Claret Parish began its ministry to East Anaheim. In 1957, Saint Cecelia Parish was established in Tustin. And in 1958, Anaheim welcomed its third parish – the second within the decade – Saint Justin Martyr in West Anaheim. In that same year, Saint Philip Benizi Parish opened in Fullerton. Throughout this decade Cardinal McIntyre and his auxiliaries were kept busy with maps, groundbreakings, and blessings.

Catholic Education

Cardinal McIntyre was a great believer in and promoter of Catholic education. In 1950, Mater

Pope Pius XII

Pope John XXIII

Disneyland

Dei High School opened in Santa Ana. In 1958, it was joined by Servite High School in Anaheim.

No less than 12 Catholic Elementary Schools opened in the 1950's. The list reads like a litany: Our Lady of the Pillar School in Santa Ana (1953), Saint Pius V School in Buena Park (1954), Saint Columban School in Garden Grove (1956), Our Lady of Guadalupe School in La Habra (1957), Saint Catherine of Siena School in Laguna Beach (1957), Saint Mary's Annex School – later known as Saint Philip Benizi – in Fullerton (1957), Saint Anthony Claret School in Anaheim (1957), Saint Anne's Annex School – later known as Immaculate Heart – in Santa Ana (1958), Saint Joachim's Annex School – later known as Saint John the Baptist – in Costa Mesa (1959), Saint

Mary's Second Annex School – later known as Saint Juliana's – in Fullerton (1959), Saint Justin Martyr School in Anaheim (1959), and Saint Joseph School in Placentia (1959).

It is very interesting to note that some of these schools actually preceded the parishes of which they would become a part. The reason was that the schools were needed right away and once their buildings were in place, they could be used for parish services until better facilities could be provided.

Healthcare

The Sisters of Saint Joseph of Orange made their own major contribution to the growth of the Church in Orange County during this time. In 1957, they added Saint Jude Hospital in Fullerton to their healthcare ministry.

A Change of Shepherds

Pope Pius XIII passed away on October 9, 1958. On October 28, the College of Cardianals elected Cardinal Angelo Giuseppe Roncalli, Patriarch of Venice, as the new pope. He chose the name John XXIII.

1950 Orange County
Population Increase: 478,811
Los Angeles
Population Increase : 1,887,084
California
Population Increase : 5,130,981

1960's

1960 Orange County
Population: 703,925

Los Angeles
County Population: 6,038,771

California
Population 14,717,204

The Context

The 1960's may be remembered as a sharp contrast between "flower power" and fear. The struggle for civil rights, the Vietnam War abroad, and social unrest at home indicated that "Camelot" was a precarious state of mind.

Fortunately, this troubled decade was not without its dreamers and doers. It was blessed with those who were convinced that worthwhile dreams weren't impossible as long as good people continued to pursue them.

The Church

Some of those good people came to the Vatican at the invitation of Pope John XXIII. Bishops of the world gathered in prayer and council to help make decisions on a broad range of issues. Inspiring the greatest church renewal of modern times, Good Pope John encouraged those gathered to open the windows, let in the fresh air of grace and seek new ways of applying the timeless Word of God to new times.

A new Pope

Pope John XXIII passed away on June 3, 1963. On June 21 the College of Cardinals elected

as his successor, Cardinal Giovanni Battista Montini, Archbishop of Milan. He chose the name Paul VI. It fell to him to lead the historic council to its conclusion and shepherd its implementation. The Second Vatican Council (1962 – 1965) was a grace-filled renewal of the Church with far-ranging ramifications for the Body of Christ.

The County

Locally, this decade might be called the "Soaring Sixties." The population of Orange County once again doubled. Over 700,000 new residents poured into the area. By the end of the decade, the county's count was well on its way to a million-and-a-half. Three more cities incorporated. Los Alamitos in 1960, San Juan Capistrano in 1961, and Villa Park in 1962.

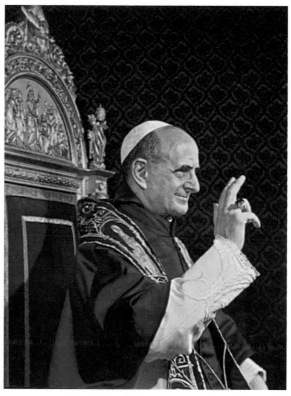

• *Pope Paul VI*

• *St. Cecilia Parish, Tustin, 1961*

In 1964, a whole new development arose in the Laguna Hills. It was a community for seniors who sought relief from their labors in "Leisure World." Who wouldn't want to live in a county claiming both Leisure World and the Happiest Place on Earth? No doubt for developers it was real estate paradise.

The Church

Out of necessity, the Church had become one of the county's best real estate customers. It had to purchase land in order to try and keep up with development. In just this decade, the Los Angeles Archdiocese established in Orange County 18 new parishes, 13 more Catholic elementary schools, two additional high schools, and two cemeteries. There would be years of growth ahead, but none would match this pace. In fact, there was nothing like it in the whole country.

There were few years that didn't see the start of a parish, or two, or three, or even four. In 1960, Cardinal McIntyre established the parishes of Immaculate Heart in Santa Ana and Saint John the Baptist in Costa Mesa. In 1961, he added Our Lady Queen of the Angels in Newport Beach, Saint Callistus in Garden Grove, Saint Irenaeus in Cypress, and Saint Polycarp in Stanton. In 1962, Saint Angela Merici Parish in Brea and Saint Barbara in Santa Ana joined the list. In 1963, Saint Norbert Parish began service to the people of Orange and Villa Park. In 1964, the Cardinal gave parish status to the existing church communities of Our Lady of Guadalupe in Santa Ana and La Purisima in El Modena. In 1965, he set up another parish foursome: Our Lady of the Pillar in Santa Ana, Saint Bonaventure in Huntington Beach, Saint Juliana Falconieri in Fullerton, and Saint Nicholas in Laguna Hills.

In 1969, the decade came to a close with the addition of Annunciation Byzantine in Anaheim and the granting of parish status to Holy Family Church in Seal Beach and Saint Edward the Confessor in Dana Point.

The Norbertines

In 1961, the Norberine Community established Saint Michael's in Silverado. This marked the beginning of a productive apostolate with lasting benefits affecting many for years to come.

Catholic Education

The amazing increases in Catholic education in the county in the 1950's were actually surpassed in the 1960's. Two more Catholic High Schools made their debut. Cornelia Connelly High School for girls, a private school operated by the Society of the Holy Childhood, opened in Anaheim in 1961. And Rosary High School for girls opened in Fullerton in 1965.

Another 13 Catholic Elementary Schools reinforced the Church's education ministry: Saint Hedwig's School in Los Alamitos (1960), Saint Jeanne de Lestonnac School in Tustin (1961), Saint Cecelia School in Tustin (1961), Saint Callistus School in Garden Grove (1963), Saint Irenaeus School in Cypress (1963), Saint Barbara School in Santa Ana (1963), Saint Polycarp School in Stanton (1963), St. Angela Merici (1964), Our Lady Queen of the Angels School in Newport Beach (1964), Saint Norbert School in Orange/Villa Park (1965), Our Lady of Fatima School in San Clemente (1965), La Purisima School in El Modena (1965), Saint Bonaventure School in Huntington Beach (1966), and Saints Simon and Jude School, also in Huntington Beach (1967).

In spite of this remarkable achievement, it was still difficult in many places to accommodate all those parents who hoped to send their children to Catholic School.

Final Things

While new things predominated in the "Soaring Sixties," final things were not ignored. In 1962, the Archdiocese of Los Angeles opened the gates to Good Shepherd Cemetery in Huntington Beach. And in 1965, additional accommodations were made available at Ascension Cemetery in El Toro (Lake Forest). Holy ground in Orange County would provide dignity, peace, rest, and perpetual care for remains awaiting the resurrection.

1960 Orange County
Population Increase: 716,461
Los Angeles
Population Increase : 1,017,029
California
Population Increase : 4,235,930

• James Francis Cardinal McIntyre

1970's

1970 Orange County
Population: 1,420,386
Los Angeles
County Population: 7,055,800
California
Population 19,953,134

The County

In the 1970's, Orange County population growth began to slow down for the first time since the Great Depression. However, it was not much of a setback. In fact, it was hardly noticed. More than half a million more newcomers made Orange County their home during this decade.

Development began to shift to the south county. In the midst of the vast Irvine Ranch holdings, the City of Irvine incorporated in 1971. While cattle still roamed their hills, surveyors began to replace cowboys. Modest beginnings were preparing for major change.

The Church

The shepherd and architect of the dramatic rise in church services to Orange County had been James Francis Cardinal McIntyre. Following his resignation because of age and infirmity in 1970, Archbishop Timothy Manning, his coadjutor, became the chief shepherd of the Archdiocese of Los Angeles.

Several new parishes were established in Orange County during the early '70s. In 1970, Saint Kilian Parish opened in the south county community of Mission Viejo. That same year, Saint Martin de Porres Parish opened in the north county city of Yorba Linda. In 1972, Holy Spirit Parish began its service to the people of Fountain Valley. And the following year, Holy Cross Melkite Church opened in Fullerton. This was a strong beginning for the new decade, but the greatest change was yet to come.

Behind the scenes Church officials had been discussing larger plans for the Church in Orange County. Rumors were rampant that Orange was ripening and ready to be on its own.

• *Cardinal Timothy Manning*

8 The Diocese of Orange in California

On Tuesday, March 30, 1976, Archbishop Jean Jadot, Apostolic Delegate, announced in Washington, D.C. that Pope Paul VI had approved the creation of the new Diocese of Orange in California and the appointment of Bishop William R. Johnson as its first bishop. The new diocese would include all of Orange County.

• Pope Paul VI and Bishop Johnson

On the same day at a press conference in Los Angeles, Cardinal Timothy Manning expressed his congratulations to Bishop Johnson and his joy at, "The creation of a new community of the people of God."

Bishop Johnson stated that he accepted the appointment, "With gratitude to God and the Holy Father. It is a real joy and a challenge." He then issued this formal statement: "God has filled the years of my priesthood with happiness and the landscape of my life with his loving people. To serve Him and them as Bishop in the new Diocese of Orange is a privilege I look forward to with joy. I am grateful to God for the opportunity this represents and to our Holy Father, Pope Paul VI, for the trust he has placed in me.

The task that lies ahead is God's work and He who begins it in us will sustain it and make it fruitful if only we make ourselves the willing instrument of His hands.

The very name "Orange" suggests a golden treasure and the new diocese is all of that in its physical characteristics, its people and its traditions. The area is small enough to be unified as a true community and large enough to encompass a substantial number of generous hearted people. These along with the dedicated priests and religious who serve them are the richest endowment one could hope for.

Orange County has a fine tradition of faith whose seeds were planted at Mission San Juan Capistrano just two centuries ago. That tradition has been nurtured and strengthened through the years by a long list of priests and prelates, not the least of whom are the recent Archbishops of Los Angeles: Archbishop John J. Cantwell, Cardinal James Francis McIntyre, and Cardinal Timothy Manning.

Each in turn has seen the area grow and has husbanded its resources toward the day when this new diocese could begin. To them and to the clergy and laity who have cooperated with them belongs the credit for the many churches, schools, health and social service agencies that now become our heritage.

The role of the bishop is to rule the Church as a shepherd of souls together with the Holy Father so as to make effective in a particular time and place the work of Christ the eternal Shepherd in teaching people, in sanctifying them in truth and in nourishing them in faith. That role is properly filled as "diakonia," ministry, service.

The prayerful support of the clergy, religious and laity of the new diocese is a gift I earnestly seek so that I may use the office of bishop in that fashion and in pursuit of that ideal. Working and praying together, we can become what God calls us to be – a Community of Faith, a visible yet mystical presence of Jesus Christ, a living testimony of His redeeming love."

Most Reverend William Robert Johnson, D.D., A.C.S.W.

First Bishop of Orange

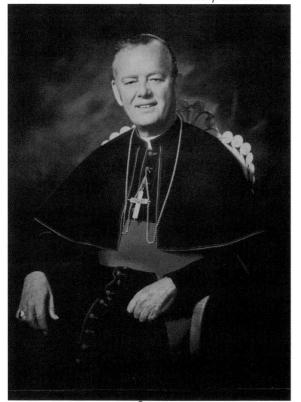

• Bishop Johnson

William Robert Johnson was born in Tonopah on November 19, 1918. He was the son of native Nevadans Jorgen and Marie (O'Connell) Johnson. His father worked in the silver mines as a hoist engineer, but the hard life ruined his health. In the early 1920's the family moved to Los Angeles, seeking a better climate and better living conditions. In spite of that, Jorgen's health deteriorated and he passed away in 1926, when Bill was just eight years old. This left Marie not only grief-stricken, but also with the difficult task of raising their four children: William, Jorgen, Thomas, and Margaret. As a devoted mother she went to work as a clerk and supported her family for the next 21 years. She was a devout Catholic and made sure the children were raised in the Faith. They attended Saint Ignatius of Loyola Parish and it was there that young Bill learned to serve Mass as an altar boy.

After spending his first year at Garvena Public School, Bill received the rest of his elementary education at Saint Ignatius School where the Dominican Sisters of San Jose taught him.

Sensing a call to the priesthood, he entered Los Angeles College in 1932. At the time, this was the junior seminary for the Archdiocese. There he completed high school and the first two years of college.

In the fall of 1938, he continued his college study of philosophy at the major seminary, Saint Patrick's in Menlo Park. After just one year there, he returned to the Archdiocese, which, in September of 1939, opened its own major seminary, Saint John's in Camarillo. As a pioneer member of its student body, he finished his college education and then went on to its four-year program of scripture and theology.

During the summer vacation months he worked to earn some much-needed income. One of his jobs was with the Southern Pacific as a cleaner for its coach cars. It is interesting to note that he was responsible for the cost of his seminary education and he had to make payments on the debt until 1961.

Upon the completion of his seminary training, William Johnson, age 25, was ordained to the priesthood by Archbishop John J. Cantwell at Saint Vibiana's Cathedral on May 28, 1944.

Father Bill Johnson's first assignment was Saint Anthony Parish in Gardena where he served as assistant for a year and a half. In March of 1946, he was sent to San Antonio de Padua Parish in Los Angeles where he was encouraged to improve his Spanish language skills. It proved to be a short assignment.

In the fall of that year, Archbishop Cantwell sent Father Johnson for further studies at the Catholic University of America in Washington, D.C. For the next two years, he spent his time studying and interning in social work. In June of 1948, he completed the program and graduated with a Masters Degree in Social Work.

After his return to Los Angeles, he joined the staff of the Archdiocesan Catholic Welfare Bureau. While doing this work he was assigned "In Residence" to Saint Columbkille's where he helped out with the Masses on the weekend. After a year there, he was "In Residence" for six months at Saint John the Evangelist Parish.

In 1950, Father Johnson transferred to the Catholic Welfare office serving Santa Barbara and Ventura Counties. While there, he resided at Our Lady of Mount Carmel in Montecito. In 1951, he was also assigned as administrator of Saint Joseph Mission in Santa Barbara.

In the summer of 1953, he returned to the main office of Catholic Welfare in Los Angeles. He resided for nearly two years at All Souls Parish in Alhambra. Afterwards, in 1955, he transferred to Saint Michael's in Los Angeles.

On September 4, 1956, Cardinal McIntyre appointed Father Johnson as Director of the Catholic Welfare Bureau, succeeding Bishop Alden J. Bell. In the fall of 1958, he took up residence at Immaculate Conception rectory, a short walk to his Archdiocesan office.

On January 15, 1960, Pope John XXIII named Father Johnson a Papal Chamberlain with the title of Monsignor. That same year he was elected as a member of the Board of Directors of the National Conference of Catholic Charities.

In June of 1962, Cardinal McIntyre added to Monsignor Johnson's responsibilities, assigning him as pastor of Holy Name Parish in Los Angeles.

In 1964, the Board of Directors elected Monsignor Johnson as President of the National Conference of Catholic Charities. On January 8, 1966, Pope Paul VI honored him by promoting him from Papal Chamberlain to Domestic Prelate.

On June 11, 1968, Cardinal McIntyre transferred Monsignor Johnson from Holy Name, where he had served the inner-city parish for six years. His new assignment was the pastorate of American Martyrs Parish in Manhattan Beach – a breath of fresh air.

On April 1, 1970, Archbishop Timothy Manning appointed Monsignor Johnson to serve as rector of Saint Vibiana's Cathedral. In less than a year, on February 9, 1971, Pope Paul VI named him the Titular Bishop of Blera and Auxiliary Bishop to Archbishop Manning, who ordained him bishop at Saint Vibiana's on March 25. Bishop Johnson was 52 years old. Personally, it was a bittersweet year. Shortly after Bishop Johnson's episcopal ordination, his beloved mother, Marie, passed away on July 28, at Santa Teresita Hospital in Duarte. She was 85 years old. He presided at her funeral at Saint Dominic's Parish where she had been an active member for over twenty years. Cardinal Manning preached the homily.

Bishop Johnson continued as Director of the Catholic Welfare Bureau even while running the Cathedral Parish, taking on extra duties at the Chancery, and administering the Sacrament of Confirmation at various parishes throughout the Archdiocese.

In the spring of 1973, Archbishop Manning gave him a first-hand experience of missionary life by sending him to pay an official visit to the Archdiocesan Lay Mission Helpers in New Guinea, New Ireland, and Africa.

In the summer of that year, he left the directorship of the Catholic Welfare Bureau. He had served the apostolate of Catholic Charities for nearly 25 years. He had worked successfully to reorganize and expand services. He helped plan and supervise the construction of a new Catholic Charities building on West Ninth Street. He was

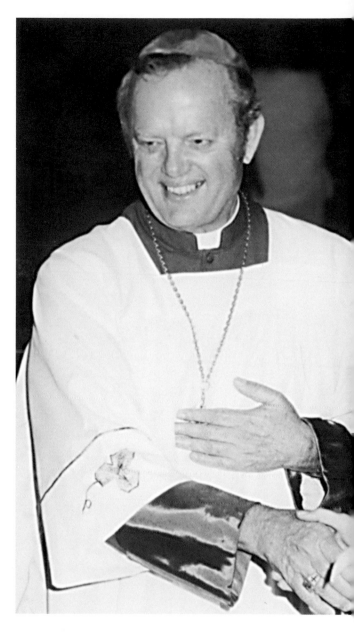

a member of the Los Angeles County Probation Committee and served on the Governor's Welfare Study Commission. He effectively promoted the mission of Catholic charities on the local, state, and national levels. His competence and love for this work earned him respect, honors, and promotion to greater duties. His motto, Caritas Christi (Love of Christ) characterized his ministry throughout his days.

When he relinquished the directorship of Catholic Welfare, he did not abandon his association with it. Neither did it lighten his workload. It just went to a higher level. In 1973, Cardinal Manning appointed him as Episcopal Vicar for Charity, Episcopal Vicar for the Black Community, and Episcopal Vicar for Los Angeles County.

Clearly he enjoyed the confidence of his superiors who entrusted him with even greater responsibilities. On March 30, 1976, Pope Paul VI created the new Diocese of Orange and appointed him as its bishop. On June 18, at Holy Family Cathedral in Orange, in the presence of the apostolic delegate, Archbishop Jean Jadot, Cardinal Manning installed his long time friend, Bishop Johnson, as the first Bishop of the Diocese of Orange in California.

Diocesan Beginnings

At the time, the Diocese of Orange was created, it already had a Catholic population larger than thirteen of the thirty-two archdioceses in the United States. It was also larger in Catholic population than four of the nine dioceses in California. It would have become a diocese sooner, but, because of its precipitous growth, it carried a lot of construction debt payable to the Archdiocese of Los Angeles. A delay allowed some of that to be paid back and a sale of some church property, originally purchased to provide for the inevitable future growth, also helped to satisfy archdiocesan interests.

Bishop Johnson and the new diocese started off with generous prayers, good wishes, enthusiasm, and potential. However, financially and botanically, the orange was not a plum. Its capital resources were humble, but in God's good providence, they would prove enough.

The challenges were many and problem solving was an unremitting agenda. Neither Bishop Johnson nor his chancellor, Father Michael Driscoll, had ever worked before in a Chancery Office. Some considered that a blessing, but for them it meant extra work learning how to proceed, especially in canonical formalities. There were a lot of phone calls to the Cardinal and his staff, taking them up on their promises to be of assistance.

Another underlying factor making things more difficult for Bishop Johnson was his poor health. Unknown to nearly everyone – initially even himself – he was to experience a slow but steady decline. People only saw a zealous, good-natured spiritual shepherd equal to his tasks. It was only in his last year that people generally became more aware of the cross of declining health that he had been carrying.

Bicentennial

The year the diocese was formed was also the year of the Bicentennial of the United States. The U.S. Catholic Church celebrated this occasion by convening at a Eucharistic Congress in the historic city of Philadelphia. The new Bishop of Orange, along with bishops from around the country, participated in this national event of prayer and thanksgiving.

Locally, it was also the Bicentennial of Mission San Juan Capistrano. On All Saints

• Bishop Johnson

• Installation Mass, June 18, 1976

Day, November 1, the actual anniversary of the mission's founding, Cardinal Timothy Manning concelebrated Mass with Bishop Johnson and preached the sermon in the Mission's historic Serra Chapel.

A Pastoral Center

The last years of the 1970's were, of course, the first years of organizing the Diocese of Orange. Even before the official ceremonies that established it, Bishop Johnson was already hard at work selecting department heads, committees, and personal staff. Initially, the diocese was run out of his car, the guest room at Holy Family rectory where he took up residence, and anywhere else where he might conveniently meet with people. Following the June 18 ceremonies, he arranged for temporary diocesan headquarters to be located in the remodeled Marian Hall on the grounds of the Motherhouse of the Sisters of Saint Joseph of Orange. He also arranged to establish his personal residence in what used to be the original rectory at Holy Family Cathedral. It was then being used as a convent for the Sisters of the Sacred Heart, but in exchange, they accepted a new residence on diocesan property owned in Santa Ana.

In 1978, the Sisters of Providence (Indiana), who owned and staffed Marywood Catholic High School in Orange, decided to put the property up for sale, since they no longer had the resources and personnel to keep the school going. The Diocese of Orange decided to acquire it as its Pastoral Services Center (Chancery Office) and as a place for retreats and educational gatherings. In the meantime, the Sisters continued to run the school until it could graduate its last class.

One of Bishop Johnson's expressed goals was to form a diocese that was efficient, but user-friendly, less intimidating than the large Church authority structures of the past. He wanted his leadership, and that of those who worked with him and for him, to be approachable and inviting. The Chancery Office (Bishop's Office) was to be named the Pastoral Services Center. He wanted people to feel comfortable and happy as members of the family of the Diocese of Orange. Of course, as the family continued to grow and expand so rapidly, it would become increasingly difficult to retain this informal feeling.

• Bishop Johnson's Office

Communications

In the beginning, diocesan communication continued through the archdiocesan newspaper, The Tidings. But in the spring of 1977, it issued its own monthly paper called The Diocese of Orange Bulletin. This was distributed for free through the parishes. The diocese also inaugurated radio broadcasts at KYMS in a program called Catholic Dimensions, hosted by Mr. Thomas Fuentes. And by 1979, it also published its own annual Diocese of Orange Catholic Directory.

Assessment

In an effort to quickly familiarize himself with the people of the diocese and allow them to get to know him, Bishop Johnson personally visited each of the parishes. He also sent his lay advisory board to meet with parish leaders to form a consensus of their problems, needs, and expectations.

For the clergy, Bishop Johnson arranged an Awareness and Needs Assessment Workshop at Mater Dolorosa Retreat Center. He also established an Office of Continuing Education for Clergy and pressed for the early organization of a Priests Council.

• Bishop Johnson Greets Children

• *First Permanent Deacon's ordination 1977*

• *Priesthood ordination Class of 1978*

• *Fr. Enrique Sera, First Priesthood Ordination*

Hispanic Ministry

Although Hispanic Ministry had already been active in Orange County, Bishop Johnson gave it greater life by enlisting the talented services of Archbishop Tomás Clavel, former Archbishop of Panama. He also established the Office for Hispanic Ministry as part of his own Pastoral Services Center. It was one of the first departments to move into Marywood as it was being remodeled for diocesan use.

Vietnamese Ministry

The Vietnamese Ministry also received early attention. Various parishes in the county and the Catholic Welfare Office in Santa Ana had already been involved in the work of refugee resettlement. A few months after the diocese was formed, Bishop Johnson, on August 15, the Feast of the Assumption, celebrated Mass with the Vietnamese Community at Saint Barbara's Church in Santa Ana. And, with the unanimous approval of the diocesan Priests Council in 1978, he established the first Diocese of Orange Vietnamese Center. The following year, at Saint Joseph Motherhouse in Orange, he presided at an awards ceremony honoring those who had participated in the on-going refugee resettlement program.

Expansion

One of the most obvious and expressed concerns in the diocese was the need for expansion of Church services throughout the growing county. The creation of new parishes was high on the list of priorities. In 1976, the first year of the diocese, Bishop Johnson established Saint Elizabeth Ann Seton Parish – the first Catholic parish in the burgeoning

community of Irvine. In 1977, he added three more parishes: San Antonio de Padua in Anaheim Hills; Saint Mary's by the Sea in Huntington Beach; and Saint Vincent de Paul, also in Huntington Beach. At the end of 1978, he gave Irvine its second parish, Saint John Neumann, in the Woodbridge area. And in 1979, he established the parish of Santiago de Compostela in the Saddleback Valley community of El Toro, now known as the city of Lake Forest.

Also during this last year of the decade, the diocese opened its first new church building and marked the beginning of another: Bishop Johnson dedicated the new church of Saint Bonaventure in Huntington Beach and presided at groundbreaking ceremonies for a church for Anaheim Hills' new parish of San Antonio de Padua.

• *Site blessing, San Antonio de Padua*

To maintain the diocese on a sound financial basis, Bishop Johnson promoted the annual campaign of "Unity and Growth through Christian Stewardship" in 1978. And to keep it on a sound spiritual basis – and to promote vocations – he established the program of Perpetual Adoration, so that this special devotion to the Blessed Sacrament would take place each and every day of the month in some designated parish of the diocese. And to encourage each individual's spiritual renewal,

● *Bishop Johnson and Fr. Michael Driscoll*

he issued a Pastoral Letter on the Sacrament of Reconciliation on Ash Wednesday, 1982.

Papal Transition

On the international scene, Pope Paul VI, who had established the diocese, passed away on August 6, 1978. Pope John Paul I, whose pontificate lasted slightly less than a month, succeeded him, on August 31. Bishop Johnson and Archbishop Clavel were to have met with him, but instead found themselves attending his funeral. Pope John Paul II, elected on October 16, visited the United States the following year. Bishop Johnson was there to greet him during the pope's visit to Washington, D.C.

● *Pope John Paul I*

1970 Orange County

Population Increase: 511,184

Los Angeles
Population Increase : 421,703

California
Population Increase : 3,715,428

● *Pope John Paul II*

● *St. Bonaventure Dedication, Huntington Beach*

Most Reverend Tomás Alberto Clavel Méndez, D.D.

Archbishop of Panama Emeritus

When the Diocese of Orange was created in 1976, Archbishop Tomás Clavel had already been working in the county for four years. The former Archbishop of Panama had come to the Archdiocese of Los Angeles in 1971. Archbishop Timothy Manning invited him to minister to the Hispanics in Orange County. And so, he took up residence with the Brothers of Saint Patrick in Midway City where he served as their chaplain and spent time improving his English-speaking skills. While living there, he organized a Community Center in the La Bonita Barrio at Our Lady of Lourdes Mission in Santa Ana.

In 1973, Archbishop Clavel returned to Panama where he served as a missionary among the Indian people on the Bayano River. From 1974 through 1977, he divided his time between Panama and Orange County: six months in the Panamanian missions and six months working with the Hispanics in Orange County.

After the Diocese of Orange was formed, Bishop William Johnson asked him in 1978 to work full-time in the diocese. Archbishop Clavel accepted the offer, feeling that his missionary work in Panama was sufficiently staffed and organized to continue without him.

The archbishop's background was certainly impressive. He was born December 21,1921, into a middle class family of 12 in Cañazas, Veraguas, Panama. His parents were César Clavel and Josefina (Méndez) Clavel. He received his formal education in Panama, Costa Rica, and Columbia. His Major Seminary training was at the Collegium Maximum de la Compañia de Jesús in Bogotá.

Bishop Francis Beckman, C.M. ordained Father Tomás Clavel to the priesthood for the Archdiocese of Panama on December 7, 1947. Afterwards, Father Clavel continued his studies at the Pontificia Universidad Javeriana, where he earned his Doctorate in Philosophy. Then he went to the United States where he studied psychology and counseling for a year at Saint John's University in Brooklyn.

Upon his return to Panama, he became chancellor for the archdiocese as well as pastor of a new parish, San Miguel, which served a large, black population.

In 1955, when he was just 33 years old, Pope Pius XII appointed Clavel the first bishop of the new Diocese of David in Panama. He was the first Panamanian to become a bishop. Moreover, just eight years later, on March 21, 1964, Pope Paul VI appointed him Archbishop of Panama City.

Both as Bishop of David and, later as Archbishop of Panama, Clavel was an active participant at the Second Vatican Council (1962-1965). He attended all sessions and served at the pope's request as a member of the Council for the Implementation of the New Liturgy and the committee for the translation of the council

● Archbishop Clavel with Mariachis

documents into Spanish. During this work, he built up personal friendships with the Bishop of Vittorio Veneto and the new Archbishop of Krakow – who later became, respectively, Pope John Paul I and Pope John Paul II.

In 1965, Archbishop Clavel was elected President of the Central American Bishops Conference. Traditionally, Church and State had worked closely in Panama. When a Military Junta seized control of the country, Archbishop Clavel felt that he could not and should not work with them. In conscience and for the good of the Church, he resigned as Archbishop of Panama in 1968. He sacrificed the prestige of office in protest of what he perceived to be a perpetuation and promotion of social injustice.

On December 18, 1968, he was translated to the Titular Archiepiscopal See of Alexanum. He then served as the representative of the Holy See to the International Institute for Colonial Art. As such, he traveled extensively throughout Latin America. He worked to make sure that the treasures of Colonial Art and Architecture were preserved as local Churches undertook modifications according to the new liturgical norms of Vatican II.

Panama's sad loss eventually became the happy gain of the Diocese of Orange. On December 1, 1978, Bishop William Johnson named Archbishop Clavel as his Episcopal Vicar for the Spanish-speaking. Shortly afterwards, he appointed him Administrator Pro Tem for Saint Joseph's Parish in Santa Ana. Then, after a pastor was appointed, the bishop sent him in residence to Holy Spirit Parish in Fountain Valley and provided for him an office at Marywood, the new Diocesan Pastoral Services Center. There he worked closely with the staff of the Diocesan Department for Hispanic Ministry. In 1980, the Archbishop moved into his own house on Baker Street in a modest neighborhood in Santa Ana. From there he continued his expanding ministry in the diocese.

On September 28, 1980, at Saint Norbert's Church in Orange, Archbishop Tomás Clavel offered a Solemn Mass of Thanksgiving on the occasion of his 25th anniversary as a bishop. The joyous presence of laity, religious, clergy, and hierarchy was a testament of appreciation for the blessing of his ministry. At the time, Bishop Johnson declared: "We want to say a heartfelt thank you for being the man, the priest, the bishop that you are. Your generous and zealous service to all the people of the diocese is a source of inspiration to your brother priests and a source of great joy to our people."

For this Silver Jubilee, the Archbishop returned to celebrations in his honor at the Diocese of David (which was also celebrating its 25th anniversary) and also at the Archdiocese of Panama City. Thousands turned out to celebrate with him.

In 1983, Pope John Paul II honored him by personally inviting him to accompany him on his Central American tour, which he did on March 2 through March 6.

During the nearly ten years that Archbishop Clavel served as Episcopal Vicar for the Hispanic Community, he was a whirlwind of pastoral activity throughout the diocese. He assisted in administration when necessary, but he preferred direct ministry to the people whenever possible. He was a Diocesan Consultor and a member of the Priests Council. He attended bishops meetings on the state, regional, and national levels. He was very active in Cursillo, Search, and other pastoral programs. He traveled extensively throughout the diocese administering Confirmation and other sacraments. He made himself available for spiritual exercises, retreats, days of recollection, and various parish celebrations. He was comfortable in the presence of both the affluent and the poor, but it was the needs of the poor that drew his unfailing attention. His genuine interest in people made him a popular shepherd of souls.

Although he contemplated an eventual return to Panama to spend his last years living with family and ministering to the poor, it was not meant to be. On October 13, 1988, he suffered a fatal heart attack and passed away at Saint Joseph Hospital in Orange. He was 66 years old.

Auxiliary Bishop John Steinbock, with Bishop McFarland presiding, celebrated Mass for him in Spanish at Saint Anne's Church in Santa Ana on October 17. Hundreds of mourners prayed their respects.

On October 18, at Holy Family Cathedral in Orange, Bishop McFarland celebrated a Mass of Christian Burial. In his homily, he spoke of Archbishop Clavel as a "man of gentle voice and strong example." He spoke for all when he added, "We remember him as a great priest with a warmth and charity and interest in God's people, exhibited with an unassuming style and grace and generosity."

On October 21, Archbishop Marcos McGrath, C.S.C. led the funeral services at Panama City's Metropolitan Cathedral. At last Archbishop Tomás Clavel had come home to remain among the people he had loved and served with courage.

1980's

1980 Orange County
Population: 1,931,570

Los Angeles
County Population: 7,477,503

California
Population 23,668,562

The Church

For the Church at large, a number of notable events took place during this decade that give relevant context to the happenings in the Diocese of Orange. First of all, we nearly lost our Holy Father. In 1981, a would-be assassin shot him while he was greeting the crowd in Saint Peter's Square. Although the pope was seriously injured, he gradually recovered. He later stated that he felt he had been spared for further work by the intervention of Our Lady of Fatima for whom he had a great devotion. Indeed, he would continue ministry for a very long and effective pontificate.

In 1984, California celebrated the Bicentennial of Fray Junipero Serra, the Apostle of the Californias. In the fall of 1987, Pope John Paul II, having recovered from his injuries, made a pilgrimage to California and while visiting the Diocese of Monterey, prayed at the tomb of Father Serra. Later, at the Vatican in 1988, he presided at Father Serra's beatification ceremony.

Closer to home, Bishop Roger Mahony succeeded Cardinal Manning as the new Archbishop of Los Angeles in 1985. Cardinal Manning was the last Archbishop of Los Angeles to have had direct jurisdiction over Catholics in Orange County. He died of cancer in 1989.

The Local Church

Within the Diocese of Orange, various events stand out during this decade. In 1980, Bishop Johnson and his Pastoral Services Center moved into their new offices at Marywood Center in Orange. That same year, Archbishop Clavel celebrated his 25th Anniversary as a bishop. Bishop Johnson accompanied him to Panama for a Mass of Thanksgiving. After their return, another celebration was held at Saint Norbert's in Orange so that local bishops, clergy, and friends could participate.

• *Pope John Paul II with Bishop William Johnson*

In 1983, Bishop Johnson traveled to the Vatican where he met with Pope John Paul II and presented his five-year Ad Limina report to curial officials. The following year, the Holy Father appointed Monsignor John Steinbock, a long time friend of Bishop Johnson's, to help him as auxiliary bishop in the ever-growing Diocese of Orange. Steinbock was ordained bishop on July 14, 1984.

Most Reverend
John Thomas Steinbock, D.D.

John Thomas Steinbock was born in Los Angeles on July 16, 1937. He is the youngest of three sons born to Leo and Thelma Steinbock. John was baptized at Holy Cross Church, but grew up in Nativity Parish where he received his elementary education and, like his brothers Leo and Robert, learned to serve Mass.

After graduating from Nativity School, he began his studies for the priesthood: first, at the Archdiocesan Junior Seminary, and then at Saint John's Major Seminary in Camarillo. Following his studies, Cardinal James Francis McIntyre ordained him to the priesthood at Saint Vibiana's Cathedral on May 1, 1963.

Father Steinbock had always hoped to work in poor, Spanish-speaking parishes. He had studied Spanish at the seminary and also, for a summer, in Mexico City. His wishes were respected and for the next ten years he was assigned to parishes in East Los Angeles. He spent nearly eight of those at his first assignment, which was at Resurrection Parish. From there, in 1971, he went to Our Lady of Guadalupe Parish on Hammel Street. After almost two years there, he was assigned for several months as Administrator Pro Tem for Saint Isabel Parish.

On April 24, 1973, Cardinal Timothy Manning called him to work in the inner city. He appointed him associate pastor as Saint Vibiana's Cathedral, where he himself resided, and Bishop Johnson served as Rector. For Father Steinbock, living and working with the Archbishop and his Auxiliary brought about the kind of respect and friendship that would significantly change his life. When Bishop Johnson became the Bishop of Orange in 1976, Father Steinbock remained on at the Cathedral as associate administrator under the new rector, Bishop Manuel Moreno. He gained a reputation of being able to effectively work with the poorest of the poor on skid row, while also dealing well with the dignitaries and special events associated with the Archdiocesan Cathedral. Honors and greater responsibilities soon followed.

Pope Paul VI honored him in 1978 by naming him a Papal Chamberlain with the title of Monsignor. Cardinal Manning appointed him to his Board of Consullers in 1979, the same year the Archdiocesan Priest Senate elected him as their President. Two years later, on February 1, 1981, the Cardinal appointed him as his Rector of the Cathedral.

Early in 1983, Bishop Johnson petitioned the Holy See for an auxiliary bishop to assist him with his continually growing diocese. On May 29, 1984, Pope John Paul II appointed Monsignor Steinbock Titular Bishop of Midila and Auxiliary Bishop to Bishop Johnson in the Diocese of Orange.

Cardinal Manning expressed the sentiments of all:"He is a precious priest and God's gift to the jurisdiction of Orange. We of the Cathedral Parish in Los Angeles will miss him much – the Cardinal who held him as a dear friend, but especially the poor of the parish, the street people, the little ones, the senior citizens. He has been a father and protector of his flock."

Bishop Johnson welcomed him and expressed his delight to be assisted by his close friend and collaborator from Saint Vibiana's.

On Saturday, July 14, 1984, Cardinal Manning – with Bishop Johnson and Bishop Moreno as co-consecrators – ordained Monsignor Steinbock to the order of bishop at Saint Columban's Church in Garden Grove.

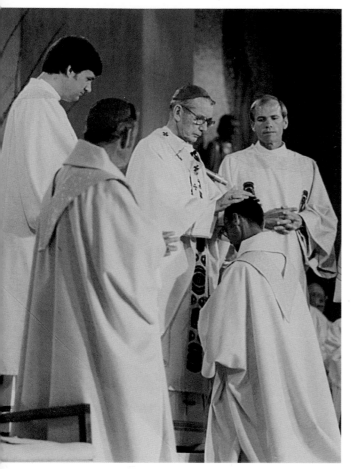

● *Bishop Steinbock's ordination*

● *Bishop Steinbock at podium*

On July 18, Bishop Johnson appointed Bishop Steinbock as his Vicar General. For the next two years the new bishop assisted Bishop Johnson in his many administrative and pastoral duties. These duties increased as Bishop Johnson's health declined.

When Bishop Johnson passed away on July 28, 1986, the Diocesan Consultors unanimously elected Bishop Steinbock as the Diocesan Administrator. He governed the diocese until the papal appointment of Bishop Norman McFarland as second Bishop of the Diocese of Orange.

Not long afterwards, Bishop Steinbock was placed in charge of his own diocese. On January 27, 1987, Pope John Paul II appointed him as Bishop of the Diocese of Santa Rosa. Then several years later, the Holy Father sent him to the larger Diocese of Fresno. He was officially installed there as the fourth Bishop of Fresno on November 25, 1991.

Although the Diocese of Orange enjoyed Bishop Steinbock's genial presence for only a few years, his dedicated ministry as its first auxiliary bishop, and then as administrator, is remembered as a real blessing, especially in the sad and difficult time of Bishop Johnson's failing health.

Changes in Leadership

Although Bishop Johnson remained active, his health steadily worsened over the next two years. Bishop Steinbock and Archbishop Clavel increasingly carried more of the leadership burdens. On July 28, 1986, the first Bishop of Orange, William R. Johnson, passed away of heart failure due to complications of advancing kidney disease. His good friend, Cardinal Manning, though then retired, presided and preached at his funeral that was held at Holy Family Cathedral on August 1, 1986. Bishop Steinbock served as Diocesan Administrator pending the appointment of a successor.

At the end of the year, on December 29, Pope John Paul II appointed Bishop Norman McFarland, Bishop of Reno-Las Vegas, as the second Bishop of Orange. Archbishop Roger Mahony presided at McFarland's installation in ceremonies at the UCI Bren Center in Irvine on February 24, 1987. In the meantime, Bishop Steinbock was appointed Bishop of Santa Rosa. He was formally installed there at the end of March.

● *Chrism Mass, 1986*

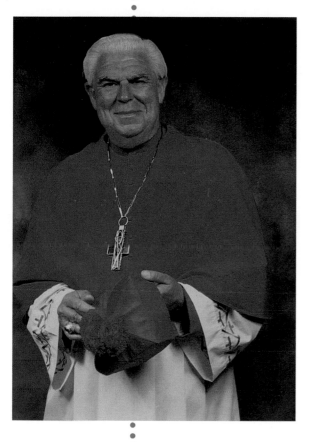

Most Reverend Norman Francis McFarland, D.D., J.C.D.

Second Bishop of Orange

Norman Francis McFarland was born in the Contra Costa County town of Martinez, California on February 21, 1922. He was the oldest of three sons born to Francis and Agnes (Kotchevar) McFarland.

Norman began his formal education in the public schools of Martinez. He became interested in the priesthood and entered Saint Joseph Seminary in Mountain View as a clerical candidate for the Archdiocese of San Francisco. After completing his studies there, he went to Saint Patrick Major Seminary in Menlo Park where he earned his Bachelor of Arts Degree in 1943 and then went on to complete the required courses in scripture and theology. On June 15, 1946, Archbishop John J. Mitty ordained him to the priesthood.

Father Norman McFarland, age 24, became assistant pastor at Saint Andrew's Parish in Oakland. After two years, Archbishop Mitty, who had a reputation for requiring special studies for his brightest and finest, sent Father McFarland to the Catholic University of America in Washington, D.C., where he earned a doctorate in canon law.

Upon his return to San Francisco, he worked for many years in the Archdiocesan Chancery Office in the Matrimonial Tribunal – primarily processing marriage cases. Besides these administrative activities, he helped out in the parishes where he resided; taught at San Francisco College for Women (1951-1958); and served for a time as Chaplain to the Cosmas and Damian Guild of Catholic Pharmacists.

On June 5, 1970, Pope Paul VI appointed forty-eight year old Monsignor McFarland the Titular Bishop of Bida and Auxiliary of San Francisco. On September 8, Archhbishop Joseph McGucken ordained him bishop. He then appointed him as Vicar for Finance, Vicar for Seminaries, and Pastor of Old Mission Dolores (San Francisco de Asis). The following year, Bishop McFarland celebrated his Silver Anniversary as a priest.

Four years later, on April 4, 1974, the Holy See sent Bishop McFarland as the Administrator for Temporal Affairs to the Diocese of Reno, then encompassing the entire State of Nevada. That diocese was in a major crisis due to extremely poor investments. Indeed, the Securities and Exchange Commission was demanding that it come up with 3.8 million dollars in cash (roughly $15 million in 2006 dollars) by April 12, or face bankruptcy proceedings. Bishop McFarland spent the next eight days on the phone, calling bishops around the country pleading for grants or low interest loans to bail them out. Thanks to his efforts and a spirit of compassion and collegiality among the bishops, he was able to raise four million dollars and meet the deadline. However, this amazing accomplishment was not the end of the problem. The diocese still faced millions of dollars in additional debt that also had to be paid, although the time requirements were not as immediate. McFarland continued searching for sources of financing to meet all these obligations. He was successful, but it would be ten years before the diocese would be debt free. It was a long, painful, up-hill climb.

In the meantime, with the official retirement of his predecessor, Bishop McFarland was appointed the Apostolic Administrator of the Diocese of Reno by Pope Paul VI on December

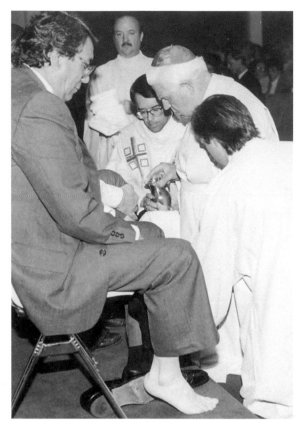

• Holy Thursday, 1989

• In the office

6, 1974. A little more than a year later, confident that the problems were in capable hands, the Holy Father appointed him Bishop of Reno. Archbishop Joseph McGucken, in the presence of Archbishop Jean Jadot, the Apostolic Delegate, formally installed him as such on March 31, 1976, in Reno's Pioneer Auditorium. It is unlikely anyone envied him the position and the tasks that lie ahead.

[Note: Just the day before, Archbishop Jadot had announced the creation of the new Diocese of Orange.]

Acknowledging the growth of the diocese and the centering of its population in the main cities to the north and the south, Bishop McFarland requested the Vatican to rename the diocese, which it did on October 13, 1976: It became the Diocese of Reno-Las Vegas. He tried to divide his time between the two major cities, but also traveled extensively throughout the 110,829 square mile state, visiting its far-flung parishes and missions. Besides traveling to administer the Sacrament of Confirmation, he made it a goal to spend weekends in different parishes, where he celebrated Mass, preached, and showed his personal support for their priests and people.

Although he had to keep an eagle eye on the budget, he was careful not to jeopardize essential programs. In fact, he increased the number of projects aiding the less fortunate. Actually, during his tenure the budget for Catholic Charities went from $360, 000 to $4.5 million.

Bishop McFarland is also remembered for his many writings: He contributed articles to various newspapers and published, six times a year, the Frontier Shepherd, which provided a wealth of historical and pastoral information on the Church in Nevada. He also delivered radio broadcasts reaching out to inactive Catholics and those with no religious affiliation. And he was known as a fearless promoter of Catholic values and a fierce opponent of any position contrary to them. After 12 years in Nevada, he had become a familiar part of the landscape. He was widely respected and admired, not only for rescuing the diocese from its financial crisis, but also for putting it back on a solid basis and restoring its pastoral confidence. He had become, as he used to say, "a Nevadan by adoption and affection." He expected to spend the rest of his days there and was content with the prospect. By 1986, he had already been a priest for 40 years and a bishop for 16. He had even secured a burial plot so his earthly remains would literally become one with the landscape he had grown to love.

Holy Mother Church, however, had other plans. Pope John Paul II appointed him the second Bishop of Orange in California. The announcement came from Archbishop Pio Laghi, the Apostolic Pro Nuncio in Washington, D.C., on December 29, 1986. The installation was set for February 24, 1987, just three days after his 65th birthday.

The new assignment was not a simple reward for a job-well-done in Nevada. It was a major challenge given to a person of proven abilities. The Diocese of Reno-Las Vegas had grown from 90,000 Catholics to 144,000 during his time there. He now faced a Catholic population of well over a half million – although compressed into an area 141 times smaller than Nevada. There would be no leisure ministry in the Diocese of Orange, but he would not have to travel so far to shepherd his abundant flock. It was something of an understatement when he first addressed it: "I greet you with a sense of anticipation and excitement." Whatever anxiety level he may have had, there was little chance that a man of his stature would shrink from the challenge.

On his first official visit to his new diocese, Bishop McFarland paid compliment to Bishop Johnson and declared his own intention: "It is my sincere hope that I may be able to build upon the solid foundation laid by the First Bishop of Orange whom we hold in fond memory, Bishop William Johnson, your beloved shepherd and my dear friend."

Many Orange Countians had never seen or heard of Bishop McFarland. But after their first encounter, it was unlikely they would ever forget him. At six foot five and 240 pounds he was definitely a bishop to be looked up to. For many the first introduction came by way of the various words and phrases used to describe him in the interviews and articles written about him at the time:

"A big bear of a man with a full head of silver white hair...a shocking white cloud of hair...husky, white haired and bushy browed...a large man with a large personality...a physical and mental giant...he is a giant, especially with his mitre...he casts an imposing but kind shadow...an impressive man... big physically and big intellectually...well read...an avid reader and a prolific and eloquent writer...He's a bear...He's a big teddy bear...the Big Mac...the Absolute Norm...Stormin' Norman...one of a kind... a gentle marshmallow...affable...a good mixture of administrative and pastoral skills...a good sense of humor...a colorful communicator...a real son of the Church...a doctrinal conservative...orthodox... ultra loyal to the Holy Father...a strong and sure leader...a very learned priest...a lovely man...a man of faith...a firm disciplinarian...stern and intimidating...startlingly blunt...fierce...a tornado waiting to happen...fearfully, wonderfully made...a very fine gentleman...everyone who knows him loves him...you couldn't say enough good things about him."

If he was unknown to many in Orange County, that certainly didn't last long. The mosaic of opinion that preceded him pictured an impressive person, not likely to be overlooked.

On February 22, 1987, Bishop McFarland formally presented his credentials in the public Ceremony of Canonical Possession at Holy Family Cathedral in Orange. In his homily, he recognized that many might wonder "what sort of man" stood before them. He was happy to reveal this of himself: It was his absolute conviction that the strength of the Church is in the local parish communities, "where the action is." This he would hold as a priority and this is where he would focus his attention. He added that it must be understood by the local parishes, that they have their strength in their relationship to the larger Church in the diocese and in the world. He also spoke of his motto, which is "In Veritate Ambulare" (To Walk in Truth). He said he would never lie, but also added jokingly that this might not always be perceived as a virtue in his case. He would be honest with people and expected the same from them. In the larger sense, walking in the truth meant the determination to walk in the path of the Truth, the Word of God, the Spirit of Truth.

• *Msgr. Michael Driscoll and the Marywood staff welcome Bishop McFarland to the Orange Diocese*

• Bishop Mc Farland installed as second Bishop of Orange

• Knights and Ladies of Malta Knights and Ladies of the Holy Sepulcher

On February 24, 1987, Archbishop Roger Mahony, in the presence of Cardinal Timothy Manning, installed Bishop Norman McFarland as the Second Bishop of Orange in ceremonies at the Bren Center of the University of California at Irvine. In his homily, Bishop McFarland reflected on the mission ahead for himself and the people of Orange: "Now it is our turn. To us who are the Church in Orange, has been committed a sacred trust to emulate the faith and match the generosity of the past and build splendidly upon the foundation that has been laid."

The first decade of the diocese under Bishop Johnson had been a time of formation and organization. For the next ten years, Bishop McFarland worked to strengthen, consolidate, and refine that work in what he liked to call "this favored portion of the Lord's Vineyard." Although no one doubted his authority, he often joked that he was in sales, not management. He had a good product to sell, he said, and, like the best things in life, it was free. Of course the product was the gospel, the good news of Jesus Christ. It was no joke that this was the driving force that motivated his ministry as Bishop of Orange. He had declared it as a pledge from the very beginning: "It is my firm resolve that Christ alone shall fire my speech and guide my service."

Because of his outstanding ad-ministrative skills and successes, his pastoral care might be underappreciated. Aside from the fact that good administration is in itself an important pastoral service, Bishop McFarland spent many hours out of the office visiting parishes, administering Confirmations, attending religious jubilees, supporting charitable causes, blessing and breaking ground for new church projects, dedicating completed projects, and making himself available for other pastoral requests.

• Bishop Mc Farland with newly confirmed

A special example of his pastoral care stands out in his extensive writings that appeared regularly throughout the course of his ministry. In them he addressed a wide range of issues relevant both to an individual's spiritual journey, and also to the application of Christ's teaching to problems affecting the world at large. It is obvious these writings are the product of personal depth, careful reflection, and a generous commitment of time. Many have found in them food for thought and soul from a bishop conscious of his pastoral teaching ministry.

On June 18, 1996, Bishop McFarland celebrated his Golden Anniversary as a priest and his Silver Anniversary as a bishop. Among the many well wishers who attended his Mass of Thanksgiving at Holy Family Cathedral were some 200 priests and religious and 44 bishops from around the country, including Cardinal Roger Mahony, Cardinal Bevelacqua, and Bishop Tod Brown. Afterwards, at a large reception in his honor, he was thoroughly toasted and roasted by friends who thought correctly that it was now safe to do so.

In February of 1998, near the end of his time as Bishop of Orange, there was a very real danger that it might also be the end of his life. Doctors discovered a large aortic aneurysm in his abdomen, complicated by a weakened heart and lung condition. A three and a half hour surgery at Hoag Hospital proved a success. After an appropriate recovery period, he was again able to look forward to a reasonably healthy and enjoyable retirement.

Following his resignation at age 75, Bishop McFarland has remained active carrying out successfully a declaration he made to his priests in a final letter as Bishop of Orange: "I look forward to remaining in Peter's boat as it sails the See of Orange, doing whatever might be appropriate and useful."

Asked once if he might be interested in a promotion to some other assignment after Orange, he responded that he hoped his next assignment would be heaven, since anything less would be a disappointment after Orange County.

Archbishop Clavel

Archbishop Clavel continued to assist Bishop McFarland for the next year and a half, but, on October 13, 1988, he died from a sudden heart attack. Bishop McFarland presided at his funeral at Holy Family Cathedral. Clavel's remains were then flown to his homeland in Panama for funeral and burial.

Bishop Driscoll

On December 29, 1989, Pope John Paul II appointed Monsignor Michael Driscoll as auxiliary bishop for the Diocese of Orange. Driscoll's experience as Chancellor and Vicar General in the Orange Diocese suited him well for this position.

Most Reverend Michael Patrick Driscoll, D.D., M.S.W.

Michael Patrick Driscoll was born in Long Beach on August 8, 1939. He is the son of Edmund P. Driscoll and Bernardine (Jarding) Driscoll and the older brother of twins, Tom and Kay.

In July of 1952, Michael, age 12, was accepted into the prestigious Mitchell Boys Choir, famous for its work in the movies, radio, and television. He spent a year touring with the choir and attending its private school.

In pursuit of a desire for the priesthood, which he had considered as early as fourth grade, he entered the seminary for the Archdiocese of Los Angeles. (During summers at home, he sometimes worked at his parent's Long Beach grocery store.) After completing the full course of studies at Saint John's Major Seminary in Camarillo, he was ordained to the priesthood by James Francis Cardinal McIntyre on May 1, 1965 at Saint Vibiana's Cathedral.

Father Driscoll then spent the next eight years in parish ministry. He served as associate pastor at Saint Anselm's in Los Angeles, Saint Finbar's in Burbank, and Saint Brendan's in Los Angeles. His priestly talents came to the attention of Auxiliary Bishop Johnson who asked him to join him in special ministry in Catholic Charities. Initially this meant going back to school. He attended the University of Southern California where he graduated with a master's degree in social work (M.S.W.) in 1975. Afterwards, he became associate director of the Catholic Welfare Bureau. He took up residence at Saint Catherine's Military School in Anaheim.

• *Monsignor Driscoll*

• *"Guess who?"*

In 1976, when Bishop Johnson became the Bishop of Orange, he asked Father Driscoll to become his right hand man, serving as his secretary, chancellor, vocation director, vicar for charities, and anything else that might be needed. It was a far-ranging assignment encompassing much that was unknown, but, of course, he accepted the challenge in good grace and went to work helping to build up the new diocese for Orange County.

In March of 1979, Pope John Paul II honored him by naming him a Prelate of Honor with the title of Monsignor. Bishop Johnson then added to his responsibilities by appointing him pastor of Our Lady Queen of the Angles Parish in Newport Beach, where he served from 1980 to 1984.

Monsignor Driscoll faithfully carried out his broad range of duties as the diocese developed through the 1980's. He was there to welcome and assist Auxiliary Bishop John Steinbock. He was there to bid a sad farewell to his bishop, mentor, and close friend Bishop Johnson who passed away in 1987. He welcomed and served the second Bishop of Orange, Norman McFarland, who soon recognized and admired Monsignor Driscoll's effective work in the diocese. When Bishop Steinbock left Orange to become the Bishop of Santa Rosa, Bishop McFarland appointed Driscoll as his Vicar General.

On December 19, 1989, Pope John Paul II appointed Monsignor Driscoll, age 50, as the Titular Bishop of Massita and Auxiliary Bishop of Orange. The bishop-elect responded publicly saying, "I am awed and very humbled by this request, and it is with some fear as well as a great amount of trust in God that I say, yes." Bishop McFarland praised him, pointing out his "outstanding character and competence" and his "intellectual and spiritual qualities." He added,

"One immediately notes his priestliness and pastoral sense, his dedication and administrative skills."

• *Press conference*

In the presence of the Apostolic Nuncio, Archbishop Gabriel Montalvo, and Cardinal Roger Mahony, Bishop McFarland ordained Bishop Driscoll at Holy Family Cathedral on March 6, 1990. Bishop Thomas J. Connelly (Bishop of Baker, Oregon) and Bishop John Steinbock (Bishop of Santa Rosa) served as principal co-consecrators. Besides a large representation of bishops, clergy, and religious, a capacity crowd of family and friends filled the cathedral.

• *Bishop Driscoll ordained*

Following the retirement of Bishop McFarland, Bishop Tod Brown was appointed the third Bishop of Orange and was installed on September 3, 1998. The following year, on June 19, Pope John Paul II appointed Bishop Driscoll to the Diocese of Boise, Idaho, where Bishop Brown had previously served. Bishop Michael Driscoll was installed as the seventh Bishop of Boise on March 18, 1999, at Saint John the Evangelist Cathedral.

The Diocese of Orange owes much of its successful beginnings, its vitality, and strong pastoral development to Bishop Michael Driscoll. He served it faithfully and well from the start and through the next 23 years – the last nine of them as auxiliary bishop.

• *Bishop Driscoll*

House of Prayer

In order to assist the clergy in their spiritual growth, the diocese planned a retreat center for priests. The Orange City Council approved the construction of a House of Prayer for Priests at the end of 1981. It was completed in 1983 and dedicated by Bishop Johnson on November 11 of that year. Across the street from Holy Sepulcher Cemetery, the House of Prayer afforded a quiet environment where priests could readily contemplate time, accountability, and mortality.

St. Michael's Abbey

During these years, Orange County was blessed with its first abbot. Saint Michael's Norbertine Priory was raised to the level of abbey and the Very Reverend Ladislas K. Parker, O.Praem., its religious superior, was elected as its first abbot. Bishop Johnson presided at his abbatial blessing on September 19, 1984, and dedicated the abbey on the following day.

• *Confirmation*

• *Bishop Johnson and Abbot Ladislas K. Parker, O. Praem*

Meeting the Needs

For the growing diocese, expansion was an important agenda item and resulted in the formation of new parishes. Our Lady of Guadalupe (Delhi) and Our Lady of Guadalupe (Third and Grand), both in Santa Ana, were given parish status in 1980. That same year, Bishop Johnson established Saint Timothy Parish in Laguna Niguel. In 1981, the venerable Saint Edward's Chapel in Capistrano Beach became the new Parish of San Felipe de Jesus. In 1985, the mission church of Our Lady of Lourdes in Santa Ana was also given parochial status. And at the end of the decade in 1989, Bishop McFarland established the Parish of San Francisco Solano in the new community of Rancho Santa Margarita.

Building community in the 1980's was often quite literal. For the diocese, these years were a blur of planning, fundraising, groundbreakings, construction, blessings, and dedications. Indeed, the groundbreakings not only joyfully commenced new projects, they also produced an array of golden shovels.

"Bless all those who have worked to contribute to provide this site on which a church is to be built. Today may they rejoice in a work just begun, soon may they celebrate the sacraments in your temple, and in time to come may they praise you forever in heaven."
(Rite of Blessing)

"Lord, fill this place with your presence, and extend your hand to all who call upon you. May your word here proclaimed and your sacraments here celebrated strengthen the hearts of all the faithful." (Dedication Mass)

Site Blessings and Groundbreakings

Date	Facility	City	Officiant
7/13/80	St. Vincent de Paul Center	Huntington Beach	+Johnson
11/16/80	St. Martin de Porres	Yorba Linda	+Johnson
2/22/81	St. Timothy Center	Laguna Niguel	+Johnson
1/31/82	San Juan Capistrano	San Juan Capistrano	+Johnson
12/17/82	Santiago de Compostela	El Toro/Lake Forest	+Johnson
5/1/84	Vietnamese Center	Santa Ana	+Johnson
5/20/84	Korean Martyrs Center	Westminster	+Johnson
1/20/85	John Paul II Polish Center	Yorba Linda	+Steinbock
6/1/86	Holy Spirit	Fountain Valley	+Steinbock

Dedications

Date	Facility	City	Officiant
5/31/81	St. Vincent de Paul Center	Huntington Beach	+Johnson
6/14/81	Our Lady of Lourdes*	Santa Ana	+Johnson
9/26/82	St. John Neumann	Irvine	Cardinal Krol
10/3/82	St. Timothy Center	Laguna Niguel	+Johnson
9/16/82	St. Martin de Porres	Yorba Linda	+Johnson
10/26/86	Holy Cross Melkite	Fullerton	+Tawil
11/14/86	O.L. Guadalupe (Grand)*	Santa Ana	Archbishop Clavel
2/8/87	San Juan Capistrano	San Juan Capistrano	Cardinal Manning
12/6/87	Holy Spirit	Fountain Valley	+McFarland
6/19/88	St. Cecelia*	Tustin	+McFarland
2/5/89	St. Joseph*	Santa Ana	+McFarland

[* Re-dedication of a renovated church]

St. John Neumann, Irvine

St. Martin de Porres, Yorba Linda

St Timothy, Laguna Niguel

St Joseph Parish centennial 1987. Samoan entertainment

• *Msgr. Sammon and Msgr. Driscoll at Santa Margarita High School groundbreaking*

• *Santa Margarita High School construction*

• *Bishop Mc Farland at Santa Margarita Dedication*

Catholic Education

Various milestones also marked the path of Catholic education in the 1980's. Marywood High School graduated its 45th and last class in 1980 and its facilities became the diocesan headquarters. In 1981, Saint Edward the Confessor Parish in Dana Point opened a Catholic elementary school – the first new elementary school in the new diocese. In July of 1982, the FCC granted the Diocese of Orange a license allowing it to broadcast educational television. Also in that year, the loss of Marywood High School was alleviated somewhat when the O'Neill Family of Rancho Mission Viejo donated land for a new Catholic high school to be built in their planned community of Rancho Santa Margarita. In one of his last public appearances, Bishop Johnson presided at the groundbreaking of Santa Margarita Catholic High School in 1986. The new, sprawling campus opened in September of 1987 and was dedicated by Bishop Norman McFarland on December 5. And, closing out the decade in 1989, Saint Catherine's Academy, the historic Dominican school, celebrated its centennial in Anaheim.

• *High School Campaign Cabinet*

Charity

During this decade, there were also considerable advances in charitable projects. In 1981, Columbia House opened in Garden Grove as a respite care facility. In 1982, Bishop Johnson dedicated the Casa Santa Maria Senior Housing facility in Buena Park. In 1983, Monsignor John Sammon blessed the St. Vincent de Paul Food Distribution Center in Orange. And in 1986, Bishop John Steinbock blessed the new facilities of Casa Teresa, a shelter for women in crisis pregnancy in Santa Ana. Precious Life Shelter in Los Alamitos was founded shortly thereafter. And, finally, fundraising for Catholic Charities took a swing in the right direction with the first ever Bishop McFarland Open at the Western Hills Country Club in 1988.

Spiritual Life

Special efforts promoting spiritual growth also graced this period. In 1984, the RENEW Program began in 43 parishes as an effort to inspire spiritual renewal and greater involvement in parish faith life. In 1985, the Center for Spiritual Development was dedicated on the grounds of Saint Joseph Motherhouse in Orange. And in 1988, Bishop McFarland brought Catholic professionals together by inaugurating in the diocese the custom of the Red Mass for justice and government personnel, and the White Mass for those involved in the health care professions.

1980 Orange County
Population Increase: 478,986
Los Angeles
Population Increase : 1,292,441
California
Population Increase : 6,091,459

1990's

1990 Orange County
Population: 2,410,556

Los Angeles
County Population: 8,769,944

California
Population 29,760,021

Closing the Century

The last decade of the 20th century witnessed new and important developments in the Diocese of Orange. Monsignor Michael Driscoll, who had been involved in virtually every aspect of decision-making in the diocese since its beginning, became Auxiliary Bishop for the Diocese of Orange on March 6, 1990. And Bishop McFarland, known for his skill in untangling administrative problems, was appointed by the Holy See as the Apostolic Administrator of the Diocese of Fresno in May of 1991. Until Bishop John Steinbock became the new Bishop of Fresno on November 25, Bishop McFarland governed two dioceses simultaneously – unusual, but not beyond the capabilities of a man of his stature.

Toward the end of 1993, both Bishop McFarland and Bishop Driscoll traveled to Rome to confer with Pope John Paul II and present the Ad Limina report on the status of the diocese. The Holy Father asked Bishop Driscoll if there were still any oranges left in Orange County. Obviously, the pope was aware of the county's urbanization and disappearing orchards.

In 1995, Pope John Paul II sent Bishop McFarland a letter congratulating him for his 25th anniversary as a bishop. Bishop McFarland deferred its public celebration until the following year when, on June 18, the 20th anniversary of the diocese, he offered a Mass of Thanksgiving, followed by a festive reception. This commemorated both his Golden Anniversary as a priest and his Silver Anniversary as a bishop. No doubt, he also took fiscal joy in the fact that he had spared the diocese the cost of two individual celebrations.

A New Shepherd

Not long after achieving these personal, ministerial milestones, Bishop McFarland also arrived at his 75th Birthday (February 21, 1997), and in accord with Church policy, he submitted to the Holy See his request for retirement. After a respectable period of time allowing the local clergy to engage in the ecclesiastical sport of speculation, the Holy Father, on June 30, 1998, appointed Bishop Tod David Brown, Bishop of Idaho, to succeed McFarland and become the third Bishop of Orange. Cardinal Roger Mahony, as Metropolitan Archbishop, installed Bishop Brown at Holy Family Cathedral on September 3, 1998. Later in the month, the new Bishop of Orange met with Pope John Paul II and presented the five-year Ad Limina report on the state of the diocese of which he had been bishop less than a month.

Several months later, Bishop Michael Driscoll learned that the Holy Father had appointed him to Idaho, Bishop Brown's former See. He was installed there as Bishop of Boise on March 18, 1999. Bishop Driscoll served in the Diocese of Orange for nearly 23 years.

Bishop Brown traveled widely throughout the diocese, acquainting himself with its people, parishes, and organizations. It soon became clear that the new bishop was eager to serve and possessed his own style of leadership. He was

eager to learn and also committed to lead.

One of his early decisions was to promote a greater role for women in Church leadership. In 1999, he appointed Sister Katherine ("Kit") Gray, C.S.J. as Chancellor of the Diocese, a role traditionally held by an ordained priest. Two years later when Sister Kit was elected General Superior of the Sisters of Saint Joseph, Bishop Brown appointed Mrs. Shirl Giacomi as the new diocesan chancellor.

Further Expansion

Rising costs and declining clerical personnel presented a problem in keeping up with the growing population. Nevertheless, during this decade two new parishes were created to help meet the challenge. In July of 1996, Bishop McFarland established Saint Thomas More Parish in Irvine – the third parish for Irvine since the beginning of the diocese. And in 1999, Bishop Brown established Corpus Christi Parish for the new community of Aliso Viejo.

Of course, the 1990's had its share of building projects as devoted Catholics planned for the future, shouldered their responsibilities, and worked hard to make their dreams a reality for their communities.

• *St. Pius V construction, Buena Park*

• *St. Elizabeth Ann Seton, Irvine*

• *St. Edward the Confessor, Dana Point*

Site Blessing and Groundbreakings

Date	Facility	City	Officiant
7/26/92	St. Pius V Church	Buena Park	+Driscoll
9/26/92	Vietnamese Center	Santa Ana	+McFarland
1/10/93	St. Elizabeth Ann Seton	Irvine	+Driscoll
9/8/96	St. Timothy Church	Laguna Niguel	+McFarland
7/4/98	St. Thomas More Center	Irvine	Msgr. Sammon
6/27/99	St. Callistus Church	Garden Grove	+Brown

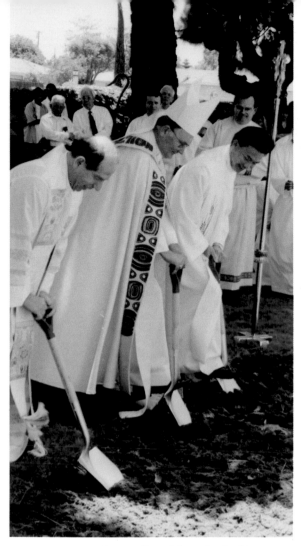

• *Groundbreaking, St. Callistus, Garden Grove*

Catholic Education

Several projects highlight advances in the diocesan Catholic education ministry at this time. In 1991, Bishop McFarland dedicated the Karcher Center at Rosary Catholic High School. In 1995, he blessed Serra Catholic Elementary School in Rancho Santa Margarita. 1995 saw the beginning of regional rather than single parish schools. Bishop McFarland blessed Serra Catholic Elementary School in Rancho Santa Margarita. This regional school originally served the parishes of San Francisco Solano, St. Kilian and Santiago de Compostela. Today it also serves Holy Trinity in Ladera Ranch. And in 1998, Bishop Brown blessed St. Francis of Assisi Catholic Elementary School in Yorba Linda. This school served St. Martin de Porres and San Antonio de Padua in Anaheim Hills. Today it also serves Santa Clara de Asis in Yorba Linda. And in 1999, as the decade came to a close, Mater Dei Catholic High School began a multi-year, multi-million dollar project to completely renovate and update its aging facilities.

In 1998, following state regulations and warnings, Bishop McFarland called for a diocesan wide policy of seismic studies and earthquake related retrofitting where necessary. Public safety would take precedence over all other proposed construction projects.

• *Mater Dei High School*

Dedications

Date	Facility	City	Officiant
9/12/93	Blessed Sacrament*	Westminster	+McFarland
3/26/94	Vietnamese Center	Santa Ana	+McFarland
11/6/94	St. Pius V Church	Buena Park	+McFarland
12/11/94	St. Edward the Confessor	Dana Point	+McFarland
11/5/95	St. John Maron	Anaheim	+Chedid
5/26/96	San Francisco Solano	Rancho Santa Margarita	+McFarland
12/5/99	St. Norbert Church*	Orange	+Brown

[* Rededication of a renovated church]

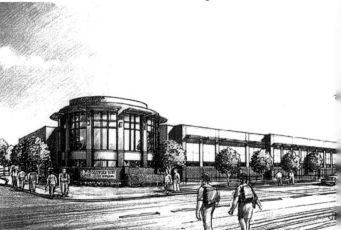

Developments in Ministry

Other areas of ministry in the diocese also showed great progress. Mary's Shelter a home for unwed teen mothers was established in September of 1994. In that same year, Mission Hospital in the Saddleback Valley became a major addition to the St. Joseph Health Care System. Saint Francis Home in Santa Ana, operated by the Franciscan Sisters of the Immaculate Conception, celebrated their Golden Jubilee in 1995. The successful Saint Vincent de Paul Food Bank gained the advantage of national affiliation, becoming the Second Harvest Food Bank of Orange County. In 1997, the Catholic Worker Organization celebrated ten years of committed service to the poor and homeless in Orange

* Bishop Brown with Pope John Paul II

County. These and many other good works gave evidence to a lively Catholic spirit by "Doers of the Word" throughout the diocese.

Spiritual Life

An active Catholic life needs constant spiritual renewal, an on-going mission for every faith community. Several new resources for this renewal emerged during this period. In 1990, Bishop McFarland broke ground in Santa Ana for the Heart of Jesus Retreat Center, staffed by the Sisters Devoted to the Sacred Heart. In 1997, the SCRC (Charismatic) convention in Anaheim drew some 10,000 participants, the largest such gathering in the United States. In 1998, Bishop Driscoll presided at the solemn blessing of the Jesuit run Loyola Institute for Spirituality at St. Joseph's Center in Orange. And of course as the 1990's came to a close, special spiritual preparations were underway for the end of the century and the beginning of a new millennium – all time and all ages consecrated to the Lord: "Christ yesterday and today, the beginning and the end...to Him be glory and power, through every age forever" (Easter Vigil).

1990 Orange County
Population Increase: 435,733
Los Angeles
Population Increase : 749,394
California
Population Increase : 4,139,979

Most Reverend Tod David Brown, D.D.

Third Bishop of Orange

Tod David Brown was born on November 15, 1936, in San Francisco. He was the first of two children born to George and Edna Anne Brown. His father worked as an accountant and also in food services. His mother was a homemaker and later became a social worker. In 1940, another boy, Daniel, was born into the family.

The boys attended various Northern California schools for their early education. Tod received his First Holy Communion at Saint Anne of the Sunset Parish in San Francisco. Later, he learned to be an altar server.

Eventually, the Brown family made their home in Santa Cruz, where Mary Star of the Sea became their home parish. Tod had various thoughts about what he might do in life. He considered law and medicine. He also had early thoughts about the priesthood. It was a calling that was neither clear nor sudden, but a vocation that gradually developed as time and grace provided.

In 1950, Tod Brown entered Ryan Preparatory Seminary in Fresno. It was a six-year seminary consisting of four years of high school and two years of college. The classes were very small and the Jesuit professors well trained, so it was a quality educational experience. His vocation continued to be nurtured by the inspiration and example of members of the faculty, as well as by good priests he had known earlier.

In 1956, Tod graduated from Ryan Prep and moved to Saint John Seminary in Camarillo to continue his priestly formation. It is interesting to note that among his new classmates were Roger Mahony, Bill Levada, and George Niederaurer – later known as Cardinal Roger Mahoney, Archbishop of Los Angeles; Cardinal William Levada, Prefect of the Congregation for the Doctrine of the Faith; and Archbishop George Niederaurer, Archbishop of San Francisco.

Following his graduation from college at Saint John's, Tod's bishop chose him to attend the North American College in Rome. William Levada was also among his classmates there. Both of them studied theology at the venerable Gregorian University under the professorship of such highly respected luminaries as Joseph Fuchs and Bernard Lonergan.

While he was in Rome, he witnessed an important event in Church history. He was present in Saint Peter's Square for the announcement and the presentation of the successor to Pope Pius XII, Pope John XXIII. Later on, he was privileged to have an audience with the new pope, the one who would soon call together the bishops of the world to convene at the Second Vatican Council. As a seminarian in Rome, Tod was present at the Basilica of St. Paul's Outside the Wall when the Holy Father first announced his intention to call the Council.

After receiving his bachelor's degree in Sacred Theology, Tod returned to California. He finished his preparation for the priesthood at Saint John's Seminary and on May 1, 1963, was ordained to the priesthood. Father Brown celebrated his first Mass with family, friends, and fellow parishioners at his home parish, Star of the Sea, in Santa Cruz.

These were exciting times. The Vatican Council was just underway and the world watched its deliberations and developments. Pope John XXIII passed away on June 3, 1963, and a new pope, Paul VI, was elected on June 21. The Council would conclude its formal sessions

The Most Reverend Tod David Brown, D.D.
Installed as Third Bishop of Orange
September 3, 1998

in 1965, but its ideals, its renewal, and even its inevitable controversies would have long lasting effects that would make life as a priest in the Church considerably different from when teenager Tod Brown entered the seminary in 1950.

Young Father Brown's first priestly assignment took him to a place very different from his Monterey home. He was appointed associate pastor (now known as parochial vicar) of Our Lady of Perpetual Help Parish in Bakersfield, the sunny southern gateway to the great San Joaquin Valley. For four and a half years he labored and learned there, carrying out his duties, as he would later recall, among "many wonderful people." During this time he also enjoyed serving as Campus Minister at Bakersfield College.

From Our Lady of Perpetual Help – true to her title – the young, but now experienced Father Brown, transferred to Seaside, California on the Monterey Peninsula where he became parochial vicar of Saint Francis Xavier Parish.

On December 14, 1967, Pope Paul VI separated Monterey and Fresno (merged into one in 1922) into two separate dioceses. This restored Monterey, the first diocese in California, back to its former status as a diocese. This was anticipated and regarded as a long looked forward to and welcome change. At the official ceremonies presided over by the Apostolic Delegate, Father Brown served as the master of ceremonies.

Father Tod Brown's 25 years in the Diocese of Monterey were a succession of appointments to greater, more demanding responsibilities. He became the Pastor of Saint Francis Xavier Parish in Seaside. He also became the Diocesan Director of Religious Education, and later Director of Education; held various positions in the Diocesan Curia; participated in the Presbyteral Council; and served on various important committees: Vocations, Catholic Charities, Building, Finance, and the Priests' Pension Plan.

Monsignor Brown assisted the bishop as Consultor, Moderator of the Curia, Chancellor, and Vicar General. There was very little that went on in the pastoral leadership of the Diocese of Monterey that did not in some way involve his influence. Because of his abilities and hard work, he became, in fact, the bishop's right hand man.

In 1988, the year of Monsignor Brown's silver jubilee as a priest, Pope John Paul II appointed him Bishop of Boise, Idaho, succeeding Bishop Sylvester Treinen who had retired. He was ordained Bishop and installed as the sixth Bishop of Boise on April 3, 1989, in the Boise State University Pavilion.

Of course, as a bishop he received the honor of the fullness of the priesthood, but he also received the fullness of responsibility that went along with it. In addition, he had to distance himself from what had been familiar, and take over a leadership role in a place where he had to overcome the disadvantage of being a stranger.

While proclaiming the Good News of Christ remained the common denominator, there were many changes facing Bishop Brown; the Diocese of Boise represented quite a contrast from the Monterey experience. Geographically, it was ten times larger – 84,290 square miles, the whole State of Idaho. Over all, it had a quarter of a million more people, but only half as many Catholics as the Monterey Diocese. For its new spiritual shepherd it meant a far greater pasturage with far fewer Catholic sheep. It was an assignment much in need of his experience, enthusiasm, and energy.

During his first years in Idaho, Bishop Brown participated in two important historical commemorations. The first was the 150 Anniversary of the First Mass in Idaho. This celebration was held in 1990 at Henry's Lake in Eastern Idaho. The second was the celebration of the Centennial of the Diocese that took place in 1993. These events marked both the pioneering and ongoing presence of the Church in the development of Idaho's rich history.

Besides the normal duties of a diocesan bishop – visitations, pastoral vigilance, confirmations, endless meetings, and both spiritual and temporal administration – various highlights stand out in Bishop Brown's Idaho ministry. He brought his religious education leadership experience to bear by emphasizing retreat ministry in programs for youth and young adults. He championed life issues by campaigning to preserve the lives of the unborn; working to eliminate the death penalty; and expanding diocesan wide efforts to better meet the needs of the sick, the imprisoned, the poor and homeless.

In an effort to encourage better consultation and collaboration, Bishop Brown initiated a study called "Continuing Our Journey." This process resulted in a network of pastoral councils, six deanery councils, and a diocesan pastoral council – each level offering wider opportunities for advising the bishop on pastoral and other significant issues.

He also broadened the Office of Hispanic Ministry, changing it to Multicultural Ministry, making it more inclusive and better addressing the needs of Native Americans, Basques, and a growing number of Asian and other immigrants.

In 1995, he launched a strategic planning process called the "Vitality Project." This project was designed to keep the Church in Idaho vital as it approached the new millennium. It encouraged greater lay participation in the life and mission of the Church and the formulation of new approaches to the recruitment of candidates for the priesthood and permanent diaconate. It also led to the development of vision and mission statements by each parish, encouraging clearer priorities and better focus. In some cases it resulted in the difficult but wise decision to consolidate some parish communities in order to more effectively employ diocesan human and material resources. Mainly, it engaged a larger number of people – laity, religious, and clergy – in both the popular and unpopular decisions required to promote and advance the church's pastoral mission.

While exercising his spiritual leadership in the Diocese of Boise, Bishop Brown was known for his willingness to face the difficulties and make the hard decisions. This sense of responsibility and courage matured him into a seasoned and experienced bishop ready for even greater responsibilities.

While attending the U.S. Bishop's Spring Meeting in Pittsburgh on June 19, 1998, Archbishop William Levada of San Francisco, his former classmate, tapped him on the shoulder and told him the Apostolic Nuncio, Archbishop Agostino Cacciavillan, wanted to see him outside in the hall. It was there that Bishop Tod Brown was informed that Pope John Paul II was appointing him the third Bishop of Orange in California.

• *Religious Education Congress Mass*

• *Blessing of Our Lady of Peace Center*

• *Press conference*

• *Bishop Brown at canonical reception*

• *Installation Mass*

The announcement was made public on June 30. On this day, Bishop McFarland and Bishop Brown hosted a joint press conference at Marywood Center. It was there that the new Bishop of Orange proclaimed a personal mission statement: " My goal is to be a successful shepherd of the Church; to lead our people into an even deeper spiritual life, and to enable our community to continue to give witness to the Gospel values we cherish."

After two months of hastily settling affairs in Idaho, rearranging his life, and moving to Orange County, Bishop Brown formally presented his canonical appointment at a ceremony of reception and welcome at Holy Family Cathedral on September 2, 1998. The following day, Cardinal Roger Mahony, in the presence of the Apostolic Nuncio and many bishops, clergy, religious, and laity, formally installed his friend and classmate, Tod Brown, as the third Bishop of Orange in California.

Like Bishop McFarland before him, he found himself shepherding a much larger flock in a far more concentrated area. More than a hundred Orange Counties could fit into Idaho's vast boundaries, yet Orange County contained more than five times as many Catholics. Although the number of hours in the day and the number of days in the week remained the same, the needs and expectations had increased significantly. Although the challenge must have seemed daunting, he accepted it with the trust of the Holy Father, the advantage of previous experience, the talents and dedication of those who welcomed him, and the confidence that the Lord whose providence led him to these new responsibilities would companion him with His grace.

• *Huntington Beach*

9 The Millenium and Beyond

2000-2007

2000 Orange County
Population: 2,846,289

Los Angeles
County Population: 9,519,338

California
Population 33,900,000

• Jubilee 2000

The millennium began with measured hope and optimism. It was a new beginning with new opportunities for a better world and a better life. Yet, even though there had been centuries of history, there was a general awareness that all its lessons had not been learned. A better world would require better efforts. Pope John Paul II proclaimed Jubilee Year 2000 a Holy Year and called on people everywhere to a greater spiritual growth by a deeper relationship with the Lord of all time. Bishop Tod Brown invited Catholics in Orange County to come and pray at the designated Pilgrimage Churches where they could receive the special blessings of the Church available during the Holy Year.

In the north was the church of our patroness, Our Lady of Guadalupe, La Habra; in the middle was our cathedral church, Holy Family, Orange; and in the south was Mission San Juan Capistrano, which the Holy Father honored with the title of "Minor Basilica" earlier in the year.

Bishop Brown celebrated Jubilee Year Masses at various times and places around the diocese. Naturally, Holy Family Cathedral was the principal site, but he also chose to celebrate the Holy Year with the Vietnamese community at the UCI Bren Center. And he closed the Jubilee Year with representatives of some 17 nations at the annual, multi-cultural Migration Mass at the Bren Center in January of 2001. In addition, as a special gesture for the Holy Year, he relieved various parishes of heavy burdens of debt by forgiving some $800,000 worth of loans. These surprised beneficiaries were truly jubilant.

Of course, as expected, the new millennium was not the commencement of a perfect era, nor did it leave all problems in the past. The national scandal of clerical sexual abuse carried over and increased as shocking revelations played out in the media and the courts. Extreme political tensions also continued and caught the whole world's attention in 2001 with the 9/11 terrorist attacks causing the loss of thousands of lives. Consequent wars in Afghanistan and Iraq, as well as terrorist activities in other parts of the world, were also a testament that the world of the new millennium was still very much in need of spiritual reform.

Disgrace and Reform

The unforeseen and greatest challenge that faced the Church of Orange was the unfolding of a clerical sexual abuse scandal. It was an ugly disappointment and a profound embarrassment. Faithful Catholics were in disbelief. Yet with increasing accusations and revelations, the hard truth began to set in. It wasn't anything that people wanted to hear about, but hear about it they did. Moreover, there were the victims. These victims deserved a hearing – and more.

From the mid 1980's, accusations of clerical sexual molestation began to emerge throughout the country. This shocking news prompted others to come forth with their own tragic stories until it became apparent that this was a major national scandal. A Church sponsored, independent report by the John Jay College of Criminal Justice indicated that there were more than 10,000 claims against clerical sex abusers nationwide during a period of five decades.

Bishop Tod Brown reacted to the report with great disappointment and an even greater determination to move forward to address the crisis: "This report will serve as a wake-up call, not only for us, but for the larger society. The numbers are shocking for people, shocking for me. Now we have to accept it and respond to it."

Suppressed anger turned to unsuppressed demands for retribution and reform. Even though these incidents represented only a small percentage of the nations clergy, the very thought that any clergy were guilty of such crimes against children was met with anger and disgust.

Victims not only went after the individual perpetrators, they also went after the bishops and religious superiors who governed them. They accused them of covering up for known molesters and simply placing them in other assignments where it was likely they would offend again. This was regarded as criminal negligence and somebody had to pay.

Church officials naturally wanted to protect the Church's good name and spare the faithful from scandal. Offenders were viewed as sick morally and mentally. It was believed that they could be quietly sent away for medical and spiritual rehabilitation, after which, with professional recommendations, they could be safely re-assigned and carry out their pastoral ministry. With the advantage of hindsight, it is obvious that this belief and practice proved disastrous for the Church's good name and the welfare of its people.

The Diocese of Orange, although still fairly new, had its share in the national scandal. There had been incidents that were dealt with quietly and settlements were reached with victims. Subsequently, the national scandal prompted new accusations and investigations. Eventually, a group of 90 victims, their representatives, and attorneys charged the diocese with the misconduct of 31 priests, ten lay employees, one religious brother, and two women religious. The complaints went back as far as the 1930's.

After a long and painful series of negotiations, a mediated settlement in principle was reached on December 2, 2004. The formal settlement, agreed on January 3, 2005, required the Diocese of Orange and its insurance carriers to pay the victims $100 million dollars – the largest payout of its kind in history – and to release relevant personnel files. Bishop Brown spoke to the victims: " I want to extend on behalf of the diocese and myself a sincere apology, a request for forgiveness, and a heartfelt hope for reconciliation and healing."

One cannot undo the past and the most credible apology is genuine reform. From the beginning, the Diocese of Orange put in place policies and practices to make that happen. To facilitate reporting, information was provided to all its parishes and on the diocesan website. An independent counselor, a Victim Assistance Coordinator (VAC), was hired. She oversaw a telephone reporting line where reports were received and she helped victims report to authorities. To provide healing, the VAC arranged for professional counseling and offered victim support groups guided by a licensed therapist.

A Sexual Misconduct Oversight and Review Board, with a majority of lay people, was organized to review and evaluate individual charges. To help prevent abuse, clergy and diocesan employees were required to undergo background checks. They had to accept a policy of zero tolerance – even an accusation would cause an individual to be removed from ministry, pending a thorough independent investigation. If a cleric was accused of sexual misconduct, the accusation would be made known at all his previous places of assignment so that, if there were other victims, they might come forward.

To further education, literature on "Respecting the Boundaries" was provided to all parishioners throughout the diocese at Sunday Masses. Educational programs on sexual misconduct recognition and reporting were required for all volunteers who worked with children. Age appropriate material was presented to all children and youth including children in Catholic schools and religious education programs. That same year, "Breaking the Silence" a teen prevention interactive DVD program was produced in English and Spanish when it was found that good teen resources on the subject were lacking. It has been purchased

nationally for inclusion in other diocesan prevention programs.

Bishop Brown frequently preached on the topic, issued apologies, and called for a policy of transparency and reform that would lead to a humbler, but holier Church. His commitment to this cause was dramatically illustrated by nailing to the doors of the cathedral a seven thesis "Covenant With The Faithful" pledging to promote healing, promote an atmosphere of openness and trust, and to fully implement policies of reform.

The survey commissioned by the National Council of Catholic Bishops reported in 2004 that the Diocese of Orange was in full compliance with all measures contained in its "Charter for the Protection of Children and Young People." In fact, diocesan policies exceeded those requirements.

Bishop Brown declared: "I hope that what we have done – the changes we have made in our policies and our personnel practices – will guarantee that, as much as is humanly possible, these things will never happen again."

In January of 2006, FADICA, a major national Catholic philanthropic organization, presented Bishop Tod Brown with its prestigious Distinguished Catholic Leadership Award for his excellence in pastoral care and for his courage and faith, especially in dealing with the clerical sexual abuse scandal and implementing its remedies.

• *FADICA Distinguished Catholic Leadership Award*

I, TOD BROWN, BISHOP OF ORANGE, CA AND MY BROTHER BISHOPS OF THE DIOCESE PLEDGE

THE COVENANT WITH THE FAITHFUL

consisting of seven theses

(1) We will continue to do everything possible to help the healing process of the victims of sexual abuse.

(2) We will implement in every respect the American Catholic Bishops' *The National Charter for the Protection of Children and Young People* and our own diocesan policies for the prevention of the abuse of children and young people.

(3) We will endeavor to heal the hurt among the clergy, religious and laity, who have been humiliated, scorned and disgraced by the actions of those priests who sexually abused children and young people and the leaders who failed to appreciate the severity of these actions and failed to respond appropriately.

(4) We will work collaboratively with all members of the Diocese to promote an atmosphere of openness and trust, and empower them as partners in parochial affairs and thereby create a new era for our Church in Orange County.

(5) We will be open, honest and forthright in our public statements to the media, and consistent and transparent in our communications with the Catholics of our Diocese.

(6) We will restore confidence in our role as Bishops.

(7) We will lead the rededication of the Diocese of Orange as an Ambassador of God's Love that cares about the welfare of the entire county, especially the disenfranchised and the poor.

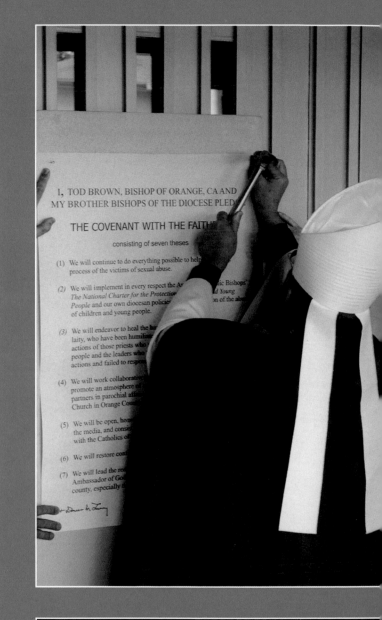

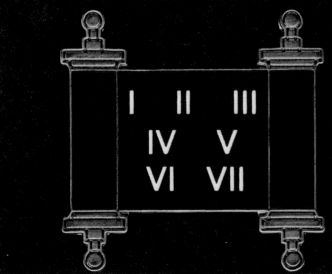

Papal Transition

Pope John Paul II had promoted the gospel cause of peace and justice during his long and inspiring pontificate. When he passed away in April 2, 2005, his mantel and mission were passed on to Pope Benedict XVI (former Cardinal Joseph Ratzinger) whose first encyclical, Deus Caritas Est (God is Love), points to the One who is the only way and authentic source of peace and justice.

Pope John Paul II gifted the diocese with a Holy Year bishop. On March 23, 2000, he appointed Monsignor Jaime Soto as Auxiliary Bishop for the Diocese of Orange. He was the first priest ordained for the diocese to be called to the episcopacy. Long active in Catholic Charities, Hispanic Ministry and an articulate advocate for social justice, his new role as a bishop would prove an important help to Bishop Brown and a real blessing for the growing diocese. He was ordained bishop on May 31.

Most Reverend Jaime Soto, D.D., M.S.W.

Jaime Soto was born at Daniel Freeman Hospital in Inglewood on December 31, 1955. He was raised in Stanton where the family moved the following year. He is the oldest of seven children born to Oscar and Gloria Soto. He attended elementary school at Saint Polycarp parish, where the Sotos were active members.

Testing thoughts of the priesthood, he entered Our Lady Queen of the Angels Junior Seminary in San Fernando. He left there early in 1973 and attended Mater Dei High School where he graduated in 1974. He then entered Saint John Seminary College in Camarillo. While he was there

the Diocese of Orange was created in 1976 and he then became one of its seminarians. (It was also there that he first began to study Spanish). He graduated with a bachelor's degree in philosophy and then spent the next four years at the theologate of Saint John's, completing the required courses and earning a master's degree in divinity. As part of his formation, he experienced parish life as a deacon at Saint Bonaventure Parish in Huntington Beach (June – August, 1981) and at Saint Joseph Parish in Santa Ana (January – May, 1982). Having successfully completed all this training, he was ordained to the priesthood by Bishop William Johnson at Holy Family Cathedral, Orange, on June 12, 1982. The following day, he had the joy of celebrating a Mass of Thanksgiving at his home parish, Saint Polycarp's, with family and friends.

Father Soto returned to Saint Joseph in Santa Ana and served there as associate pastor until July of 1984. Bishop Johnson then sent him to the Columbia University School of Social Work in New York, where he graduated in 1986 with a master's degree in social work (M.S.W.). Following his return to the Diocese of Orange, he served as the associate director of Catholic Charities. In December of that year he became Director of Immigration and Citizenship Services for the diocese and was involved in the implementation of the Immigration and Reform and Control Act of 1986. It was not long before he became widely recognized as an outspoken and skilled activist promoting Catholic values, defending immigrants, and advocating the rights of the poor.

On March 3, 1989, Bishop Norman McFarland appointed him as his Episcopal Vicar for the Hispanic Community – a major responsibility in a diocese where the percentage of Hispanics was rising dramatically. The following year, Pope John Paul II honored him as a Prelate of Honor with the title of Monsignor. Monsignor Soto served on an impressive number of public and church boards, councils, and committees. Awards came his way as various groups showed their appreciation for his zealous and effective participation in important social causes. He became known as a prominent "voice for the voiceless poor."

In 1999, Bishop Tod Brown appointed Monsignor Soto as his Vicar for Charities. And on March 23, 2000, Pope John Paul II appointed him Titular Bishop of Segia and Auxiliary Bishop of Orange. The episcopal ordination took place at Saint Columban's Church in Garden Grove on May 31. Bishop Brown was the Principal Consecrator and Bishop McFarland and Bishop Michael Driscoll served as Principal Co-Consecrators. Nearly 30 bishops participated, along with over 200 priests, religious, and a capacity crowd of family and friends.

Bishop Jaime Soto, the first priest of the Diocese of Orange to become a bishop, chose as a motto "Gozo y Esperanza" (Joy and Hope). It speaks of the joy and hope that are found by living in the Spirit of Christ, but also appropriately reflects the blessings the Diocese of Orange has received through Bishop Soto's Christlike ministry.

• *Bishop Soto*

Most Reverend Dominic M. Luong, D.D.

Surprising many, Pope John Paul II also surprised Monsignor Dominic Mai Luong of New Orleans by appointing him as a second Auxiliary Bishop for the Diocese of Orange. He is the first native Vietnamese priest to become a bishop in the United States. He was ordained bishop on June 11, 2003 – a real gift for the diocese, which is blessed with a large and vibrant Vietnamese population.

Dominic Dinh M. Luong, also known as Daminh Luong Thanh Mai, was born on December 20, 1940, in Ninh Cuong – about 50 miles from Hanoi – in the Province of Nam Dinh, formerly known as Bui Chu, in North Vietnam. He was the second youngest of the 11 children of Dominic Vy Ngoc Mai and Maria Khuou Thi Pham. His father was an official primarily involved in real estate transactions. The family, devout Catholics, belonged to Our Lady of the Holy Rosary Parish. Unfortunately, because of the dangerous political instability plaguing the country, the family was forced to move a number of times beginning in 1954.

Young Dominic received a quality elementary education from a French-Vietnamese school. He and other minor seminarians for the Diocese of Bui Chu attended Ho Ngoc Can secondary school in Trung Linh.

In 1956, Dominic's bishop sent him to the United States to continue his formation for the priesthood. Of course, this meant a long, difficult separation from his family and his country. He was just 16 years old. He would not be able to return home until 1969.

After passing comprehensive studies testing by the State of New York, he studied for six years at the Diocesan Preparatory Seminary in Buffalo where he received his high school diploma and an Associate of Arts degree. After that, he went on to Saint Bernard's Major Seminary in Rochester, New York where he studied for six years. Besides the expected studies in philosophy, scripture, and theology, he also took science classes during summer vacations.

On May 21, 1966, Bishop James A. McNulty ordained Dominic M. Luong to the priesthood for the Diocese of Da Nang at the Basilica of Our Lady of Victory in Lackawanna, New York. Of course, he was unable to return to his home diocese because of the war raging in Vietnam at that time.

Following his ordination, Father Luong completed his formal science studies, adding a bachelor's degree in physics and master's degrees in biology and psychology. He then returned to the junior seminary in Buffalo where he taught biology for nine years and also served as a chaplain to Saint Francis Hospital. For a time he also was associate pastor at Saint Louis Parish, also in Buffalo.

Father Luong's experience as a Vietnamese trained for the priesthood in America providentially suited him to be a leader when, at the fall of South Vietnam, many refugees came to the United States. A large portion of them went to the New Orleans area where Archbishop Hannon worked to help resettle them. He persuaded Father Luong, whom he met visiting in a refugee camp, to move to New Orleans and become Director of the Archdiocesan Vietnamese Apostolate. He accepted and served in this capacity from 1976 to 1983, when he became the Founding Pastor of Mary, Queen of Vietnam Parish.

On the national level, Father Luong served as the Director of the National Center for the Vietnamese Apostolate, under the Pastoral Care for Migrants and Refugee Office belonging to the National Conference for U.S. Bishops. He traveled throughout the country assisting various Vietnamese immigrant groups. Because of this important work, Pope John Paul II honored him with the title of Monsignor.

Although Vietnamese immigrants settled in many places around the country, another very large concentration made their home in Southern California, principally in Orange County. The Vatican was aware of this circumstance, and so, when Bishop Tod Brown petitioned for a second auxiliary bishop to assist him in his growing diocese, Pope John Paul II, on April 25, 2003, appointed Monsignor Dominic M. Luong Titular Bishop of Cebaredes and Auxiliary Bishop of Orange. He was to be the first native-born Vietnamese Roman Catholic Bishop in the United States.

Bishop Brown welcomed him and in his formal statement to the media noted: "Not only is he a person with deep spirituality and dedicated heart, but he also possesses well-honed leadership skills that will be very useful in his ministry here."

For his part, Bishop-elect Luong acknowledged: "By calling me the first Vietnamese priest to the office of episcopacy, His Holiness in particular, and the Church in the United States in general, recognize the many contributions with which 400,000 Vietnamese Catholics, over 600 priests, and more than 500 religious have enriched the Church in the United States, especially in the area of vocations to the priesthood and religious life."

In the presence of Cardinal Roger Mahony, Bishop Tod Brown ordained Bishop Dominic M. Luong to the fullness of the priesthood on June 11, 2003, at Saint Columban

Church in Garden Grove. Archbishop Alfred C. Hughes of New Orleans and Bishop Jaime Soto served as Principal Co-Consecrators. Among the many bishops in attendance were two from Vietnam: the Bishop of Thai Binh and the Bishop of My Tho. A very special guest was Bishop Luong's older brother, Father Dominic Loi Mai, who had arrived just in time after an exhausting flight from Vietnam.

In an article written for the Orange County Catholic, retired Bishop Norman McFarland observed: "This is a happening of major historical significance and brings the greatest joy to all. It recognizes the enormous growth of the Church in Orange County in its brief life span, calling for additional assistance on the hierarchical level, and it speaks no less graphically of the role of the Vietnamese community as a burgeoning and integral part of the local Church."

• *Ordination Day*

• *Meeting With Pope John Paul II*

25 Years and Counting

In 2001, the Diocese of Orange celebrated its Silver Jubilee. After a Mass of Thanksgiving at Holy Family Cathedral, Bishop Brown announced plans for a new cathedral to better accommodate services for the diocese's much larger Catholic population. The following year, he purchased property in Santa Ana for that purpose from the Segerstrom family. He later decided to postpone the project because of a serious economic down turn and also the prospect of considerable legal liabilities due to pending abuse cases. To ease the situation, it was also necessary to make painful budget cuts, seriously downsizing diocesan operations. By 2006, however, with an improved economy and the resolution of principle legal claims, the diocese was once again able to explore the possibility of a new cathedral and other worthwhile pastoral projects.

Communications

Diocesan communications were seriously improved during these first years of the 21st century. Instant access to important diocesan information via the Internet was provided by the creation and maintenance of a Diocese of Orange website: www.rcbo.org. Also, the diocesan newspaper, The Diocese of Orange Bulletin, was reformatted and expanded, becoming the Orange County Catholic. This tabloid size paper was enhanced with color printing and, later, also contained a Spanish language insert.

Shared Grace: Respect and Understanding

From the beginning of the diocese, Bishop William Johnson sought to promote better relations with people of other faith traditions by establishing an Office for Ecumenical and Interreligious Affairs. However, since Bishop Brown became the Bishop of Orange, his personal interest and gift for this work has became apparent. He has sponsored and participated in regular interfaith and interreligious services. The annual Week of Christian Unity has been an occasion for Celebrations of the Word: joint prayer, scripture, reflection, and song. He has accepted invitations to special events at various places of worship in the county; participated in educational panel discussions; and promoted greater understanding and respect among Orange County Catholics for people of other faiths. His Muslim-Catholic Dialogue Programs have been especially helpful during times of heightened suspicions and tendencies toward violence.

Evidence of success in these endeavors became apparent in the Inter-faith Prayer Service held at Holy Family Cathedral following the 9/11 terrorist attack and the Memorial Tribute to Pope John Paul II following his death. The impressive participation in these events are a clear indication of the desire among good-hearted people of diverse faiths to search for and celebrate common spiritual values.

Bishop Brown's work in inter-faith ministry has been local, national, and international. Besides serving as a member of various inter-faith organizations, he has served nationally as the Chairman of the National Conference of Bishops Commission.

for Ecumenical and Interreligious Affairs. And internationally, Pope John Paul II appointed him to serve as a member of the Vatican's Pontifical Council for Interreligious Dialogue.

Interfaith Memorial for Pope John Paul II

• *Christian Unity Service*

• *Orthodox and Catholic Bishops*

Where charity and love prevail, there God is ever found.

• *9/11 Interfaith service for Peace*

• *9/11 Interfaith service for Peace*

Continued Growth

The first decade of the new millennium proved to be every bit as active as the earlier years in the Diocese of Orange. While people deplored the revelations of scandal, they did not permit either their own good work or their spiritual needs to be paralyzed by them. There was still much to be thankful for and much more work to do. Bishop Brown established three new parishes to serve expanding communities: Santa Clara de Asis in Yorba Linda (2001); Holy Trinity in Ladera Ranch (2005); and Christ Our Savior Cathedral Parish in Santa Ana (2005). The small parish of Our Lady of Lourdes became the multi-cultural parish of Our Lady of La Vang, with a new site and a much larger church building. Parishioners of Saint Philip Benizi in Fullerton, whose church was destroyed by arson, gathered for a long time in a large tent, until a new church could be built to accommodate its congregation. The same was true for parishioners of Saint Justin Martyr in Anaheim. Their church was severely damaged by arson and they too worshiped in a tent while their church underwent extensive renovation. At any given time, at various places around the diocese, good hearted and hard working people were making good things happen by their prayers and generous support.

"These groundbreakings and dedications are all concrete signs of the growth and the vitality of our local Church and should be beacons of hope for all of us." (+Brown: June, 2005)

• St. Philip Benizi, Fullerton, Fire destruction

• Tent Mass

• Church construction

• *San Juan Capistrano School*

Site Blessings and Groundbreakings

Date	Facility	City	Officiant
8/24/00	St. Vincent de Paul	Huntington Beach	+Brown
1/28/01	Immaculate Heart of Mary	Santa Ana	+Brown
6/14/03	St. Philip Benizi	Fullerton	+Brown
6/28/03	La Purisima	Orange	+Brown
10/3/04	Santa Clara de Asis	Yorba Linda	+Brown
6/19/05	Corpus Christi	Aliso Viejo	+Brown
12/19/04	Our Lady of La Vang	Santa Ana	+Brown

• *Corpus Christi, Aliso Viejo*

Dedications

Date	Facility	City	Officiant
10/15/00	St. Callistus Church	Garden Grove	+Brown
2/2/02	St. Vincent de Paul	Huntington Beach	+Brown
6/8/02	Immaculate Heart of Mary	Santa Ana	+Brown
3/12/05	St. Philip Benizi	Fullerton	+Brown
6/4/05	La Purisima	Orange	+Brown
7/1/05	St. Catherine of Siena*	Laguna Beach	+Brown
2/26/06	St. John the Baptist*	Costa Mesa	+Brown
3/5/06	Santa Clara de Asis Center	Yorba Linda	+Brown
8/10/06	St. Justin Martyr*	Anaheim	+Brown
8/20/06	Our Lady of La Vang	Santa Ana	+Brown

[* Rededication of a renovated church]

• St. Vincent de Paul, Huntington Beach

• La Purisima, Orange

• St. Catherine of Siena, Laguna Beach

• Our Lady of La Vang, Santa Ana

• St Philip Benizi, Fullerton

• St John the Baptist, Costa Mesa

• St. Justin Martyr, Anaheim

• Christ Our Savior Cathedral Parish inaugural mass

• *New Mission School*

• *Serra High School Agreement*

Catholic Education

Diocesan schools were also challenged trying to adjust to growth and decline, changing demographics, and aging facilities. Saint Francis of Assisi School, Yorba Linda, completed a middle school wing in 2000. Bishop Brown presided at groundbreaking ceremonies for a new K through 5 building for Serra Catholic Elementary School at Rancho Santa Margarita in 2002. It opened for students in September of the following year and is now the largest elementary school West of the Mississippi. The aging Mission School at San Juan Capistrano and St. Joachim in Costa Mesa were replaced with completely new buildings – San Juan in 2000 and St. Joachim in 2005. On the other hand, changing demographics, low enrollment and struggling finances called for re-thinking the situations of several other schools. Saint Philip Benizi Catholic School and Saint Mary Catholic School, both in Fullerton, combined in 2003 with Saint Mary's as a middle school and Saint Philip's as K through five. Since this experiment did not work out, the two schools became one in 2005. This combination was located in the school buildings at Saint Philip Benizi Parish in Fullerton and was named Annunciation Catholic Elementary School. That same year, Immaculate Heart of Mary and Our Lady of Pilar School merged at the IHM campus and was renamed School of Our Lady. And Nativity School, a private coed Catholic school serving grades 6 – 8 for the at risk poor, moved into the Pilar campus. Saint Boniface School in Anaheim, after years of decline and no realistic rescue plan, closed in June of 2006.

In June of 2001, Bishop Brown signed an agreement with the founders of J Serra High School in San Juan Capistrano, sanctioning it as a private Catholic High School governed by a lay board. It opened in 2003 and has been steadily expanding. In May of 2006, Bishop Brown presided at ceremonies blessing its state-of-the-art sports facilities.

From the beginning of the decade to the present, Mater Dei Catholic High School in Santa Ana has been undergoing a major, $60 million campus makeover. By the spring of 2000, it had a new chapel and campus ministry center. At the beginning of the school year in 2002, a new library, academic services center, and a student activities center were added. In November of 2004, its athletes enjoyed the facilities of a new, lighted baseball field and outdoor athletic complex. And in 2006, it opened an $18 million gymnasium and aquatic center. In the future, Mater Dei High School hopes to transform its old gym into a modern performing arts center.

As a special fundraiser for Catholic Education Assistance, the Diocese of Orange inaugurated, on May 4, 2003, an annual Conference on Business Ethics and Morality at Marywood Center. Michael Novak, the famous Catholic author and lecturer, was the featured speaker.

Health Care Ministry

A major expansion of Saint Joseph Hospital is underway in Orange. On Saint Joseph's Day, March 19, 2004, ground was broken for a $132 million patient care center. This new facility will provide 150 beds and 14 operating rooms.

Katrina

Hurricane Katrina devastated the Gulf Coast in 2005. Bishop Dominic Luong, a Vietnamese leader and former pastor in New

Orleans, returned there and helped with relief efforts. In May of 2006, he led a delegation there from the Diocese of Orange to meet with Church officials, view the devastation, and assess its needs. As a result, in late June, a second team that included young adults went back to help with the rebuilding efforts in Biloxi.

Cemetery Improvements

Since the beginning of this decade, the Diocese of Orange has pursued plans to improve its Catholic cemeteries. A ten million dollar program seeks to provide mausoleum facilities and semi-private, enclosed gardens for family plots.

Call to Spiritual Renewal

Business, buildings, and even outreach programs are a part of our daily existence in this temporal world. But there is no renewal without spiritual renewal. It is the foundation of all that has been done and all that is hoped for. The new millennium began as a Holy Year and Pope John Paul II called for dedication to gospel values. In that spirit, the diocese promoted a three-year parish renewal program called Disciples in Mission. The Year of the Eucharist (October 2004 – October 2005) proclaimed by the Holy Father, prompted a pastoral letter on the Eucharist by Bishop Brown. In it, all are reminded that the presence of Christ among us is central to our Catholic identity and purpose. In his most recent pastoral letter, Learning, loving, and Living our Faith, he challenged all to reflect on what it means to be a true follower of Christ in a time and place where secular values and worldly concerns easily entice us in a direction other than the privileged path to which all are personally called, "Come follow me."

"I am inviting you to willingly work with me in renewing the Catholic
faith in Orange County. I cannot reach out to those who want to deepen
their faith without your willing support and collaboration. We will all
have to work together to become the wise, loving and giving Catholics
that our Lord has called each of us to be."
(Bishop Tod Brown, September, 2006.)

"May the God of peace himself make us perfect in holiness. May he preserve us whole and entire, spirit, soul, and body, irreproachable at the coming of our Lord Jesus Christ."

(1 Thes. 5: 23)

COME LORD JESUS

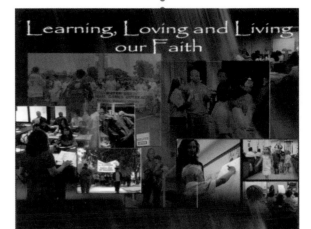

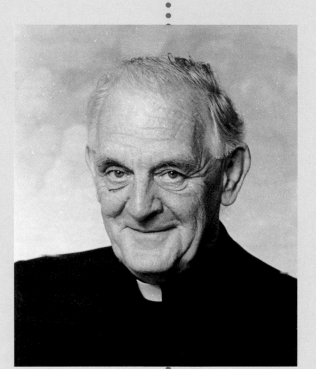

Rt. Rev. Monsignor John Francis Sammon, P.A.

John Francis Sammon was born in Pittsfield, Massachusetts on December 10, 1915. He is the son of Maurice Henry Sammon, a plumber, and Mary Agnes (Flanagan) Sammon, a homemaker. John was the oldest of three children. He had a younger brother, Joseph, and a sister, Mary Margaret.

The Sammons lived in Pittsfield and their home parish was Saint Joseph's. It was there that young John was baptized, received his First Holy Communion, learned to be an altar boy, and received the Sacrament of Confirmation.

John began his elementary education at Saint Joseph Parish School in 1921 – tuition was just a dollar. When he was in "about the fourth or fifth grade," his mother suffered a serious accident at home and severely injured her back. Whatever carefree youth he might otherwise have had, it was severely curtailed at this time. John and the rest of the family had to spend much of their time tending to her needs.

Saint Joseph Parish also had its own high school. John studied there from 1929 to 1933. The family struggled along financially; and things didn't get any better as the whole nation entered the years of the Great Depression. What they did have, though, was a rich sense of humor. That got them through difficult times and became a wonderful asset to John's later ministry as a priest.

The Sammon family also had pets – a cat and a dog. As a young man, John found employment as a veterinarian's assistant. Perhaps, this along with his sense of humor, enkindled in him his later interest and delight in Charles Schultz's "Snoopy" – a cartoon character that often became a popular and pet example of many of his priestly talks.

Following high school, John studied for a year at Boston College. After that he went to work helping out at Saint Luke's Hospital. In 1935, he attended Holy Cross College in Worcester, Massachusetts. The Jesuits arranged something of a scholarship for him, but he was required to do office work there every night. Studying and holding down a job didn't leave much time for anything else. The scholarship wasn't free.

John entered Saint Mary's Seminary, Roland Park, Baltimore, Maryland in 1938. He had been inspired by various priests he had encountered and admired the work they did. He later recalled that the seminary, though challenging in some ways, was a great relief from his college days when he had to attend classes during the day, work at night, and find some time in between to do homework. The seminary regimen of prayer, study, and suitable time for recreation was a welcome balance in contrast to his previous highly pressured experience.

John finished his seminary studies at Saint Mary's Seminary and was ordained a priest on May 30, 1942, by Bishop Thomas O'Leary at St. Michael's Cathedral.

The bishop, however, had made it clear that he had no place for him in his home Diocese of Springfield. A sympathetic parishioner encouraged him to write to her brother who was a priest in Los Angeles – Monsignor Bernard Dolan. The monsignor wrote back and told him that Archbishop John J. Cantwell would welcome him as a priest for the Archdiocese of Los Angeles. Young Father Sammon was happy to be accepted, even though it meant leaving home and family. He arrived in Los Angeles as a kind of Massachusetts missionary, something of a stranger in a strange land, ready to faithfully serve an unknown flock shepherded by an archbishop he had never

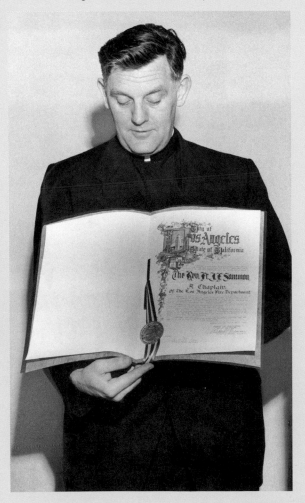

• *Msgr Sammon Fire Chaplain Award*

met. In retrospect, this certainly is one of those situations where their loss was Orange's gain, and then some.

Although it was wartime, the position of military chaplain was not an option. The requirement at the time was that you had to be at least five years ordained. So, instead of being sent to combat, he was sent to Compton. His first assignment was as assistant pastor to Our Lady of Victory Parish, whose patroness was especially appropriate considering the times. He served there from July 2, 1942 to July 6, 1944. His next assignment took him to Saint Gregory Parish in Los Angeles where he was assistant pastor for nearly ten years. In 1954, he also served for several months at St. Vibiana's Cathedral. In April of that year, he was sent as assistant pastor to Saint Monica's Parish in Santa Monica, where he served with Father Jack Siebert, a fellow priest from Massachusetts and later pastor of Saint Mary's Parish in Fullerton. While at Saint Monica's, he also spent time teaching in the parish high school. His next assignment promoted him to Administrator of Our Lady of the Rosary in Paramount on May 31, 1960. It seems that no one had the nerve to communicate this to the existing pastor, or that he blissfully failed to take the hint. He was outraged that Father Sammon had the audacity to have a second telephone installed in the rectory without his permission! Mercifully, the Chancery Office rescued Father Sammon who somehow had managed to survive almost two months in the lion's den.

Whatever favor Cardinal McIntyre did for Father Sammon, he did Orange County an even greater favor by appointing him as the pastor of Saint Cecilia's in Tustin on July 23, 1960. Although this was considered a promotion, it was at the time a very difficult assignment. The parish was involved in a long, drawn out lawsuit, there was very little available money, and its boundaries made it the largest parish responsibility in the county. A lesser man would have cowered at the prospect. He himself admitted that it was the most difficult assignment that he had experienced. Nevertheless, over the next 16 years, the parishioners knew that they had a very loving pastor and the whole county grew to appreciate his priestly involvement in a wide variety of Church and civic endeavors. His name even appeared on official Church inquiries seeking recommendations for bishops. In 1974, the Holy Father honored his work by naming him a Prelate of Honor, with the title of Monsignor.

In his early years as a seminarian working at a hospital, he had seen and admired police, firemen and paramedics as they carried out their work. Later as a priest, he kept running into them as he carried out his own priestly ministry. He recognized that they needed spiritual help too, so he took on chaplaincies in both police and fire services.

His genuine appreciation for their work, his admiration for them as a group, and care for them as individuals won the deep respect of both Catholics and others among their ranks. Statewide they saw in him a person who could both laugh with them and, by his wit, make them laugh. They also saw in him a person who could share in their tears and bring authentic words of comfort and wisdom in their darkest hours. Not surprisingly, Chaplain Sammon became the recipient of walls full of awards of appreciation. Some of them were considerably larger than others: He had three fire engines dedicated in his honor – two of them were named respectively, "Little John" and "Big John."

In 1976, when the Diocese of Orange was formed, he was embarrassed to receive as a gift from Fire Services a gold, Cadillac. He

• Msgr Sammon with Mother Mary Felix Mongomery, C.S.J.

asked Bishop Johnson what he should do since he neither wanted to disappoint the donors, nor did he want to scandalize the faithful by driving around in a luxury car. The bishop assured him that it was a credit to his priestly work and told him he should keep it. But, just to be on the safe side, Monsignor Sammon made sure that "Chaplain of Fire Services" was painted on both sides of the car.

Monsignor Sammon was also involved as priest and chaplain for many other occasions, projects, and organizations. He was gifted and he generously put those gifts to good use. Public recognition followed accordingly. His presence lifted hearts and guaranteed smiles.

At the beginning of the Diocese of Orange, Bishop Johnson called together certain members of the clergy to help him by accepting leadership roles over the various departments and ministries needed in a new diocese. He asked Monsignor Sammon what he was already involved in. As he responded with each area in which he was working, Bishop Johnson simply said, "Okay, you're in charge of that." By the end of the meeting, there were so many things that Monsignor Sammon was already doing, Bishop Johnson decided to assign him to work with him full time as a kind of all-purpose cleric, giving him the unique title of Vicar for Pastoral and Community Affairs. The general nature of the title left him open for just about anything and everything, which, of course, was his specialty.

When he left Saint Cecelia's, he left many parishioners who were sad to see him go, but were happy that he would have such an important position in the new diocese. He moved in with Bishop Johnson and was indispensable in helping to organize the diocese. In fact, he has been involved in practically every important decision-making meeting the diocese has had since its beginning. His subsequent imprisonment in diocesan meetings did not prevent him from his numerous public appearances at Church and civic functions. His fellow clergy often called him the "Vicar for Invocations" because of all the opening prayers and remarks he made at ceremonies humble and grand throughout the county.

A look at his duties in the Diocese of Orange reveals something, but not all, of his work as Vicar for Pastoral and Community Affairs. For nearly 30 years, Monsignor John Sammon has been a member of the bishop's College of Consultors. He was the organizer of the Council of Priests and has always been a member. He has been diocesan liaison and Chaplain to the Fire and Police Agencies. He has also been diocesan Director of the Propagation of the Faith (Missions), the Holy Childhood Association, Mission Groups, the National Organization for Decent Literature, and the Boy and Girl Scouts of America. In addition, he has served as chaplain to the First Friday Friars, the Holy Name Society, and the Knights of Columbus. Over the years, he has been a valued Church presence at numerous civic events and the meetings of various organizations. How he does all this is a mystery he reduces to the simple statement, "Each day I try to be a good priest." On November 21, 1985 Pope John Paul II honored him a Protonotary Apostolic, the highest rank of monsignor.

Each of the three successive Bishops of Orange reappointed Monsignor John F. Sammon P.A. to his unique office as Vicar for Pastoral and Community Affairs. This priest, rejected by the Diocese of Springfield, Massachusetts, has in many ways been the cornerstone for the spiritual growth of so many people whose lives have been privileged to be touched by his extraordinary priestly ministry.

• Chaplain John

• On the scene

• 85 th Birthday

• Consoling Snoopy

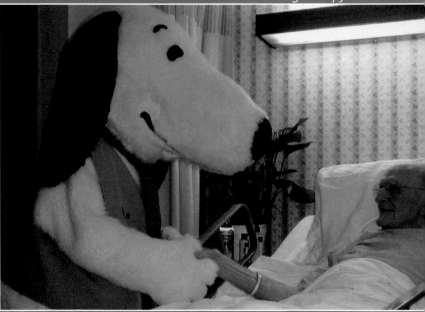

• Pastoral Services Staff 1982

• Pastoral Services Staff 2006

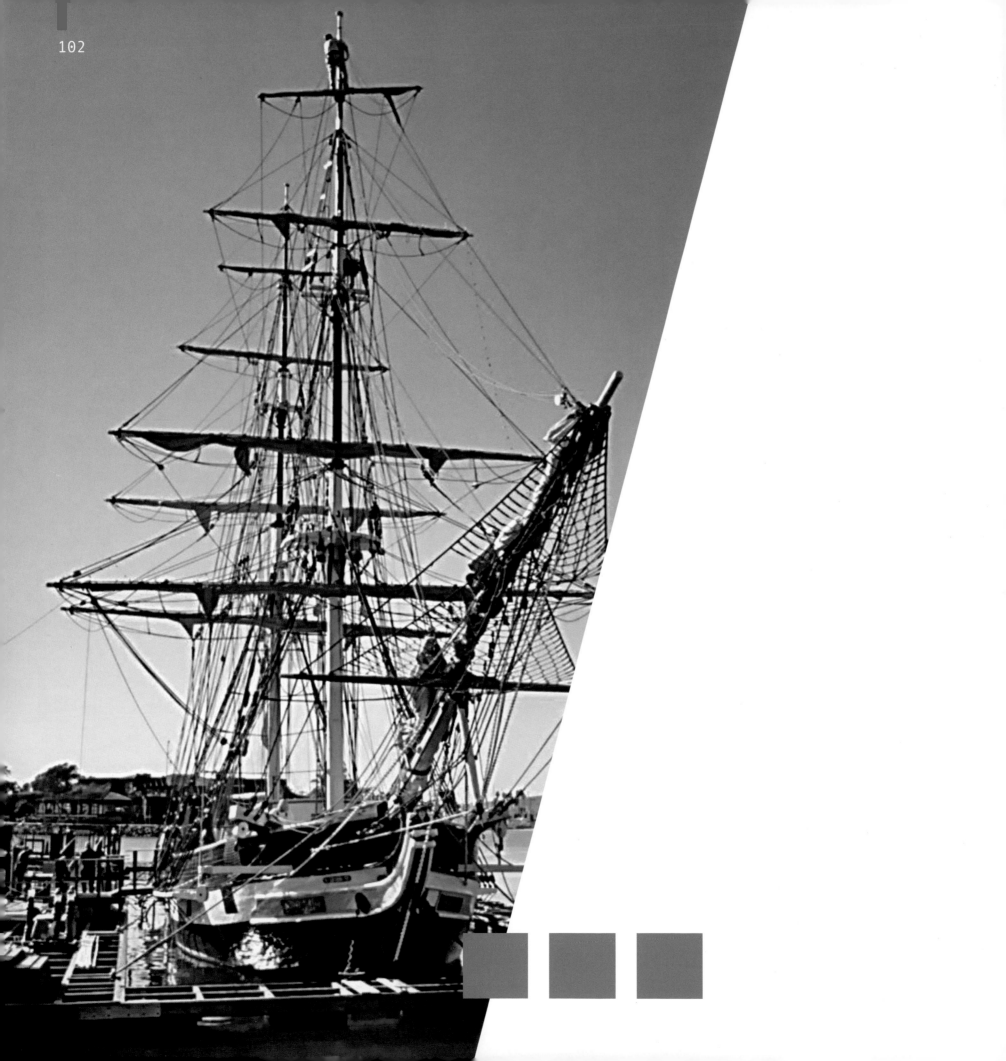

10 Demographics

• Hockey Center

• Angel Stadium

• Knott's Berry Farm

Population Growth

The history of the Church in Orange County is characterized by the growing need to provide for the spiritual needs of growing communities. To use a contemporary and very California metaphor, our Church History surfs the steadily rising swell of Orange County's population. It has been and continues to be an ever more challenging ride.

Orange County, comprising an area of 798.3 square miles, was established on March 11, 1889.

Orange County Population Progression

Year	Population	Increase
1890	13,589	-
1900	19,696	6,107
1910	34,436	14,740
1920	61,375	26,939
1930	118,674	57,299
1940	130,760	12,086
1950	216,114	85,354
1960	703,925	478,811
1970	1,420,386	716,461
1980	1,931,570	511,184
1990	2,410,556	478,986
2000	2,846,289	435,733
2006	3,047,054	200,765

Source: United States Census

2006 is an estimate of the California State Department of Finance

Ten Most Populous Cities In Orange County

1) Santa Ana	337,977
2) Anaheim	328,014
3) Huntington Beach	189,594
4) Garden Grove	165,196
5) Irvine	143,072
6) Orange	128,821
7) Fullerton	126,003
8) Costa Mesa	108,724
9) Mission Viejo	93,102
10) Westminster	88,207

Source: 2000 United States Census

Catholic Population Growth Diocese of Orange

1976	333,860
1986	417,590
1996	595,101
2006	1,131,464

Source: The Official Catholic Directory
P.J. Kenedy & Sons

The October Mass Count

The October Mass Count is a Mass attendance census taken every year. Each weekend during the month a count is made of all those who participate in Sunday Mass or its Saturday Vigil. A record is also made of the language in which the Mass is celebrated.

By 2006, Orange County was the second most populated county in California, after Los Angeles County. It was the fifth most populated county in the nation and had a greater population than 20 of the United States. (2006 Orange County Progress Report)

● *Garden Grove*

A Comparison

Year	Average Attendance	English	Spanish	Vietnamese	Other	Bilingual
1989	175,155	116,514	42,879	12,596	3,166	-
2006	218,928	119,790	70,500	25,154	1,846	473

DEMOGRAPHICS

Hispanics in Orange County

Hispanic Population in Orange County		
1970	160,168	11%
1980	286,331	15%
1990	564,828	23%
2000	875,579	31%
Note: Percent = Percentage of O.C. Total		

Source: 2000 U.S. Census

It is generally believed that the census figures for Hispanics are too low because of the reluctance of undocumented people to participate.

Latino Population

The 2000 Census figure for Hispanic origin, 875,579, is made up of the following components: Mexican (712,496), Puerto Rican (8,877), Cuban (6,703), and Other Hispanic (147,503 – This includes U.S. born and others).

Latino Conclusions:

• The Hispanic population of Orange County has grown by 55% since 1990.
• 31% of the county is of Hispanic origin.
• 25% of the county is Spanish-speaking.
• Orange County has the second largest Hispanic population in California, after Los Angeles County.
• Orange County has the fifth largest Hispanic population of all U.S. counties.
• Santa Ana is the most Hispanic city in Orange County with a 76% Hispanic population.

• Santa Ana ranks first in the nation among large cities for the largest population of Spanish-speakers at home.
• Anaheim, the second largest city in Orange County, had the biggest increase (15%) in Hispanic population.
• 28.7% of the Hispanic Population in Orange County is under the age of 18 as compared to 25% in the United States and 26% in California.*
(Source: U.S. Census and the 2006 Orange County Progress Report)
*Source: U.S. General population figures 2000

• Our Lady of Guadalupe Mass, Santa Ana Stadium, 1983

• Bishops Soto and Luong, Guadalupe Procession

Ten Most Hispanic Cities In Orange County	
Santa Ana	257,099
Anaheim	153,379
Garden Grove	53,606
Orange	41,428
Fullerton	38,015
Costa Mesa	34,519
La Habra	28,920
Huntington Beach	27,794
Buena Park	26,224
Tustin	23,113
Source: 2000 United States Census	

DEMOGRAPHICS

Asians in Orange County

Since the 1980 U.S. Census, there have been six separate categories for Asians: Asian Indians, Chinese, Filipino, Japanese, Korean, and Vietnamese. The 2000 Census added another category for "Other Asian."

The Asian population of Orange County in the year 2000 was 386,344 or 13.5% of the county. This represents a 59% gain since 1990. Westminster had the biggest increase with a 16% gain, followed by Irvine with a gain of 12%.

Asian Population in Orange County

Vietnamese	136,197	4.7%
Korean	57,487	2%
Chinese	49,820	1.7%
Filipino	48,920	1.7%
Other Asian	93,920	3%

Source: 2000 United States Census

Top Ten Cities in Orange County Asian Population

Garden Grove	52,152
Irvine	42,864
Anaheim	40,706
Fountain Valley	35,196
Westminster	34,039
Santa Ana	30,924
Fullerton	20,551
Huntington Beach	18,163
Buena Park	16,885
Orange	12,302

Source: 2000 United States Census

Top Ten Cities in Orange County Vietnamese Population

Garden Grove	35,406
Westminster	27,109
Santa Ana	19,226
Anaheim	10,025
Fountain Valley	7,088
Huntington Beach	5,422
Irvine	4,414
Orange	3,743
Stanton	3,010
Tustin	2,197

Vietnamese Population In Orange County

1980	19,333
1990	71,822
2000	136,197

Census Reports: Orange County Board of Supervisors 1980 &1990

The Vietnamese in Orange County

In the spring of 1975, a little more than a year before the Diocese of Orange was established, an event happened some 8,000 miles away that would have major, unforeseen, and lasting effects on Orange County. The government of South Vietnam collapsed and thousands fled for their lives as North Vietnamese communists seized control. In mid-April of 1975, the U.S. Military evacuated some 40,000 refugees to a hastily prepared "Tent City" at Camp Pendleton, just south of Orange County. In this first wave of Indochinese, predominantly Vietnamese, some 130,000 arrived to a very uncertain future in America. They had their lives, but many had very little else.

To its lasting credit, Orange County opened its arms in welcome. Many Catholic parishes generously took up the cause especially Saint Barbara's under the leadership of Monsignor Michael Collins. They sponsored families and worked to get them started in a new and independent life. Initially about 12,000 refugees were resettled in Orange County. Within a year, this was up to about 18,000.

In 1977, another wave of desperate Indochinese, sometimes called the "Boat People," fled the area on their own. They hoped and prayed to reach safety somewhere, somehow.

Many perished in the process, but for those who survived, many eventually found refuge in the United States. By 1982, the refugee population in Orange County had tripled and counted more than 54,000.

At the beginning, the vast majority settled in Westminster and Garden Grove, a portion of which became known as "Little Saigon." At present, Garden Grove claims the largest concentration of Vietnamese at 35,406. However, it is increasingly evident that this growing population is spreading out. Vietnamese are making their way into wider areas of the county as they seek higher education and better business opportunities. And like others, many are looking for homes in safer neighborhoods with better school systems.

There are more Vietnamese in California than in any other state and the largest concentration is in Orange County. In fact, Orange County has the largest number of Vietnamese second only to Vietnam. In just one decade (1990 – 2000) the Vietnamese population in Orange County has nearly doubled to 136,197.

In response to their spiritual needs, Pope John Paul II appointed Msgr. Dominic Mai Luong as Auxiliary Bishop to Bishop Brown in the Diocese of Orange. Historically, he is the first Vietnamese bishop to serve in the United States.

Increasingly a new generation of Vietnamese-Americans have been born here, grown-up here – many having never seen Vietnam – and are as much a part of the fabric of Orange County as anyone else.

It is a special blessing to Orange County Catholics that many Vietnamese Catholics are very devout and active in their faith. This has been an inspiration to the rest of the Orange Diocesan Catholic community and has produced an impressive number of vocations to the priesthood and religious life.

• *Bishop Johnson with Vietnamese leaders*

• *Bishop Mc Farland at Vietnamese Center groundbreaking*

• *Bishop Driscoll and Msgr. Peter Tien at dedication*

• *Bishop Luong with Archbishop Montalvo, Apostolic Nuncio*

Leadership

Bishops of Orange in California

Most Rev. William R. Johnson, D.D.	1976 - 1986
Most Rev. Norman F. McFarland, D.D.	1987 - 1998
Most Rev. Tod D. Brown, D.D.	1998 - Current

Auxiliary Bishops of Orange

Most Rev. John T. Steinbock, D.D.	1984 - 1987
Most Rev. Michael P. Driscoll, D.D.	1987 - 1998
Most Rev. Jaime Soto, D.D.	2000 - Current
Most Rev. Dominic Mai Luong, D.D.	2003 - Current

Vicars General

Rev. Msgr. Donald J. Strange	1976 - 1978
Rev. Msgr. Harry J. Trower	1978 - 1985
Most Rev. John T. Steinbock	1984 - 1987
Most Rev. Michael P. Driscoll	1988 - 1999
Rev. Msgr. John Urell	2000 - 2004
Rev. Michael Heher	2005 - Current

Chancellors

Rev. Msgr. Michael P. Driscoll	1976 - 1987
Rev. Msgr. John Urell	1988 - 1999
Sr. Katherine Gray, C.S.J.	2000 - 2001
Mrs. Shirl Giacomi	2002 - Current

Secretaries to the Bishop of Orange

Rev. Msgr. Michael P. Driscoll	1976 - 1980
Rev. Daniel J. Murray	1981 - 1984
Rev. Msgr. John Urell	1984 - 1998
Rev. J. Michael McKiernan	1999 - 2005
Rev. Tuan Joseph Pham	2005 - Current

• Diocesan Pastoral Council

• Fr. Michael Heher, Bishop Tod D. Brown, Shirl Giacomi

Note:

• Father Driscoll became a Monsignor
in 1979 and a Bishop in 1990.

• Father Urell became a Monsignor in 1990.

Judicial Vicars

Rev. Msgr. Peter Scannell	1976 - 1990
Rev. Msgr. Daniel Brennan	1991 - 1997
Rev. William J. Vohsing, J.C.L.	1998 - 2002
Rev. Douglas Cook, J.C.L.	2003 - Current

Vicars for Religious Education

Rev. Msgr. Michael Duffy	1978 - 1988
Rev. Christopher Smith	1989 – 2004

Vicar for Faith Formation

Rev. Gerald M. Horan	2005 - Current

Directors of Religious Education

Sr. Mary Irene Flanagan, C.S. J.	1976 - 1977
Ms. Carol Cowgill	1978 - 1989
Rev. Christopher Smith	1990
Ms. Ruth Bradley	1991 - 2004

Office of Faith Formation

Rev. Gerald M. Horan, O.S.M.	2005 - Current

Director of Parish Faith Formation

Ms. Nancy C. Hardy	2006 - Current

Coordinator of Youth and Young Adult Ministries

Deacon Guillermo Torres	2006 - Current

Orange Cathechetical Institute

Ms. Carol Cowgill, Director	1979 - 1983
Mr. James Campbell, Director of Religious Studies	1980 -1987
Ms. Carol Cowgill, Director of Religious Studies	1988
Ms. Joan Kulik, Director of Religious Studies	1989 - 2004
Ms. Nuria Chekouras, Associate Director	2000 - 2004

Institute of Pastoral Ministry

Ms. Joan Kulik & Sr. Leticia Salazar, O.D.N.	2005
Sr. Leticia Salazar, O.D.N.	2006 - Current

Ministry to Priests / Vicar for Priests

Msgr. Wilbur L. Davis	1978 - 1982
Rev. Michael Pecharich	1983 - 1989
Rev. Michael Heher	1990 - 1993
Rev. Eamon O'Gorman	1994 - 1999
Rev. Kerry Beaulieu	2000 - 2004
Rev. Christopher Smith	2005 - Current

Diaconate

Rev. Msgr. Donald J. Strange, V.G.	1976 - 1978
Rev. Kenneth Krause	1979 - 1982
Rev. Gary Kinzer, Associate	1981 - 1982
Rev. Gary Kinzer	1983 - 1988
Deacon Jack Brennan, Associate	1986 - 1998
Sr. Marianna Gemmet, C.S.J.	1989 - 1991
Sr. Jo Ann Tabor, C.S.J.	1992 - 1999
Deacon Frank Chavez, Associate	1999
Deacon Frank Chavez	2000 - Current

Vocations Directors

Rev. Michael P. Driscoll	1976 - 1978
Associate: Sr. Paul Damiano, S.P.	1978 - 1983
Rev. Richard Kennedy	1978 - 1980
Rev. Daniel J. Murray	1981 - 1999
Rev. Msgr. Wilbur Davis	2000 - Current

Director for Women's Religious Vocations

Sr. Paula Damiano, S.P.	1978 - 1983
Sr. Marianna Gemmet, C.S.J.	1986 - 1991
Sr. Jo Ann Tabor, C.S.J.	1992 - 1994
Sr. Rina Cappellazzo, O.P.	1995

Office of Worship

Rev. Kenneth Krause	1976 - 1979
Rev. Arthur Holquin, S.T.L.	1980 - 1989
Rev. Rod Stephens	1990 - 2002
Ms. Lesa Truxaw	2003 - Current

Ecumenical and Interreligious Affairs

Rev.Msgr. Lawrence J. Baird	1978 - 1999
Rev. Raphael Luevano	2000 - 2005
Rev. Al Baca	2006 - Current

Office of business Management

Mr. Al Pesqueira	1976 - 1982
Deacon Lee Meyer	1983 - 1988
Mr. John Sauer	1989 - 1991
Mr. Phil Ries, CPA	1992 - Current

Solemn liturgy

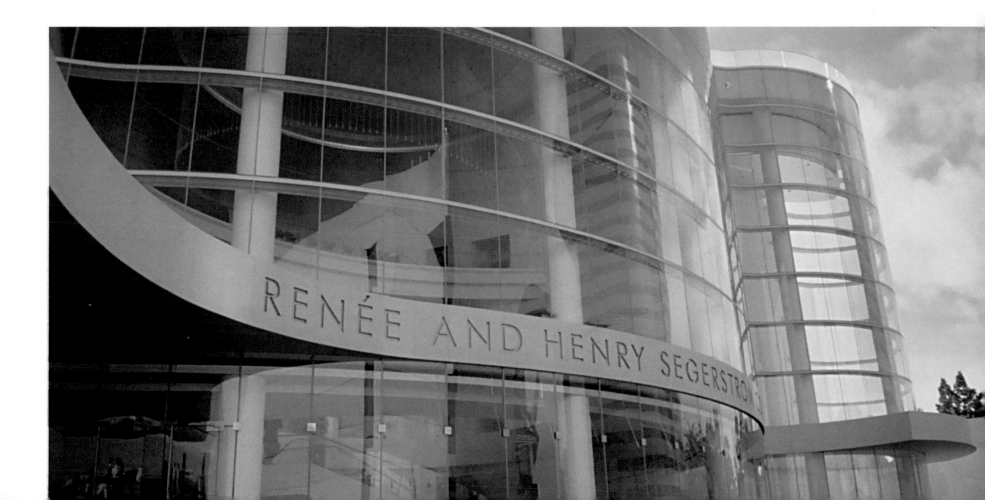

Religious Communities

Vicar for Religious

Rev. Msgr. Harry J. Trower, P.A.(1978 –1985)
Most Rev. John T. Steinbock, D.D. (1986-1987)
Most Rev. Michael P. Driscoll, D.D. (1988-1998)
Sr.Eymard Flood, O.S.C. (2000 – Current)

Associate Vicars

Vicar for Religious Men
Rev. Charles Motsko, O.S.M. ((1979-1988)

Vicar for Religious Women

Sr. Briegeen Moore, O.S.C. (1979-1991)
Sr. Rina Cappellazzo,O.P. (1992-1995)

The Religious Communities of Men and Women serving in the Diocese of Orange have been a vital force in its Gospel mission. Their contribution has included a wide variety of important ministries: Faith Formation, Spiritual Direction, Retreat, Vocation, Charity, Education, Health Care, Social Service, Detention, Ethnic, and Parish Ministry.

• Norbertine Fathers

Sisters of St. Benedict, OSB*
Religious Sisters of Charity – RSC
Sisters of Charity of the Blessed Virgin Mary – BVM
Sisters for Christian Community – SFCC
Sisters of the Company of Mary – ODN
Missionary Sisters of St. Columban – SSC*
Dominican Sisters, Adrian – OP
Dominican Sisters, W. Australia - OP
Dominican Sisters, Mission San Jose – OP
Dominican Sisters, Rosarian – OP
Eucharistic Missionaries of Most Holy Trinity
      – MESST
Felician Sisters – CSSF*
Franciscan Missionary Sisters of the Immaculate
Conception – OSF
Franciscans, Syracuse (NY) – OSF
Franciscan School Sisters of St. Francis – SSSF
Sisters of the Holy Child Jesus – SHCJ
Congregation of the Sisters of the Holy Cross – CSC
Lovers of the Holy Cross (Los Angeles) – LHC
Sisters of the Holy Family – SHF
Sisters of the Holy Names of Jesus and Mary
      – SNJM
Sisters of the Little Company of Mary – LCM
Religious Sisters of Mercy of the Americas – RSM
Sisters of Mercy of Ireland – RSM
Medical Missionary Sisters – MMS
School Sisters of Notre Dame – SSND
Sisters of Our Lady of Perpetual Help – SOLPH
Poor Clare Missionary Sisters of the Blessed
      Sacrament – MC
Presentation Sisters of the Blessed Virgin Mary
      – PBVM
Sisters of Providence – SP
Sisters of Providence (Seattle) – SP
Religious Sisters of the Sacred Heart of Mary – RSHM
Society Devoted to the Sacred Heart – SDSH
Sisters of St. Clare – OSC
Sisters of St. Joseph (Carondolet) – CSJ
Sisters of St. Joseph of Orange – CSJ

• 2006 Jubilarians honored at Mass for Consecrated Life

Sisters of Notre Dame - SND
Sisters, Servants of the Immaculate Heart of Mary
      - IHM
Sister Servants of Jesus - SJP
St. Joseph, Sisters of the Third Order of
      St. Francis – SSJ, TOSF
Sisters of St. Louis – SSL
Sisters of Social Service – SSS*
Family of Mary of the Visitation – FMV
Secular Institutes of the Apostolic Oblates
* No longer ministering in the diocese.

Augustinian Fathers – OSA
Augustinian Recollects – OAR
Brothers of St. Patrick – FSP
Brothers of the Christian Schools – FSC
Carmelite Brothers – OCD
Columban Fathers – SSC
Crusade of the Holy Spirit – CHS
Divine Word – SVD
Franciscan Fathers – OFM
Jesuits – SJ
Legionnaires of Christ – LC
Marianists – SM
Missionaries of the Holy Spirit – M.Sp.S.
Missionaries of the Sacred Heart – MSC
Norbertine Fathers – O.PRAEM.
Salesians of Don Bosco – SDB
Servite Fathers and Brothers – OSM

Sisters of St. Joseph of Orange

Mother Bernard Gosselin established the Sisters of St. Joseph of Orange in 1912. She and eight other sisters left La Grange, Illinois, near Chicago to establish a school in Eureka, California. They were able to sustain themselves with a meager income from their teaching and by growing most of their own food.

The flu epidemic presented a new challenge to the community. Although none of the sisters were trained in medicine, the people of the area needed nursing care. The sisters responded the best they could at the time, but realized that by establishing a hospital, they could provide a health care service that would effectively address the personal, social and spiritual needs of the area as well. In 1920, the Sisters opened St. Joseph Hospital in Eureka.

As the numbers continued to grow, the Sisters not only expanded their ministries but traveled to other areas as well.

By 1922, the Sisters were teaching in several areas and recognized that the community could better develop its ministries by moving the Motherhouse to Orange. The first ministries of the Sisters were in education and health care. St. Joseph Hospital was opened in 1929, followed by the opening of St. Jude Hospital in 1957. More recently, the St. Joseph Health System, incorporated in 1981, was established to enable the Congregation to direct, support and conduct its health care ministry more efficiently and responsibly. The Sisters describe their relationship to the St. Joseph Health System as a sponsorship. The latest

Orange County-based hospital to join the Health System is Mission Hospital, acquired in 1994. Today, 15 hospitals as well as many other health care entities (including home health, hospice programs and other health care and community outreach programs) are affiliated with the St. Joseph Health System.

While health care may be one of the most visible ministries, it is by no means the Sister's only one. In 1988, the CSJ Education Network was established to support principals and teachers in 12 Catholic schools throughout California. Today, the CSJ Education Network works with 22 schools throughout the state.

The Congregation's ministries have expanded beyond education and health care. In Orange County, the Sisters sponsor the Center for Spiritual Development, a retreat and conference center; Bethany, a residence for women in transition; Taller San Jose, and educational and vocational center for young adults; and the St. Joseph Justice Center. Sisters of St. Joseph of Orange minister to the poor, participate in prison ministries, work to enhance cultural development of the communities in which they serve, and minister to the elderly. The Sisters' outreach efforts include not only the United States, but also Mexico, El Salvador, and Australia.

> *Statement of Promises*
>
> *We promise to be women of unity.*
> *We promise to stand with people who are poor.*
> *We promise to promote ecological justice.*
> *Through these promises we witness that:*
> *Our God is in love with the world.*
> *Our God is alive in the world through all persons of good will.*
>
> July 2006

• *Sisters of St. Joseph of Orange Leadership*

Orange Diocesan Council of Catholic Women

The Orange Diocesan Council of Catholic Women (ODCCW), affiliated with the National Council of Catholic Women, is a coordinating unit for action for all women of the Diocese of Orange. It seeks to gather, educate and promote awareness of the needs and works of Catholic women through commissions that encourage involvement in important issues.

ODCCW Presidents

Diane Abati	1976 - 1977
Gerry Andert	1978 - 1979
Carol Berger	1980 - 1981
Helen Vohsing	1982 - 1983
Jackie Reed	1984 - 1985
Margery Doolin	1986 - 1987
Harriet Hizon	1988 - 1989
Bonnie Powers	1990 - 1993
Mary Jane Mueller	1994 -1995
Gwen Murphy	1995 - 1996
Doris Cantlay	1997 - 1998
Jackie Reed	1999 - 2001
Gerry Monahan	2002 - 2003
Mary Hayes	2003 - 2004
Theresa Sherrin	2005 - 2006
Marie Romanski	2006 -

ODCCW Moderators

Rev. Msgr. Emmett McCarthy	1976 - 1984
Rev. William Vohsing	1985 - 1989
Rev. Joseph Robillard	1990 - 1997
Rev. Douglas Cook	1998 - 2000
Sr. Eymard Flood, O.S.C.	2001 - Current

Catholic Schools

• *St. Pius V School, Buena Park*

• *St. Columban School, Garden Grove*

Catholic Schools

Catholic Schools	
Superintendent: Brother Dominic Beraradelli, F.S.C.	1976 - 1980
Associate: Sr. Celine Leydon, S.S.L.	1978 - 1980
Superintendent: Se. Celine Leydon, S.S.L.	1981 - 1991
Associate: Sr. Margaret Zimmerman, P.V.M.	1981 - 1986
Associate: Brother William Carriere, F.S.C.	1987 - 1991
Superintendent: Brother William Carriere, F.S.C.	1992 - 2004
Associate: Sr. Mary Catherine Evans, O.P.	1992 - 1999
Associate: Mrs. Sally Todd	2000 - Current

Office of Faith Formation

Superintendent: Rev. Gerald M. Horan, O.S.M.	2005 - Current

Note: *In 2005, St. Philip Benizi and St. Mary School merged and became Annunciation School located in the school buildings at St. Philip Benizi Parish. That same year, Immaculate Heart School and Our Lady of the Pillar School merged and became the School of Our Lady located in the school buildings at Immaculate Heart of Mary Parish. Nativity School, a private school- grades sixth through eighth - for the at risk poor, opened in the school buildings at Our Lady of the Pillar Parish.*

Serra Catholic School in Rancho Santa Margarita belongs to three parishes: San Francisco Solano in Rancho Santa Margarita, St. Kilian in Mission Viejo, and Santiago de Compostela in Lake Forest.

St. Francis of Assisi School in Yorba Linda belongs to two parishes: St. Martin de Porres in Yorba Linda and San Antonio de Padua in Anaheim Hills.

1889	St. Catherine's Academy	Anaheim
1912 (1934)	St. Joseph's Academy	Anaheim
1914	St. Joseph's School	Santa Ana
1923	St. Mary's School*	Fullerton
1928	Mission School	San Juan Capistrano
1930 (2006)	St. Boniface School	Anaheim
1934 (1945)	Sacred Heart Academy	Laguna Beach
1945	St. Anne's School	Santa Ana
1948	Blessed Sacrament School	Westminster
1949	Holy Family School	Orange
1949	St. Joachim School	Costa Mesa
1953	Our Lady of the Pillar School *	Santa Ana
1954	St. Pius V School	Buena Park
1956	St. Columban School	Garden Grove
1957	Our Lady of Guadalupe School	La Habra
1957	St. Mary Annex (St. Philip Benizi)*	Fullerton
1957	St. Anthony Claret School	Anaheim
1958	St. Anne Annex (Immaculate Heart)*	Santa Ana
1959	St. Joachim Annex (St. John the Baptist)	Costa Mesa
1959	St. Mary Second Annex (St. Juliana)	Fullerton
1959	St. Justin Martyr School	Anaheim
1959	St. Joseph School	Placentia
1960	St. Hedwig School	Los Alamitos
1961	St. Jeanne de Lestonnac School	Tustin
1961	St. Cecelia School	Tustin
1963	St. Callistus School	Garden Grove
1963	St. Irenaeus School	Cypress
1963	St. Barbara School	Santa Ana
1963	St. Polycarp School	Stanton
1964	Our Lady Queen of Angels School	Newport Beach
1964	St. Angela Merici School	Brea
1965	St. Norbert School	Orange
1965	Our Lady of Fatima School	San Clemente
1965	La Purisima School	Orange (El Modena)
1966	St. Bonaventure School	Huntington Beach
1967	Saints Simon and Jude School	Huntington Beach
1981	St. Edward the Confessor School	Dana Point
1995	Serra Catholic Elementary	Rancho Santa Margarita
1998	St. Francis of Assisi School	Yorba Linda
2005	Annunciation School*	Fullerton
2005	School of Our Lady*	Santa Ana
2005	Nativity School*	Santa Ana

Catholic High Schools

1934 (1982)	Marywood High School	Anaheim/Orange
1950	Mater Dei High School	Santa Ana
1958	Servite High School	Anaheim
1961	Cornelia Connelly High School	Anaheim
1965	Rosary High School	Fullerton
1961	St. Michael Preparatory School	Silverado
1987	Santa Margarita Catholic High School	Rancho Santa Margarita
2003	J Serra High School	San Juan Capistrano

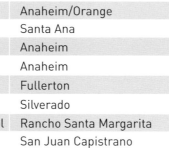

Cornelia Connelly
School of the Holy Child

Established in 1961 by the Sisters of the Society of the Holy Child Jesus, Connelly is Orange County's only independent, college preparatory Catholic high school for girls, and is committed to the educational mission of the Catholic Church through the philosophy and spirituality of Cornelia Connelly and the Society of the Holy Child Jesus. As one of ten Holy Child Schools in the United States, Connelly is part of the Holy Child Network of Schools, a national network and international community of schools that offer an education with a distinctive spirit.

Connelly's student body consists of over 300 students who represent a multitude of religious and cultural traditions from Orange, Los Angeles Riverside and San Bernardino Counties. With an average class size of 15-18, Connelly offers a highly personal approach to education, which encourages independent thinking and responsible decision making. Connelly's caring and committed faculty strives to engage each student's intellectual curiosity, and to challenge each student to test her abilities. Cornelia Connelly School believes in providing a supportive educational environment that nurtures spiritual and personal development as well as academic achievement.

JSerra High
School

Tim Busch, co-founder of St. Anne School in Laguna Niguel, a K-8 private Christian school, organized a group of parents and business leaders in South Orange County as Founders of JSerra High School. Their concerted effort has been focused on establishing a private Roman Catholic high school that will ultimately house 1,800 to 2,000 students.

The Program of Study of JSerra is a quality, college preparatory curriculum integrated with the traditions and beliefs of the Roman Catholic doctrine. Religious education is a priority, with prayer and worship serving an important role during each day. The school is authentically Catholic yet warmly ecumenical, open to students of all faiths. Teachers are credentialed and specially selected for their ability to work well with students and colleagues. The faculty has created a learning environment where students, parents and administration unite in a quest for knowledge.

God, family, community, and training for life: JSerra has its path charted and is on its way!

Mater Dei
High School

The students, faculty, staff, administration and alumni of Mater Dei High School are proud of its traditions of Honor, Glory, and Love. A school built by faith, dedication, and help from the families and community around them, Mater Dei was and still is a thriving commitment to Catholic education in the heart of Orange County.

Mater Dei High School first opened in September, 1950. The original 111 students endured less-than-comfortable conditions, but they believed in the Mater Dei High School that was yet to come. They started the foundation that we continue building on today.

In 1960, the school looked back on the first ten years that added 1300 students and a waiting list for more. They added a theater arts department in the 1970's and performed the first senior musical. Enrollment hit 2,150, making Mater Dei the largest Catholic high school west of Chicago.

During the 1980's, they broadened their curriculum, including technology, and further heightened academic standards in order to provide the excellent education the students needed for success in college and life.

As the Mater Dei community continues its second 50 years, they are in the midst of the largest redevelopment project in the school's history. The" MD 2000 Capital Campaign" has funded the construction of Phase I (Fall 1999 – Fall 2002): a student parking lot, the Gordon & Gail Lee Family Chapel and Campus Ministry Center, the Antone & Anna Borchard Family Library, the Reed & Angela LeVecke Student Activities Complex, the Shamrock Student Plaza, the Josef D'Heygers Academic Services Center, including the Muth Family Learning Center, and the Ward Family Multi-Media Center. Phases II & III will include a state-of-the-art Athletic & Aquatics Complex and Performing Arts Complex, respectively. "MD 2000" builds on the tradition of excellence inspired by its founders in 1950.

Rosary High School

Rosary High School, located in Fullerton, California, is a Catholic diocesan college preparatory secondary school for young women. Founded in 1965 under the administration of the Sisters of St. Joseph of Orange, Rosary's mission is to provide an empowering educational environment in which her graduates can become integrated and holistic women who think critically, communicate effectively, and embody their religious faith. 100% of Rosary graduates proceed to schools of higher education.

Rosary offers a diversified college preparatory curriculum enhanced by technological capabilities and complemented by extensive co-curricular programs. Some of these are

• Campus Ministry and Service Leadership
• ASB Leadership
• California Scholastic Federation and National Honor Society
• Athletics which include ten sports and 25 teams participating in the Trinity League
• Award winning Cheer and Dance teams
• A full array of clubs
• Tri-School Theatre
• The O'Connor Institute for Ethics and Leadership.

A unique and popular educational experience at Rosary is the annual Red and Gold event. This 37 year old cherished tradition is a school wide endeavor in which students create, develop, direct, and perform in a musical theatre production based on an assigned theme. As a friendly competition, the Red and Gold process unifies the school community, profoundly deepens school spirit, loyalty, and pride, and supports the mission of educating and empowering learners, believers, and leaders.

Santa Margarita High School

Santa Margarita Catholic High School began as a dream of the late Bishop William R. Johnson. He saw the need and possibility of a Catholic high school in south Orange County. The dream then became the vision of many who shared his ideas. They caught his enthusiasm and the campaign began. Beginning in 1985, the Church and business community worked together to fund and build an extraordinary educational facility. With God's blessing, a handful of dedicated people, and the generosity of donors, the campus one can see today became a reality. The school opened in the fall of 1987 and the Charter class graduated in June 1991. In 1990, the school added a new three story classroom building. In 2006, plans were approved for SMCHS to complete the campus.

Servite High School

In 1957, the Archdiocese of Los Angeles invited the Friar Order Servants of Mary (Servites) in Chicago to come to Orange County to open an all-male Catholic high school in Anaheim. Father Maurice Gillespie, OSM, arrived in May, 1958, with a small band of Friars as well as equipment, supplies and personnel from St. Philip High School in Chicago. They purchased an unfinished brick building and 110 boys comprised the inaugural freshman class.

From the beginning, Servite has emphasized developing very well-rounded young men prepared for success in college and life. Servite teaches young men to seek excellence in academics, athletics, the arts and Catholic spirituality. Servite men become leaders in business, medicine, law, non-profits, military and civic service, and in the Church.

Servite has one of the most challenging academic programs in Southern California and often leads Orange County private schools in the number of National Merit scholars.

With 7,500 alumni in 45 graduating classes, the Servite alumni, parent and benefactor network is very strong in Southern California. Servite men are leaders of billion-dollar businesses; are among the best attorneys and physicians in the nation; are leaders of federal and local governments; have started important non-profits like Corazon; and have served with distinction in the Church and military.

As Servite approaches its 50th anniversary, it continues to seek excellence in developing the faith-filled leaders needed in our society for the future.

St. Michael's Preparatory High School

St. Michael's Preparatory School is a Roman Catholic boys' boarding, college preparatory school run by the Norbertine Fathers of St. Michael's Abbey. The school serves families whose sons demonstrate moral commitment and academic potential. St. Michael's Prep offers a classical sequence of courses of College Prep, Honors, and Advanced Placement levels.

The school, located in southern Orange County, has an enrollment of approximately 60. It is the primary apostolate of the priests of St. Michael's Abbey. The Norbertine Fathers have a tradition that spans over eight centuries of experience in Catholic education.

The Catholic Welfare Bureau

The beginnings of Catholic Charity as a formal organization in Orange County can be traced back to the 1930's and the Great Depression. Many of the impoverished people of the time turned to the church communities for help. St. Boniface Parish in Anaheim and St. Joseph Parish in Santa Ana, situated in the main population centers, were inundated with requests for assistance. The Catholic Welfare Bureau in Los Angeles assisted them by hiring (albeit at $10 a month) an experienced layperson from each parish to organize and coordinate relief efforts. Mrs. Florence Burrows from Anaheim and Miss Schovalier of Santa Ana worked to provide the basics: food; clothing; and where possible, shelter. Initially, they worked out of their homes. Later, Mr. James Murphy, a Santa Ana realtor, donated the use of his office on Tuesday and Thursday mornings.

In 1940, the Catholic Welfare Bureau of the Archdiocese of Los Angeles placed Mrs. Burrows in charge of their charitable operations in Orange County. To her goes much of the credit for building up important working relationships with county, Red Cross, and other service oriented agencies. The Bureau accepted its cases regardless of race or religion. At the time, it was the only agency in Orange County licensed for the placement of children. During World War II, it was a key element in the county's efforts to provide war relief. Father Alden J. Bell, who had been Director of the Catholic Welfare Bureau since its inception in Orange County, joined the military as a chaplain in 1942. Mr. Richard Carter succeeded him during the war years.

In the 1950's, the Catholic Welfare Bureau in Orange County grew sufficiently to warrant its own office, telephone, and its paid secretary. Father William Barry, Assistant Director of the Bureau in Los Angeles, was in charge of Orange County operations. Later, when Father Bell became an auxiliary bishop, Father Barry, was called to the Los Angeles office and Father John Keenan was placed in charge in Orange County. As the county population increased following the war, the Santa Ana office grew to include satellite offices in Fullerton, Huntington Beach, and Laguna Beach.

In 1956, Father William Johnson succeeded Bishop Bell as Director of the Archdiocesan Catholic Welfare Bureau. 20 years later, when he became the first Bishop of Orange, he brought with him the experience, familiarity, and personal interest that guaranteed the continued growth and strength of Catholic Charities in Orange County.

Over time, the Catholic Welfare Bureau in the county has changed names to suit its growth and focus. It has been known as Catholic Community Agencies and Catholic Social Services. It is now known under the simple, but accurately encompassing title of Catholic Charities. Its outreach efforts have been wide-ranging and have adjusted as changing circumstances call for change in priorities. During the years since the Diocese of Orange began, it has done remarkable work in helping to resettle refugees desperately in need of new beginnings. The continual population increase and its growing cultural diversity guarantee that Catholic Charities will be busy long into the future. Its accomplishments and its continuing mission underline its importance and call for its generous support.

Catholic Charities

The Mission of Catholic Charities is rooted in the Gospel: To feed the poor, clothe the naked, care for the ill, visit the imprisoned, shelter the homeless and welcome the stranger in our midst.

Vicar for Charites	
Most Rev. Michael P. Driscoll, M.S.W.	1976 - 1998
Most Rev. Jaime Soto, M.S.W.	2000 - Current

Director of Catholic Charities	
Mr. William E. Ericson, A.C.S.W.	1976 - 1905
Mr. Allen Andrew	1986
Ms. Kristan Schlichte, M.S.W.	1987 - 2002
Ms. Catherine Spear, M.S., C.F.R.E.	2003 - 2004
Ms. Theresa Montminy, M.S.H.S.	2005 -

Catholic Charities Auxiliary

Mrs. Thomas Heffernan, Mrs. Martin Melanson, and Mrs. Peter Muth founded the Catholic Charities Auxiliary on February 27, 1974. It is an organization of volunteer Catholic women dedicated to support the programs and activities of Catholic Charities. Their primary fundraising activity is an annual Catholic Volunteer Woman of the Year Luncheon. This event not only raises funds for charity, it also highlights the exemplary work of many outstanding women throughout the diocese.

Catholic Woman of the Year:

1976	Genevieve Nutto	1992	Rennea Connelly
1977	Olga Valenzuela	1993	Myldred Jones
1978	Diane Abati	1994	Dolores Cervantes
1979	Delores Larson	1995	Carolyn Pryor
1980	Mary Schmitz	1996	Shirley McCracken
1981	Theresa Martin	1997	Cynthia Coad
1982	Millie Ronca	1998	Jackie Dudek
1983	Rose Callahan	1999	Emelia Kua
1984	Lorrie R. Lopez	2000	Jean Eslinger
1985	Jennie Castillon	2001	Mary Jean Niklas
1986	Phyllis Ann Coleman	2002	Gerry Stacy
1987	Sandra Salgado	2003	Mary Ann Ringkamp
1988	Therese McAndrew	2004	Diane Halal
1989	Theresa Sherrin	2005	Elizabeth Smith
1990	Linda Smith	2006	Gerry Monahan
1991	Kathleen Ivankay		

• 2006 Catholic Woman of the Year
Gerry Monahan

Mardi Gras Ball

Each year Catholic Charities of Orange County organizes a fundraiser dinner and auction called the Mardi Gras Ball. At this event it honors people who have distinguished themselves as leaders in Catholic charity. These honorees are the Kings and Queens of the Mardi Gras Ball.

• Regina and Dick Hunsaker

Their Majesties:

1988	Mary and Peter Muth
1989	Gail and Gordon Lee
1990	Gayle and Arthur Birtcher
1991	Deanne and Alfred Baldwin
1992	Margaret and Carl Karcher
1993	Jill and Patrick Ortiz
1994	Susan and Timothy Strader
1995	Thomas and Emma Jane Riley
1996	Sherry and Richard Van Meter
1997	Bishop Norman F. McFarland
1998	Gail and Roger Kirwan
1999	Rita and Eugene Deiss
2000	The Sisters of St. Joseph of Orange
2001	Valetta and Kenneth Tait
2002	Betty and Terrance Barry
2003	Tracy and Patrick Powers
2004	Steph and Tim Rusch
2005	Theresa and Stan Pawlowski
2006	Regina and Dick Hunsaker
2007	Maria and Gabriel Ferrucci

• *Bishop Mc Farland with Peter and Mary Muth*

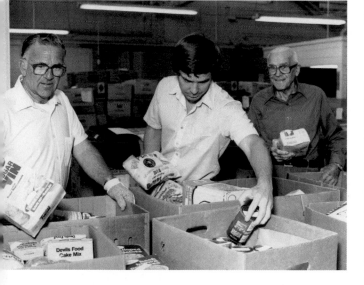

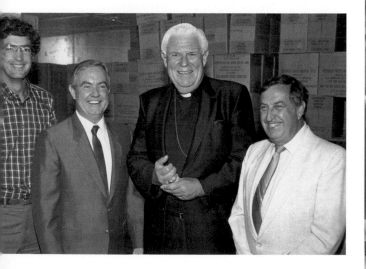

Society of Saint Vincent de Paul

The Saint Vincent de Paul Society is an international Catholic organization of lay persons dedicated to charity. It has four main missions: spirituality, fellowship, helping the poor, and giving others the opportunity to help the poor. The Council of Orange began as a part of the Los Angeles Council. The first Conference of the Saint Vincent de Paul Society in Orange County was established in 1954 at Saint Pius V Parish in Buena Park. When the Diocese of Orange was established in 1976, there were 16 active Conferences in Orange County. On November 2 of that year, members of the society incorporated as the Council of Orange County, a non profit charitable entity.

Currently there are 29 Parish Conferences in the county. Services include a wide variety of charitable programs and activities. The "Second Harvest Food Bank," formed in 1983, distributes a million pounds of food each month through nearly 400 non-profit agencies. The St. Vincent de Paul Center for Community Reconciliation coordinates two services for the incarcerated, their families, and the victims of crime: "Friends Outside," the "Institute for Conflict Management," and St. Vincent's Haven. Six St. Vincent de Paul Thrift Stores provide customers with inexpensive – in some situations free – household and clothing items, as well as opportunities for employment for those in need. More than 11,000 volunteers help to make the St. Vincent de Paul Society a vital resource for the poor and homeless in Orange County.

Respect Life

Birth Choice

Birth Choice is an international pregnancy service that supports pregnant girls and women who need help. Services include free pregnancy testing, shelter homes, counseling, aid, and referrals to medical care, adoption and legal advice. There are four offices in Orange County: Placentia, founded in 1997; Irvine; founded in 2004; Mission Viejo, founded in 1981; and Santa Ana, founded in 2006.

Life Centers

The Life Centers of Orange County Chapter of International Life Services offer free pregnancy testing, counseling and other aid to women facing a crisis pregnancy.

Santa Ana Life Center:
Founded in 1975 by Ruth Rozak, Olive Meehan, Harriet Hizon, and Judy Kelly.

La Habra Life Center:
Founded in 1984 by Mecki Grothues.

Shelter/Homes

Casa Teresa
Casa Teresa was founded in 1976 by Deacon Neal and Sally Sullivan. It is a temporary nondenominational home for single pregnant women 18 years old and over. Its program includes counseling and support. Participants may stay until the baby is two months old.

Precious Life Shelter
The Precious Life Shelter was founded in 1989 by Don and Theresa Sherrin. It provides residential and support services for adult pregnant women. There are three phases: an emergency program providing immediate shelter for up to 30 days at no cost; a transitional program providing shelter during pregnancy and up to two months after the birth of the baby; and a single parent efficiency program allowing a stay of up to 24 months after the birth of the child – providing the mother is working or in job training.

Mary's Shelter
Mary's Shelter, incorporated in 1985, is the vision of Jan Lindsay. It was implemented under the leadership of Joan and Dick Basile and opened in 1994.

Mary's Shelter is a residential care facility in central Orange County for pregnant girls under 18 and their babies. It provides individual, group and family counseling, job training, parenting education, continuing education, and medical referrals.

Hannah's House
In 1995, the Board of Directors of Casa Teresa established Hannah's House as a home for women 18 years old and older, who are single, pregnant and planning to place their baby for adoption. Lisa Callahan was its first director.

Toby's House
Toby's House was founded by Cathleen Eaton in 1998. It is a non-denominational program, operated by Birth Choice of Orange County, offering love and support for expectant mothers who are in crisis and have

children. Women may stay through their nine months of pregnancy and approximately six months after the child is born. It is a two year transitional living adoption home for support and shelter for women placing children for adoption. This program includes appropriate counseling and other support services.

The Knights of Columbus

The Knights of Columbus were chartered in Orange County on September 30, 1906. The Honorable Joseph Scott, State Deputy, presided over its first initiation and installation meeting. Mr. Charles F. Grim was elected the first Grand Knight for Anaheim Council Number 1154. The first meetings were held in the Anaheim Odd Fellows Hall (no negative reflection on its membership).

Since this beginning, the Knights of Columbus in Orange County have been an active social and charitable organization dedicated to supporting the Church at large and in the local parishes. They are known for their strong support of pro-life issues and their generous acceptance of Bishop William Johnson's invitation to adopt aid to the handicapped as their special charity.

Mercy House

Mercy House Ministry, founded by Father Jerome Karcher and a group of concerned friends, provides shelter, care, and counseling for the poor, marginalized, and homeless. The first Mercy House opened in Santa Ana in 1990 as a shelter for men willing to work towards self-sufficiency. Its purpose inspired a growing number of caring donors and volunteers to support and build up this ministry. Mr. Larry Haynes became Executive Director and Lisa Mastropietro took on the role of Director of Development. As the positive reputation of Mercy House Ministry grew, so did its facilities and programs. The original Mercy House eventually became Joseph House, a larger facility accommodating more residents. In 1994, Regina House opened providing similar assistance to homeless mothers and their children. In 1999, Mercy House Center opened as a walk-in outreach program providing crisis intervention, food and shelter referral, clothing vouchers, transportation, and hygiene items. In 2001, Emmanuel House opened as a 21-bedroom facility housing adult men and women living with HIV or AIDS. Backed by the generosity of a growing number of compassionate individuals and organizations, Mercy Ministry allows many men, women and children to experience their God-given dignity through programs leading to self-sufficiency and independent living through work and education.

Scott Fitzgerald

Catholic Worker

Catholic Worker (Isaiah House) is an all volunteer religious organization that provides food, clothing and housing which belongs to a network of 150 independent "houses of hospitality" throughout the country. The Orange County Catholic Worker community was established in 1987 at a home on Main Street. Today it is headed by Dwight and Leia Smith at a new facility on South Cypress Street. Today the shelter serves about 2,000 meals a week and accommodates over 110 people every night in the house and backyard.

Parishes
in the Diocese of Orange

DIOCESE OF ORANGE
ESTABLISHED BY
HIS HOLINESS POPE PAUL VI
JUNE 18 1976

BISHOP

MOST REV WILLIAM R. JOHNSON   1976 - 1986
MOST REV NORMAN F McFARLAND   1987 - 1998
MOST REV TOD D. BROWN   1998 -

Holy Family Cathedral

Orange

On July 28, 1769, a Spanish expeditionary force, under the leadership of Don Gaspar Portola, cut diagonally across the county, probably crossing the Santa Ana River north of what is now Chapman Avenue. Mass was said on the day before the march resumed -- the first Mass offered in what is now the City of Orange and Holy Family Cathedral Parish.

By 1921, the number of Catholics had increased in the area and a new parish was established. Father Francis Burelback was appointed pastor. The property at the corner of East Chapman and Shaffer was acquired and on Palm Sunday, 1922, the first Mass was celebrated.

The parish flourished and outgrew the site. In July 1943, Fr. Bernard Collins became pastor. After several disappointments, Fr. Collins found a desirable location for a new church building at the corner of

La Veta Avenue and South Glassell. Plans for a four-room school were developed; two weeks later, work began. On September 12, 1949, the school, still under construction was opened, staffed by the Sisters of St. Joseph. Next, a large auditorium was built.

In September of 1952, Fr. Robert McEvoy was appointed Pastor. He oversaw the remodeling of the auditorium which became a temporary worship space. Under Fr. McEvoy, parish life flourished and a bulletin was started. In 1956, Fr. McEvoy planned for the construction of the present church building which was completed in April 1958. Fr. McEvoy suffered a stroke in June. In July of 1958, Fr. Robert Gara was appointed Administrator. Additional classrooms were built to accommodate 880 students. The new structure was dedicated January 8, 1961 by Cardinal McIntyre.

In June 1963, the Reverend Donald Strange was appointed to succeed Fr. McEvoy. Fr. Strange built a new rectory and a convent.

In June of 1976, the County of Orange became the Diocese of Orange led by the Most Reverend William Johnson. Holy Family Church was designated the Cathedral Parish. Msgr. Strange was its first Rector and also Vicar General for the Diocese. Msgr. Strange retired in 1978 and Fr.

Brian Coghlan, was appointed Rector. Under Fr. Coghlan's direction, the development of the parish continued with many ministries.

A new parish center was constructed to meet increasing parochial and diocesan needs.

In July of 1988, Reverend Arthur Holquin became the third Rector of the Cathedral. Fr. Holquin focused on the centrality of the sacred liturgy within the life of the Cathedral. He also oversaw the renovation of properties. Under Fr. Art's direction, the Catholic Men's Fellowship was formed. In 1997, the women formed *Hearts and Hands* which continues to provide camaraderie and spiritual nourishment.

In 2003, Fr. Donald Romito was named Rector of the Cathedral. Under Fr. Don's leadership, a Pastoral Council was formed as well as a Hospitality Ministry.

Christ Our Savior Cathedral Parish

Santa Ana

From humble beginnings, this fledgling parish is headed toward a promising and historic future. For many years the densely populated southern portion of Santa Ana lacked a Catholic Parish. When land became available in 2000, Bishop Tod Brown saw the opportunity to not only create a new parish but to purchase sufficient acres to support his vision of a new Cathedral Parish Church and buildings large enough to accommodate diocesan liturgies.

The centrally located property was acquired at the crossroads of three freeways near the cultural and business centers of Orange County – a fitting location for gathering the 1.2 million Catholics in the county.

In January 2005, Bishop Brown announced that he would establish Christ Our Savior Cathedral Parish and on July 1, 2005 he appointed Reverend J. Michael McKiernan as Rector. The first parish Masses were celebrated on September 18, 2005 in the multi-purpose room at Thorpe Fundamental School – just a block from the future parish site. From two Sunday Masses, one in English and one in Spanish, the diverse community quickly grew to three Sunday Masses and still experienced standing room only crowds at some liturgies. On October 1, 2006, the parish gathering site moved one step closer to its final destination, meeting in the large theater at Segerstrom High School.

Assisting Father Michael are Deacon Frank Chavez, Deacon Francisco Martinez and (for the first 10 months) Seminarian Benjamin Tran, now Fr. Tran. Sue Kirrer handles Administration, Lesa Truxaw coordinates Liturgy and Lauren McCall and Bob De Carlo provide Music. At the end of September 2006, the parish hired Lisette Fernandez as its Director of Religious Education.

Parishioners, eager to help build up this new parish, immediately stepped forward to volunteer for liturgical, catechetical and outreach ministries. The first Pastoral Council and Finance Council are in formation. A sense of belonging was easily created since parishioners of all ages help set-up for Mass each Sunday, and meetings and sacramental preparation are hosted in the intimacy of parishioners' homes.

Beginning as a small faith-sharing community, in just over a year, the people of Christ Our Savior Cathedral Parish have already become a "church" and are developing a charism for servant hospitality. In the coming years, they will – with the help of people throughout the Diocese of Orange – build a large Cathedral structure from which to minister to all of the people of the Church of Orange.

Mission Basilica – San Juan Capistrano

School continues a 77 year old tradition of fostering of the faith in the hearts and minds of its students. Under the pastorate of Rev. Msgr. Paul Martin, the magnificent new Mission Church was completed and eventually raised to the status of a Minor Basilica in the Great Jubilee Year of 2000. It has also been designated a National Shrine by the United States Conference of Catholic Bishops. In 2003, Very Reverend Arthur A. Holquin was appointed the 34th successor to Blessed Serra as pastor of the parish and Rector of the Minor Basilica. Under his leadership, the new Parish Pastoral Center was completed as well as a restoration and renovation of the Basilica Church. In 2007, a Grand Retablo was installed in the Basilica Church. The Retablo is artistically reminiscent of the great Spanish Colonial Retablos of the 17th and 18th century. The Retablo was solemnly blessed in July 2007 by His Eminence William Cardinal Levada, Prefect of the Congregation for the Doctrine of the Faith, to the honor and Glory of God and His Most Blessed Mother.

San Juan Capistrano

The historic Mother Church of the Diocese of Orange, Mission San Juan Capistrano was founded on November 1, 1776 by Blessed Junipero Serra. It was the seventh Mission founded by Serra himself. The great restorer of the Mission was Rev. Msgr. St. John O'Sullivan (1910-33). Working tirelessly to "resurrect" this Jewel of the California Missions, Mission San Juan has become a place of pilgrimage and peace for visitors from around the world. Today, the vibrant parish consists of over 3000 households and is enriched by its multi-ethnic character. The Mission Parish

Blessed Sacrament

In 1942, as World War II was underway, many Diocesan priests also had military assignments. Archbishop John J. Cantwell of the Los Angeles Diocese petitioned the Columban Missionary Fathers for priests. As a result, Columban missionary, Father John McFadden SSC, was given the charge to establish a mission in the undeveloped rural area of Westminster. After saying Mass in a home, then in a larger dirt-floored shed, he acquired a tiny Methodist chapel with 16-small pews with a capacity of 100 persons. It was bought and moved to land procured by the Los Angeles Diocese at the direction of Archbishop Cantwell. With the end of World War II, the population began to grow with the influx of ex-servicemen and the expansion of aircraft and electronics industries.

Westminster

In 1947, the parishioners built a convent and a school building which were immediately staffed by the Columban Sisters. The school was dramatically expanded in 1955 to a capacity of over 600 students.

Of course, the tiny chapel was too small for the growing community and in 1950, the parishioners again volunteered their skills and completed the Church building that exists today. Because of the overflowing

attendance at Mass, the structure was expanded in 1955 by adding two wings and an enlarged sanctuary. Blessed Sacrament became the mother parish for nine parishes in the surrounding area. With the end of the Vietnam War, many refugees settled into Southern California. The resultant mix of parish families are now about evenly divided between Anglo, Latino and Vietnamese with a total family count of 4600. Throughout the time of major growth between 1942 and 1986, the Columban Fathers staffed the parish. Then in the year 1986, the Diocese of Orange assumed responsibility. The Columban Sisters continued their teaching mission through the year 1979. Today the accredited school has an enrollment of over 320 with a staff of credentialed lay teachers,

and excellent science and computer classes.

The student body is a mix of Vietnamese, Latino and Anglo children and is known for its student achievement and level of preparedness for high school.

Blessed Sacrament Parish has continued to prosper. In addition to those enrolled in the school, there are over 1,290 students attending the after school religious education programs. The Sunday Masses constitute five in English, two in Spanish and four in the Vietnamese language. There are thirteen choirs contributing to the celebration of Mass. The annual Blessed Sacrament Parish festival began in 1946 and has continued since that time as a successful multi-cultural celebration well known in the wider community.

Corpus Christi

Aliso Viejo

stablished on June 6, 1999 by Bishop Tod David Brown, Corpus Christi Catholic-Christian Community began its story at the Oak Grove Elementary School auditorium as a 'Pastoral Outreach of St. Timothy's to the People of Aliso Viejo.' Having quickly outgrown the elementary school, Aliso Viejo Middle School Auditorium was fortuitously available and it was here that the community's viability as a potential parish was proven and validated.

A few years later, Corpus Christi leased 14,000 square feet of an undeveloped office structure and consolidated both offices, meeting rooms and worship space into a single, integral space. Flourishing within the newly formed City of Aliso Viejo, Corpus Christi has exhibited a willingness to explore new manners of ministerial outreach and celebration of our time-honored Roman Catholic Christianity. Faith Formation of children, with appropriate oversight by parish representatives, is entrusted to families, thus insisting on 'whole family catechesis.' Outreach to both High School and Middle School – aged youth is offered through HAVEN and Jams (Jesus and Me), with our Good Shepherd Ministry providing valuable catechetical moments for pre-Eucharist-aged children. 2007 will see the introduction of the 'Christi Kid's Club', a weekly gathering opportunity for all elementary-aged children. Pastoral Outreach to our Sister-parish, weekly feeding of the homeless and other chosen charities is overseen by our 'Hands Across the County' Ministry, funded through the dedication of 1/40 of each week's Stewardship/Offertory collection, the same level of 'First Hour' tithing recommended to parishioners in support of the parish. Seasonal outings amidst the diversity of the Southern California landscape have become welcome additions to the parish experience.

With visioning provided by the Pastoral Council and day-to-day oversight provided by the volunteer Development Team, in 2006 Corpus Christi completed construction of the permanent Grand Hall, Parish Offices and Meeting Rooms. Comprising three floors, inclusive of a full basement, the new construction of 37,000 square feet has been designed in the Craftsman-style of architecture, a style which flows from the Arts and Crafts movement of recent centuries. Looking ahead, the Staff, Pastoral Council and parish community anticipate exciting and varied ways in which the newly completed structures will allow Corpus Christi Catholic-Christian Community to grow in our 'intentional discipleship of Jesus Christ.'

MISSION STATEMENT

'Through the indwelling of the Holy Spirit, our Catholic-Christian Community seeks to fully understand, embrace and live as God's children and disciples of Jesus Christ.'

Holy Family

Seal Beach

Holy Family Parish began as a mission on property donated to the Archdiocese in 1963 by Ross W. Cortese, builder and developer of Leisure World. This parish serves a senior community, 55 years and older. This is a very unique parish comprised of seniors who come from all over the country.

In November 1963, Father William Mullane was named the first administrator of the Leisure World Catholic mission. At that time, two societies were initiated; the Holy Name Society for men, and the Little Flower Guild for women.

In September 1969, the mission was raised to a parish status and Father Patrick Kelly was appointed Pastor. He died suddenly on October 15th while he was in Ireland. His successor was Father Anthony Kelly who later became the first Monsignor to serve the parish. Msgr. Anthony Kelly added the 5 p.m. vigil Mass to the schedule of services. The use of Eucharistic Ministers was also initiated. On September 1, 1977, Msgr. Kelly became Pastor Emeritus when Father James Pierse became Pastor. Many new parish activities, such as Parish Council, Holy Communion to shut-ins, Christian Service, and expanded duties for the Lectors, were initiated. After Father George M. Breslin became Pastor, Msgr. James Pierse became Pastor Emeritus and is still in residence. Father Breslin died in 1994 and Msgr. Brian P. Coghlan became the new Pastor. During Father Brian's tenure an extensive building project was launched to remodel the rectory and church bulding, and he personally donated the ambo. He retired in 2005 and is also Pastor Emeritus, in residence. Father James Hartnett is the current Pastor.

Holy Family's church building has a distinctive A-frame design and holds a capacity of 500 which adequately serves its 841 registered households. Although Holy Family has no meeting hall the clubhouses inside Leisure World serve the purpose for various meetings such as adult education classes and The Little Flower Guild/Altar Society. The primary purpose of this Guild is to contribute to the support of the parish, through altar care and fund raising activities.

Our Lady of Africa Guild, supports the needs of the missions through prayer and fund raising. Christian Service welcomes new parishioners and visits those unable to leave their homes.

A "Welcome Home Program" was started by Fr. James Hartnett to invite people who have been away from the practice of their faith to "come home."

Because of the advanced age of the community, there is a very active group of Extraordinary Ministers to the sick. There is also a 200 bed convalescent home which the parish is responsible for and where a monthly Mass is celebrated. The parish supports many social justice outreach efforts: a monthly donation to the Shelter for the Homeless in Westminster, monthly support towards a parish in New Orleans, and a yearly collection of blankets and clothes for the homeless.

Parishioners strive to be a friendly welcoming community to all.

Holy Spirit

Holy Spirit's mission statement was published for the first time in January 2006 and is as follows: "We, the Parish Community of Holy Spirit Catholic Church, are a family of many cultural backgrounds. Our mission is to enrich the spiritual life of all parishioners through the active participation in prayer and the sacraments, promoting opportunities to grow in faith and hope and providing a place to come together in the love of God and neighbor. We are committed to the needs of our parishioners and to reach beyond to serve the needs of others. We are called by the Spirit to witness the forgiving, healing and saving presence of Jesus as one Church and one people."

Fountain Valley

Holy Spirit Parish was established in June of 1972 with Monsignor Timothy J. Doyle serving as the first pastor. Under Msgr. Doyle, the parish community progressed from Mass in the local high school cafeteria to the erection of a two-stage multi purpose building, a rectory and a beautiful, 850 seat church which was dedicated on December 6, 1987 by Bishop William R. Johnson.

After Msgr. Doyle's retirement in July 1994, Fr. Joseph Knerr was named pastor. By this time, large numbers of Vietnamese refugees had settled in the community and the parish welcomed the many Catholics among them. The parish demographics were also changing from the founding Hispanic farm families and young middle class families, to many 'empty nesters' as well as the large extended Vietnamese families. All found a welcoming place to worship.

Fr. Knerr oversaw the retrofitting of the church structure, the renovation of the parish hall and the addition of the Parish Center which added much needed classrooms.

In July 2003, Fr. Marito Rebamontan was named the third pastor and he has continued with updating the parish facilities and care of the parishioners. As the community continues to evolve so does Fr. Rebamontan's dedication to integrate all into one parish, each respectful of the other's cultural differences. Currently there are 3,647 registered families and 907 children in English and Vietnamese Religious Education classes.

As a multi-cultural parish, the focus is always to serve the entire community while helping each member come together as one body.

Holy Trinity

The story of Holy Trinity Parish begins before the foundation of the parish itself. As a new community in south-eastern Orange County was being developed, the Bishop had the foresight to buy a piece of land for a future parish site. Over the following six years, the community of Ladera Ranch was then built around this vacant land. Then on July 1, 2005 the Parish was begun. Fr. Reynold Furrell was the founding Pastor. The parishioners were mainly composed of former members of San Francisco Solano, the Mission Basilica San Juan Capistrano and St. Killian's. Fr. Reynold took up residence and had part-time duties at San Francisco Solano Parish for the first year while Holy Trinity Parish was developing.

Ladera Ranch

Since no building was yet constructed, and Ladera Ranch had no other facilities available, the Sunday Eucharistic liturgy was first celebrated in a park – the Town Green. The first "Mass on the Grass" was celebrated July 3, 2005. More than 700 people came to celebrate the new parish. Through rain and shine these outdoor liturgies continued each Sunday for a number of months before a more suitable spot could be completed. In late October 2005, Holy Trinity liturgies moved from their "natural" venue into a newly constructed public elementary school, Oso Grande. Moving into the public school

facility meant celebrating two Sunday Masses for the first several months since the facilities were smaller than the outdoor setting. By January 2006, the parish had grown to the point of adding a third liturgy on Sunday evening. For the holidays of Christmas and Easter, the school facilities weren't available. Nor were they capable of holding the anticipated crowds, so a large tent was erected for each holiday on the polo field of "The Oaks" and the community celebrated the Nativity and Resurrection of Christ in an outdoor setting.

On July 1 2006, Fr. Reynold moved from San Francisco Solano, indicating that Holy Trinity Parish was in a position to be self-sustaining. About the same time, the first full-time employee was hired; Kathie Wickham was named the Director of Faith Formation. Religious Education classes for children began in October 2006. There were 240 children from grades 1-8 registered in the first year of classes.

Holy Trinity Parish is continuing to grow at a rapid rate. God has blessed this young community. Southern Orange County will continue to grow for a number of years and Holy Trinity Parish is working hard to meet the needs of all who will be attracted. New buildings are being planned, ministries are budding into full blossom, and the community is looking to affect its environs by witnessing God's love, mercy and kindness to all.

Immaculate Heart of Mary

The parish and school were begun in 1958 by Monsignor Bradley, and were known as St. Anne's Annex. The first sisters arrived on August 18, 1958 from Worcester, Massachusetts. The Sisters of Mercy first to arrive were Sr. Mary Ambrose, Sr. Mary Imelda, Sr. Mary Carmel, Sr. Mary Leonard, Sr. Mary Paracleta, Sr. Mary Dolorosa, and Sr. Mary Martin. There was a general shower to provide household items for the Sisters of Mercy on January 18, 1959.

Ground breaking for the church structure was held in April 1959. The first Altar and Rosary Society for the 1959-1960 year was headed by Doris Eckler (president) and Eithne Donnelan (vice-president), along with Jennie Watwood (secretary), Connie Lozano (treasurer), and Carol Askins (historian).

Dedication of the church building and school was held on January 17, 1960 by Cardinal James McIntyre. The Reverend Martin C. Hiss was appointed the first pastor in May 1960 and a reception was held on June 5. Four new classrooms were added to the school in the summer of 1960. Two sisters were added to the faculty, Sr. Mary Innocentia and Sr. Mary Celene. Sr. Mary Germaine was appointed principal of the school. Mother Mary Ambrose became Reverend Mother.

Fr. John Wehmhoefer was pastor when the Diocese of Orange was founded and he remained pastor until 1977 when Fr. Brian Coghlan was named Administrator. He was named pastor in April 1978 but was reassigned as the rector of Holy Family Cathedral in July of that same year. He was succeeded by Fr. Francis Moran. Rev. Enrique Sera was appointed pastor in July 1, 1987. Because the population had outgrown the present church structure, he began planning for a new building in 1998.

The ground-breaking for the new church building was held in January 2001, and the dedication was celebrated on June 8, 2002. That same year, a Vietnamese mass was added to accommodate the growing Vietnamese population. In July 2004, Fr. Ed Poettgen was appointed pastor and began overseeing the seismic retrofitting of the

Santa Ana

"old church" building (currently used as a parish hall) and plant refurbishment.

There are 5,787 registered households and with over 20,000 individuals, most masses are filled to capacity. 1,815 children attend religious education.

La Purisima

In 1872, two brothers from New York, Stephen and Robert McPherson, purchased 80 acres of Chapman land on the east side of the Santiago Creek. Two other land developers - Oge and Bond - acquired a large area of level land between the foothills and a western lower mesa area. They were able to extend Chapman Avenue eastward, then parceled out land for farming. La Purisima Parish is within the Oge and Bond tract. After several failed crops, and a blight in 1886 that killed thousands of grape vines, McPherson and Modena, two farmers, began planting orange groves. In 1888, to connect the communities, a railroad was constructed linking the Plaza in downtown Orange, to a livery stable in Modena. The fare was five cents.

World War I began and many farm workers enlisted. Mexico was asked for help, and families came to pick the crops. When the War ended, most of the migrants stayed. However, Mexican families lived in the El Modena area as early as 1895. From 1890-1910, the Catholic people in the area traveled to St. Boniface in Anaheim, or St. Joseph in Santa Ana, to attend Mass.

In 1924, Mr. Remedios Mares donated property on Center Street and a framed structure (seating 80), La Purisima Mission was erected. Later, adjoining property was purchased, the building moved and enlarged to seat 200. Fr. Jose Origel, from Our Lady of Guadalupe in Santa Ana, was assigned. Baptism records document his presence for 30 years.

In October 1957, the Missionary Servants of the Most Holy Trinity arrived. They began the first "Fiesta" in 1958.

The aerospace industry grew and the parish flourished as a bi-lingual community. Many lay groups were begun and the Sisters of St. Joseph were invited to teach religious education.

In 1962, the "old" church was built on Hewes Street. In 1964, La Purisima attained parish status. During this time, the Vietnamese immigrated and many settled in the parish. In 1983, after 25 years, the Trinitarians left and were followed by the Claretian Missionaries. At the same time, two events led to an increase in parishioners: many new Mexican immigrants settled in the area and a housing development in the foothills was built.

The people of La Purisima celebrated perhaps the very first "Tri-lingual" liturgy in the Diocese. The Vietnamese, Hispanic and Anglo communities celebrated together. Because of the popularity of tri-lingual liturgies, sometimes held outside, the parishioners saw a need for enlarging the building.

In 2000, a capital campaign for the construction of a larger structure was begun. Original plans were to remodel the current building, but Bishop Tod Brown wisely

Orange

concluded that any new church building should have seating for at least 1,200.

In July 2003, the Claretians were reassigned to other work and the diocese assigned Fr. Christopher Heath as the new pastor, along with Fr. Anh Nguyen and Fr. Ismael Silva as parochial vicars. On June 4, 2005, Bishop Tod Brown, presided at the dedication of the new church building.

Fr. Vincent H. Pham is the current administrator along with Fr. Antonio Zapata anf Fr. Tuan John Nguyen.

MISSION STATEMENT
Founded in 1924 as a mission parish, La Purisima is a Eucharistic family of socially and culturally diverse people. As a welcoming community of faith, inspired by the Holy Spirit, we reach out, evangelize and serve others in the spirit of Gospel.

Our Lady Of Fatima

San Clemente

Our Lady of Fatima Catholic Parish was established by Archbishop Cantwell of Los Angeles in April, 1947. The population of San Clemente at the time was 600, and the parish was the smallest and southernmost in the Archdiocese of Los Angeles. Father O.B. Cook, a decorated Navy chaplain from World War II, was the founding pastor, and in the intervening years there have been seven pastors serving the parish. In 1976, Pope Paul VI established the Diocese of Orange, and Our Lady of Fatima Parish became one of the 45 founding parishes of the new diocese. Today the city of San Clemente numbers 75,000 residents, and Our Lady of Fatima parish has 1250 registered families.

Our Lady of Fatima Parish is "A Eucharistic Community Living the Good News." Parish life covers the full spectrum of ministries and service. They are a multicultural parish celebrating five English Masses and one Spanish Mass each weekend. The faith community is dedicated to the formation of their children through a parish school with an enrollment of 275 students, and a school of religious education program with 385 students in both English and Spanish. There are over 50 ministries serving the spiritual, educational and social needs of the parishioners as well as caring for those beyond their walls.

The community recognizes its baptismal call to continue the mission of Jesus in the world. Nurtured by a vibrant liturgical

life, they continue to grow in stewardship – discerning, encouraging and sharing God's many gifts. The parishioners are actively involved in the local community and in the diocese caring for the poor, the homeless and the imprisoned. With God's grace, they seek to reveal Christ's light in their families, their parish and their neighborhoods.

Our Lady of Guadalupe

In 1928, construction began on Our Lady of Guadalupe Church structure. The building was overseen by Father Murphy of St. Mary's Church in Fullerton and construction was completed by the Cristobal Gomez Family. The first Mission Church was completed in 1929.

La Habra

In 1929, the Guadalupanas, the oldest church organization, raised funds to add a bell and a bell tower to the church building. In 1944, a fire destroyed the church structure and rectory. All parish records were lost. Until the completion of a new building, Masses were held in private homes or outside. In 1945, Fr. John Stapleton was assigned as parochial vicar.

In 1947, the second Our Lady of Guadalupe mission was completed at its new home on Hillcrest Street. On April 10th of 1947, the mission was proclaimed to be an official parish of the Archdiocese of Los Angeles by Archbishop John. J. Cantwell.

By January of 1951, the city of La Habra's population had risen to 7,800 residents and Father David Coleman was appointed pastor. This rapid growth in the population required the building of yet a third church building. A new location was sought for the site and under Father Coleman's direction, eight acres of land were purchased. This land on Central Avenue would also house a new eight classroom school.

The school was finally completed in 1956. The Sisters of St. Joseph of Orange came to La Habra to teach catechism to the children of the parish and in September of 1956, Sister Annette Bachard became the first principal of the school which opened with 178 students. By the end of the first year, Sister Fabian Stephenson and two lay teachers were teaching over 200 students. A convent was built for the women religious.

In 1958, Father Coleman became Monsignor Coleman.

In 1961, the enrollment of the school had climbed to 440 students and four new classrooms were added to the school plant.

In 1966, due to the fact that the congregation had outgrown the Church facility, Cardinal Francis A. McIntyre allowed Monsignor Coleman to build yet another structure. Construction was commenced in 1969 and was completed by 1970.

Bishop John J. Ward of the Archdiocese of Los Angeles consecrated the altar at the fourth site on April 19, 1971. As the new building began its life the old structure, now "Coleman Hall," became a much needed auditorium. In 1976, Monsignor Coleman retired as pastor and the parish became a part of the Diocese of Orange which had been established under the leadership of Bishop William Johnson.

Father Francis Roughan replaced Monsignor Coleman as pastor. In 1979, Fr. Roughan suffered from declining health and Fr. Justin MacCarthy became Administrator. He was named pastor in 1983. By then, the number of registered families in the parish numbered 3,883.

In June of 1991, Monsignor Coleman died. The summer of 1992, saw a major remodeling of the church's choir loft, and the installation of a new organ. In 1995, Our Lady of Guadalupe was chosen for the diocesan's first Feast of Our Lady celebration. The year 1997, saw the Golden Jubilee of the Parish and the retrofitting of the school.

In the year 2000, Our Lady of Guadalupe was chosen as one of the pilgrimage sites for Diocesan parishioners. That same year, the Life Teen program in the parish was established. In 2004, the parish hall was completed and in 2005, the convent was remodeled and became the Faith Formation Center. Today the number of registered households is 5645. Currently there are 387 in the school and 874 in the religious education program.

The parish will be celebrating its 60th anniversary in 2007.

 ur Lady of Guadalupe

Our Lady of Guadalupe was established as a Mission on March 24, 1922 to serve the needs of the Spanish-speaking community in Santa Ana. The community was first administered by clergy from Mexico. The wooden frame church was dedicated to Our Lady of Guadalupe on July 22, 1922.

On November 18, 1938, the community was entrusted to the Order of Augustinian Recollects at the invitation of the Most Rev. John J. Cantwell, Archbishop of Los Angeles. Religious assigned there lived in a mission house until 1957. OLG remained a mission of Our Lady of the Pillar Parish in Santa Ana from March 5, 1965 until it was established as a parish on April 7, 1980. That same year, the religious began to reside with the community at Our Lady of the Pillar Parish until a rectory was build in 1982.

Major renovations to the original mission church occurred in 1939, 1945 and 1967. The new parish center was built in 1986 as a multi-purpose building and was dedicated as a church structure in April, 1991.

3,000 families are officially registered and individuals number 6500; 1292 children attend the religious education program.

Parish organizations include Guadalupanas, Holy Name Society, Matrimonios Vida en Cristo, Jovenes para Cristo and St. Vincent de Paul Society. Ministries include: Eucharistic Ministers, Lectors, and Prayer Groups.

Santa Ana

Our Lady of Guadalupe Delhi

Santa Ana

Our Lady of Guadalupe Church (Delhi) began its history in the 1920s. It is located in the Delhi community in Santa Ana, California. The community was known as Gloryetta at that time. Developers from New York renamed the area Delhi and it became a part of the church name.

Guadalupe (Delhi) was first established as a mission. On June 28, 1927 the Rev. Father Jose Origel was named Rector of the Church of Guadalupe De Gloryetta (Delhi). He presided over the church until 1962 when he retired. The first baptisms registration book lists Maria Herminia Barajas as being baptized on July 02, 1927.

In 1938 a new church, which is now the present church, was constructed. Two major contributors are listed as Mrs. Catherine Meassor and Mrs. Mary Felton.

Rev. Father Adolfo Jimenez became the priest in charge of the church in 1962 and remained in the position until 1967 when Rev. Father John Coffield took over and stayed until 1973. During this time the church was instrumental in establishing the Delhi Community Center. The center worked out of two used Quonset huts obtained by Father Coffield. It gradually evolved, by December 2001, into the largest community center in this area.

The mission was established as a parish in 1979. The first pastor was the Rev. Frank J. Gallagher, S.J. Several other priests served, including priests from the Company of Jesus. Guadalupe continues to maintain as its main purpose Evangelization through the Disciples in Missions movement. Father Alonso Cáceres has been the Pastor since 1987. The church has several active groups such as Youth for Christ, Guadalupana Society, OCCCO, Saint Vincent Society, two Prayer Groups and a Religious Education Program for children and adults, which educates approximately 1000 people per year. This program has been coordinated and supervised by Rosa Teresa Castro for the past 40 years. Volunteer workers operate the church kitchen and run food sales on Sunday. The "Jamaica", an annual fiesta for benefit of the church, is held during the summer.

Our Lady of La Vang

In 1921, a small chapel was built to meet the needs of the growing population of Mexican migrant farmers. Under the supervision of St. Boniface in Anaheim, the chapel was named, "Manzanillo" in memory of their country of origin. Supervision of the chapel fell to a number of parishes as the county grew and finally rested with St. Barbara's. It was established as Mission de Lourdes in 1972; Msgr. Pedro Yrigan became administrator. He energetically made contacts with Archbishop Tomas Clavel, Sister Magali, and the Santa Clara Sisters. He became friends with Mrs. Augustina Garcia who eventually became his right hand person for 21 years.

Santa Ana

Msgr. Yrigan created La Bonita Community Center which offered ESL classes, driving lessons, cooking and sewing classes, and programs for children. Archbishop Clavel introduced the Catholic Youth Organization (CYO) which expanded services to the youth, In 1985, Msgr. Yrigan became the official pastor of Our Lady of Lourdes which was the smallest geographical parish in the Diocese. In 1990, the first deacon was ordained, Rafael Romero. Three women parishioners entered religious life: Magdalena Avalos, MC, Norma Guerrero, MC, and Luz Elena Juarez, NMC.

In 1994, Father Bill Barman succeeded Msgr. Yrigan. For the next ten years, one of the youngest pastors in the diocese significantly improved the facilities and expanded ministries.

The number of parishioners increased beyond capacity and the ministries focused primarily on the Spanish speaking population, especially recent arrivals from Mexico.

When the demographics of the area began to change to include many Vietnamese Catholics, Fr. Barman encouraged informal gatherings of Vietnamese parishioners. In 2000, a new parish was established to integrate the small Our Lady of Lourdes into a larger community under the patronage of Our Lady of La Vang. Soon, the small structure hosted a weekly Mass in Vietnamese. Meanwhile, land was acquired for a larger building. Fr. Joseph Son Nguyen, who recently returned to the diocese after graduate studies, succeeded Fr. Barman. The new pastor expanded services in Vietnamese and English while keeping services to the Spanish speaking community an integral part of the parish. Soon, another Spanish speaking Deacon, Rigoberto Maldonado, was ordained to help him. Groundbreaking was held on December 17, 2004. In July 2005, the new community rented the Plumbers and Steamfitters hall nearby and began celebrating Sunday Mass. Construction began work in October 2005, and all major works were completed by August 2006. On August 13, the

last day of services in the rented hall, Bishop Jaime Soto led a procession with a statue of Our Lady of La Vang from the hall to the new site, officially ending an era. The new Our Lady of La Vang building was dedicated in a multilingual Mass by Bishop Tod D. Brown on August 20, 2006. Thousands celebrated throughout the day in different languages.

Services are held in Spanish, English, and Vietnamese; attendees number 3,000. There are 300 children in bilingual religious education, and 80 teenagers in Confirmation preparation. To date, over 500 active families have officially registered; the number grows each week.

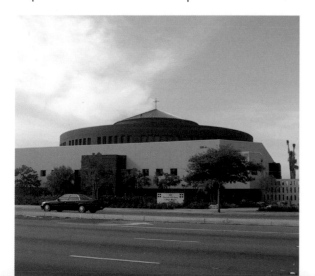

Our Lady of Mount Carmel

Newport Beach

Our Lady of Mount Carmel parish is located in the city of Newport Beach incorporated on September 1, 1906 on the Newport-Balboa peninsula which parallels California State Highway 1 between Huntington Beach on the north and Laguna Beach on the south, and encloses Newport Harbor.

As early as 1912, Bishop Thomas Conaty of the Diocese of Monterey-Los Angeles considered establishing a Catholic parish in Newport Beach, a settlement tracing its history back to 1865 when a "new port" was built to handle shipping for the area ranchos.

The first mass in Newport Beach was celebrated on Christmas day, 1912 by Father John Reynolds of St. Mary's, Huntington Beach. The first mass in the new structure of the parish was celebrated on July 16, 1923, the feastday of Our Lady of Mount Carmel, by Father Maurice Harnett of St. Mary's.

In February 1924, Bishop John J. Cantwell established the parish to serve thirty families residing year-round in

Newport Beach, Balboa Peninsula, Balboa Island, Costa Mesa, and Corona Del Mar and appointed Father Thomas Tannyane as its first pastor.

In 1941, St. John Vianney chapel was constructed and dedicated on Balboa Island as a mission of Mount Carmel and Father Peter Conroy was appointed as the first-ever assistant pastor of Our Lady of Mount Carmel.

Fathers Denis Falvey, John Stapleton, and Stephen Kiley, oversaw the construction of the present church building which was blessed on July 8, 1951 by Los Angeles Archbishop James Francis A. McIntyre.

Today's parish is a thriving Catholic family of 1300 households with many ministries. Among them is a vibrant Adult Faith Formation Speaker's series that attracts people from all over the diocese.

Our Lady of The Pillar

In the 1940's, when the Augustinian Recollect Fathers were serving the Mexican people at Our Lady of Guadalupe Parish, (Third and Grand), in Santa Ana, they saw the need for a parish on the west side of the city. Mexican families were settling there and they needed a center of worship closer to home.

The Friars purchased property on the west side of Santa Ana where a chapel was constructed from a U.S. Army Quonset hut located on West Sixth Street. It was on January 19, 1949, when at the invitation of Father Braulio Balisa, Bishop Joseph T. McGucken blessed their chapel, dedicated to Our Lady of Mount Carmel. Father Joseph Urrutia had obtained the former military barracks from the Santa Ana Air base. It would be the beginning of Our Lady of the Pillar Parish, which would take more definite form in the 1960's. The former chapel now serves as a parish hall. Father Damian Gobeo came to the parish in 1951. He was one of the Augustinian fathers' most notable "builders." Fr. Damian lost no time in erecting the school and then the rectory. A life-long devotee of the Blessed Virgin, especially under the title of Nuestra Senora del Pilar, he began to realize his dreams of building a church structure in Santa Ana. In 1960, his dreams came to life on the drawing boards of architect, Harold Gimeno, who had worked with Fr. Damian on the school and rectory. In August 1961, construction began. A year later, the building was completed and the first Mass was celebrated.

On June 21, 1964, Cardinal James Francis McIntyre officiated at the solemn dedication.

After 12 years of service, Fr. Damian's eventful pastorate came to an end in June 1963, and Father Jose Maria Santiago was appointed pastor. During his term, Nuestra Senora del Pilar became the official parish of the Mexican-Americans in Santa Ana, and the "mother-church" of Our Lady of Guadalupe (Third and Grand) was now a mission of her vigorous daughter.

The altar, made of Mexican onyx, was consecrated on December 12, 1964 by His Excellency the Most Reverend Timothy Manning, then Auxiliary Bishop of Los Angeles.

The year 1966 saw the Franciscan Sisters, who had taught in the school since its opening, move to a private residence on Washington Street.

In March 1976, construction began on a new hall; it was dedicated on August 1, 1976. The last building project at Pillar was the construction of an annex to the school. It houses the general office, the principal's office and a teachers' room.

Father Alfredo de Dios first served as associate pastor in 1979 and was named Pastor in 1984. He introduced the Neo-catechumenate to the parish in Lent of 1987. After the first catechesis, five Spanish

Santa Ana

communities formed, and shortly thereafter, one English-speaking community was added. The number has since grown to 20 communities (17 Spanish and 3 English). Fr. de Dios served as pastor the second time from 1984 to 1987 and a third time from 1997-2006. Rev. Anthony Palos succeeded Fr. Alfredo de Dios in July 2006. The Augustinians have faithfully served the Pillar parishioners from the very beginning.

Our Lady Queen of Angels

Newport Beach

On May 1, 1961, Our Lady Queen of Angels parish was established in Corona del Mar, California from the original parish in Newport Beach, Our Lady of Mount Carmel. At the time, some wondered if there were enough Catholic families to support the new parish. Forty-five years later in May 2006 OLQA has 4074 registered households! Msgr. Ralph Harvey was the founding pastor back in 1961 and worked hard to build a new Catholic community in a growing area. He was responsible for the construction of the church building, school, hall and rectory. The Sisters of St. Joseph of Carondelet along with the lay faculty staffed the parish school. Religious Education programs were established for students attending public schools.

In 1982, then Msgr. Michael Driscoll was appointed pastor to succeed Msgr. Harvey who had retired after 21 years leading the OLQA community. At this time, many of the reforms of the Second Vatican Council were implemented and the parish community blossomed with the RENEW program, Cursillo and youth ministry. Msgr. Driscoll was simultaneously Chancellor of the Diocese of Orange and went on to become Auxiliary Bishop of Orange and then Bishop of Boise, Idaho.

In 1984, Msgr. William McLaughlin began his 20 years of service to Our Lady Queen of Angels as pastor and it was during this time that the parish grew to a community of over 4,000 households. The school became so popular, a lottery had to be held to see who would be admitted and the waiting lists grew longer. The inadequate parish hall was replaced by a much larger facility called the Parish Center that included the parish hall, meeting rooms, parish offices, the school administrative offices and faculty room. The rectory was beautifully remodeled and became a priests residence. Parish Pastoral and Finance Councils work with the School Board.

Parishioners became involved with the larger Orange County community serving on many diocesan boards and committees and helped to start worthwhile organizations like Casa Teresa and SPIN that still flourish today. A series of associate pastors now called parochial vicars served the parish community along with a large parish staff. The monthly Outreach collection was started to provide support for local non-profit community organizations. In 2001, the Cornerstone campaign was begun to build a new, larger church, expand the school and add a gymnasium to the parish facilities. In 2003, Our Lady Queen of Angels received national recognition as a Blue Ribbon School for excellence in education.

Recently, a young adult from OLQ organized a trip to Biloxi to help to rebuild the community.

Fr. Kerry Beaulieu was appointed pastor by Bishop Tod Brown upon Msgr. McLaughlin's retirement. In April 2006, Our Lady Queen of Angels completed the purchase of the site of St. Mark Presbyterian Church across Domingo Drive from the present church building.

Saint Angela Merici

In 1951, St. Mary's Parish in Fullerton began as a mission to Catholics in Brea. The first Mass was celebrated in the American Legion Hall by Rev. Augustine O'Gorman, Pastor of St. Mary's in Fullerton. In 1952, the Archdiocese of Los Angeles purchased land for a new parish in Brea and in 1955, Cardinal McIntyre approved construction of a temporary hall at the corner of Fir Street and Walnut Avenue. The new pastor of St. Mary's in Fullerton, Rev. John Siebert, continued serving the mission in Brea. On January 29, 1956 ground was broken for the temporary hall and construction was completed within the same year; Cardinal McIntyre blessed the new structure on March 17, 1957. An altar society was begun in April. Five years later, Rev. Emmett R. McCarthy was appointed pastor when the Mission became a parish under the patronage of St. Angela Merici.

Brea

In 1964, the Sisters of St. Clare arrived from Ireland to teach in the new parish school which opened that same year with four grades. By 1966, a convent was erected to house the ten sisters. In September the Archdiocese approved plans for a new parish structure which included the relocation of the temporary building for future use as a hall.

In 1968, Fr. McCarthy was honored with the title of Monsignor and in 1969 the new building was completed and opened for Easter services. In 1979, the Women's Council Christmas Bell Ringer raised funds for the electric Carillon for the church building. In 1988, Fr. McCarthy retired as pastor and Fr. Gordon Pillon served temporarily as Administrator. In 1988, Msgr. Brian Coghlan was appointed as the second pastor of St. Angela Merici parish. He served until 1993 and Fr. Ted Olson was appointed as the third pastor. Major construction projects were overseen by Fr. Olson including a new parish center, a new

hall and a new kindergarten classroom. In 2003, the founding pastor, Rev. Msgr. Emmett B. McCarthy, died, and in 2005 Fr. Olson was reassigned to St. Pius V Parish after his 12 year term at St. Angela's. Fr. Michael-Dwight Galinada was appointed the fourth pastor of St. Angela's Parish. He has overseen a number of renovation projects.

Saint Anne

Santa Ana

St. Anne Parish was established in the southern portion of Santa Ana on March 14, 1923, by Bishop John J. Cantwell of the Los Angeles-Monterey Diocese. Reverend William F. Verhalen was appointed as the first pastor. In its early years, the parish saw a succession of pastors who served relatively short terms; in its first fifteen years, the parish was served by eight pastors. The arrival of Fr. Christopher Bradley, named pastor in 1939, marked significant change.

His appointment marked the beginning of the period during which St. Anne Parish realized tremendous growth and change. Fr. Bradley served as pastor of St. Anne for 28 years. The buildings on the property today, with the exception of Campbell Hall, were built during his guidance of the parish. In addition, Mater Dei High School was his dream and became the apple of his eye. Also during his tenure as shepherd of the parish, St. Anne Parish Annex was built at McFaddden and Center Streets, and later became today's Immaculate Heart of Mary Parish.

St. Anne School opened its doors in September, 1945. The Sisters of Charity of the Blessed Virgin Mary (BVM) were first entrusted with administration and teaching at the school. The Sisters of Charity served the parish families until 1980, when the Sisters of the Company of Mary, (ODN) took charge of the parish school. The Sisters of the Company of Mary have been serving the parish school for the last twenty-six years. St. Anne Parish School continues to be strong, viable, well-regarded, and is a positive asset of the parish and surrounding community.

The St. Anne Parish area has seen dramatic demographic, racial and cultural changes in its recent history. Today more than 5,500 faithful attend the nine Sunday liturgies in English and Spanish. Parish facilities are in constant use. The parish is marked by extensive lay participation, outreach, and emphasis on evangelization. Strong Religious Education programs for children and Faith Formation for adults, liturgical ministers, choirs, Disciples in Mission small groups, communities of the Neo-Catechumenal Way, Jovenes Para Cristo, Young Adults for Christ, the Guadalupanas, Adoradores, a parish conference of the St. Vincent de Paul Society, and many other groups cooperate and collaborate with the priests and parish staff in a wonderful manner. In recent years, Catholic Charities of Orange County has had a regular presence at the parish in service to the surrounding community. Every week members of the Neocatechumenate participate in 'Mission' as they conduct house to house neighborhood visits, knocking on doors, sharing faith, and inviting all to St. Anne's.

After 83 years of devotion and service, the parish community thanks God for the past, celebrates present blessings, and welcomes future challenges. The Parish of St. Anne continues to stand on Main Street as a sign of faith, hope, and service for the entire community of Santa Ana.

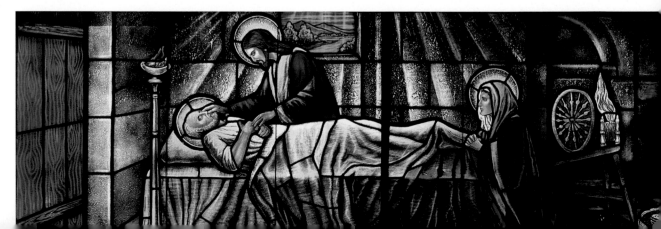

Saint Anne

St. Anne's Parish in Seal Beach, has grown amid a typically Californian pattern of development and expansion. The mission of Seal Beach was established in 1921 by the late Father Thomas Morris, pastor of St. Matthew's Parish, Long Beach. Prior to this, the Sisters of the Immaculate Heart of Mary had organized a Sunday School. Masses were then celebrated in a temporary building, a grain storehouse, located at the back of Brock's Drug Store on Electric Avenue. The Reverend Austin Fleming was named as the first pastor. A site was purchased at 317-319 Tenth Street by a few parishioners, aided by a $1,000.00 donation of a generous Chicago woman who requested that the parish be dedicated to St. Anne.

On August 22, 1937, the new church building was dedicated, dignified by the presence of the Most Reverend John Joseph Cantwell, Archbishop of Los Angeles. During the ensuing years, St. Anne's gave evidence of the ever-increasing pace of expansion and change.

In 1943, Fr. Thomas O'Sullivan assumed the responsibility of the parish. His was the longest term of service of all the priests who have left their mark upon the growth of St. Anne's Parish – spiritually and temporally.

The only private parking lot of any size in town became a reality when Fr. O'Sullivan purchased from the City, five beach lots which lie south of the rectory.

Seal Beach

In 1958-59, Fr. Thomas managed the affairs of St. Anne until he was succeeded by Fr. Louis Pick. The orderly neatness of his training as Naval Chaplain was clearly reflected in the many improvements effected during his stewardship. The church building was given a thorough renovating by way of new sanctuary fittings and furniture; the sacristies were remodeled and painted. To accommodate the increasing demand for pastoral services, the old rectory was remodeled with the addition of five new rooms. In 1965, the eastern portion of the parish became a part of the then new St. Bonaventure parish.

Fr. Robert Vidal assumed the responsibility of the parish in 1994. In 2002, the parish hall was completely remodeled along with the adjoining restrooms, and the exterior area of the church building was given a new look with landscaping and terra cotta pavers.

St. Anne's currently has a Bereavement Ministry, Peace and Justice Ministry, Youth Ministry, an active Knight's of Columbus and a newly formed Women's Group.

Many of the former pastors of St. Anne's have been called home by the Good Shepherd. May they be remembered by those who now reap what they have sown.

Saint Anthony Claret

Anaheim

Saint Anthony Claret, the son of a weaver, was born in the town of Sallent, Spain in 1807. Trained as a weaver, he chose the cloth of the Church instead of the cloth of the world. In his priestly career, he became Archbishop of Santiago, Cuba. St. Anthony Claret was a noted speaker, a prolific writer and founder of the Claretian Order. He died October 24, 1870 and was declared Venerable by Pope Leo XIII in 1889. St. Anthony Claret Parish was named after this illustrious modern saint.

Before the church structure was built, Mass was celebrated at the La Jolla Mission, Our Lady of Guadalupe, once a mission of St. Mary's Parish, Fullerton. This quaint little mission was razed to make way for the busy Orange Freeway.

St. Anthony Claret church building was erected in 1955 and the first Mass was celebrated in the new structure at Christmas Midnight Mass that year.

The parish has seen many changes over the years to accommodate the growing numbers of parishioners. Beginning in the late 1990's, the interior of the church building was renovated to include a beautiful Blessed Sacrament Chapel, a cry room for parents with small children, pews surrounding the main altar, stained glass windows and a new Baptismal font.

The parish school, built in 1957, opened its doors, September 16 to 195 students under the devoted guidance of the Sisters of St. Louis. The school enrollment has grown to 328 students, pre-school through eight grades and the Religious Education classes have 1168 students enrolled.

Over the years the physical plant grew with the addition of other buildings: the parish hall, convent, rectory, Religious Education offices and two meeting rooms, the St. James and St. Rita rooms, to accommodate the many parish group meetings and new ministry offices.

St. Anthony Claret Parish celebrated its 50th Anniversary in October 2005 with Mass celebrated on the parish grounds by Bishop Tod Brown and a delegation of priests.

The parish has grown considerably within the past 50 years to over 5000 registered families. The parishioners are all very proud to be part of St. Anthony Claret parish and welcome all who come. May this home of Christ continue to urge all on in service to God and one another.

Saint Barbara

Santa Ana

ames Francis Cardinal McIntyre, Archbishop of Los Angeles, designated Reverend Michael Collins to shepherd the Catholics of West Santa Ana in 1962. Fr. Michael came as an ordained priest from Ireland in 1944 and had assignments as an Assistant Pastor at Incarnation Parish of Glendale and St. Gregory of Los Angeles. He was now ready for the role of Pastor which meant transforming a ten acre tomato patch at Euclid and McFadden into a living Faith community. It would take time to build the facilities, and Mass was held in a rented facility, the Garden Grove Elks Lodge.

The west end of the south building served as the parish structure for two years. The rectory which started on Wisteria Avenue moved to Maxine Avenue just as Fr. Michael's first assistant arrived. At that time he was the recently ordained Fr. Frank Buckman. Fr. Michael eventually added a second helper, Reverend Erwin Bauer, SVD. This team of priests oversaw the development of the faith-life of the parish through a Catholic School program, Religious Education and adult formation classes. The Poor Clare Missionary Sisters were the first teaching order at St. Barbara School.

The priest team also leaned heavily on the laity right from the beginning. A Men's Club and a Women's Council were sounding boards for the priests for the faith life, social life and facility development. The new Church building was opened on September 24, 1965, followed by the rectory and a parish hall-gymnasium. Along with faith development, there was the need to provide sportsmanship as well as physical development. Presently, St. Barbara's has facilities for baseball, football, soccer, basketball and volleyball. A Parents Association works to support the Catholic School program.

This community also became a spring-board for the pro-life movement in the early 1970's. Probably the most significant program inaugurated in the spring of 1975 was the welcoming and resettlement of the Vietnamese peoples who left their home country under duress. Since St. Barbara's formation in 1962, there was a gradual assimilation of the Hispanic community and subsequently St. Barbara evolved into a multi-cultural parish from its earlier European rooted population.

Through the years, other Pastors such as Reverend Richard Delahunty, Reverend Gary Kinzer, Reverend John Joyce and Reverend Richard Kennedy have all added their own dimensions of change to continue and update the faith life of the parish. Two significant changes in the last ten years include the neo-Catechumanate for families and a Parish Pastoral Council.

Additional facilities added through the years include a rectory annex, a parish hall annex, and most recently a third school building. A major Christian Service program provides food on a weekly basis for those in need.

Currently there are 12 weekend liturgies attended by approximately 9,000 people.

Saint Bonaventure

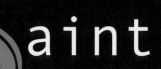

St. Bonaventure Parish in Huntington Beach was established in 1965 by Monsignor Michael Duffy. A small contingent of Catholics held their first liturgy in the living room of the temporary rectory located on Plymouth Lane on September 1, 1965. They soon moved to a warehouse on Murdy Circle and celebrated their first Mass there on October 3, 1965. The warehouse remained their place of worship until the construction of the existing church building which stands on nine acres acquired in 1967.

The new house of worship was dedicated on June 10, 1979. Prior to the construction of the parish school, students were bussed to Blessed Sacrament School in Westminster. The Presentation Sisters have been with the school since its inception. Their excellent leadership was validated in 2006 with the conferral of the Blue Ribbon Award for academic excellence, a national honor.

The current rectory was completed in 1972, the hall in 1976, the parish center and religious education building in 1984, and the kindergarten in 1990. Following Monsignor Duffy's retirement in 1988, Father Kerry Beaulieu was appointed pastor. By that time, the parish, though still largely English-speaking, was experiencing change. After the fall of Saigon, the parish had graciously welcomed Vietnamese refugees and had given them a place to call their spiritual home. Father Beaulieu expanded the reach of ethnic ministries when he initiated the Spanish Mass in 1995, and he helped found the Greater Huntington Beach Interfaith Council, an important local group that promotes tolerance, cooperation and understanding among the various local faith communities. Today, the parish has over 100 organizations and ministries, which reflect the dynamism and diversity of a parish with 5,000 registered households.

Under the current pastor, Father Bruce Patterson, who arrived in 1999, discernment began on future directions for the parish, which resulted in the current master plan. In 2006, Phase I of the master plan was completed, expanding the HOPE office Christian outreach facilities, and creating a new multi-purpose building, the

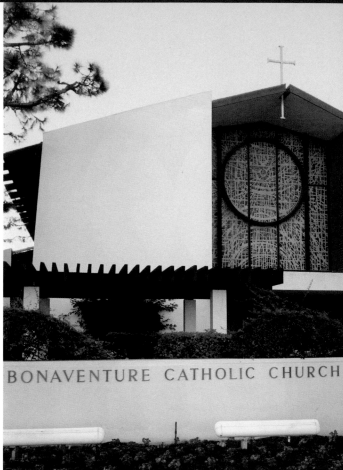

Huntington Beach

Duffy Center, named after the founding pastor. The second and third phases of the master plan include a central courtyard, a new and expanded hall, an improved playing field and a renovation of the interior of the church structure. New junior high and high school ministries have been implemented, and in response to the recent Pastoral Letter, "Learning, Loving and Living Our Faith" from Bishop Brown, new opportunities for adult faith formation are in development.

Saint Boniface

The history of Saint Boniface Parish humbly began in the home of the Rimpau Family, 19th century residents of Anaheim. A room served as a chapel and Mass continued almost monthly until the first St. Boniface Church structure was built in 1859. Priests from the San Gabriel Mission as well as Bishop Thaddeus Amat, CM, tended to the spiritual needs of Anaheim's first Catholics.

Anaheim

The first resident pastor was Reverend Victor Foran. In the year of his appointment, 1875, Saint Boniface Parish was officially established. It was named for Boniface, Apostle of Germany. Anaheim, at the time, was predominantly comprised of German settlers. It is worthy to note that local churches in the neighboring settlements were missions of Saint Boniface; at one time its territory extended over the whole of what is now Orange County.

The parish was successful and eventually outgrew its first church building. In 1902, construction began on the corner of Palm and Center Streets for a "new" Saint Boniface. Father Francis J. Dubbel oversaw his project which was completed in one year. The Gothic style church was richly decorated with numerous statues, stained glass windows, and paintings on the ceiling.

St. Boniface Church, Anaheim, Cal.

Of significant note is the foundation of the Knights of Columbus Council in 1906. They are still extant in the life of the parish. The next half century brought growth and prosperity to the parish community, albeit without challenges; earthquakes, a flood, and the Klu Klux Klan (whom the parishioners ran out of Anaheim) tested the faith of parishioners. In spite of these, the community continued to flourish with determination and undeterred faith. At this time several mission churches were served by Saint Boniface to meet the spiritual needs of the growing Mexican Community. Eventually these missions became their own parish or were absorbed by newly founded parishes.

In 1961, Father John C. Quatannens broke ground for a new church building to accommodate the growing community and it was formally dedicated on January 12, 1964 by James Cardinal McIntyre. This new structure featured exquisite stained glass windows, lofty ceilings, a larger-than-life-size crucifix, mosaics, and a 16-foot bronze statue of its patron on the façade. The church was richly decorated with marble throughout and rich terrazzo flooring. The main altar was created from a single block of marble weighing seven and a half tons.

The subsequent decades brought a great influx of Latino and Vietnamese Catholics to Saint Boniface.

The eighties and nineties proved to be years of great blessing and challenge. At the turn of the millennium, Saint Boniface served over 5,000 registered families, baptizing over 1,000 new Catholics each year, and celebrating ten Sunday Masses in three languages: English, Spanish, and Vietnamese.

As the 150th anniversary approaches, the parish of Saint Boniface continues to serve a diverse community and strives to be a sign of the living gospel for the community.

Saint Callistus

St. Callistus Parish was founded in November of 1961 under the direction of His Eminence James Francis Cardinal McIntyre. It was placed under the patronage of St. Callistus, a pope and martyr of the early Church who died in 222.

In the early 1960's, the new St. Callistus Parish met the needs of Orange County's rapidly growing population, and was located near four major cities - Anaheim, Garden Grove, Orange and Santa Ana. It was

east, Harbor Boulevard on the west and 17th Street on the south.

In the earliest years of the parish's history, Mass was celebrated at a roller rink on Garden Grove Boulevard. Next a house was purchased in Garden Grove, and used as a temporary rectory.

Bishop Alden J. Bell broke ground for a new church building and school on April 29, 1962, and the first mass was

both of the new buildings on April 21, 1964.

Over 45 years have passed since St. Callistus was first established. The parish has grown from a small community of 700 families to today's thriving parish of 4,500 families. The parish mirrors the diversity of Orange County with its rich cultural heritage of Anglo, Hispanic and Vietnamese Catholics sharing and worshiping together as one.

Many unnamed saints have passed through the doors of St. Callistus Parish over the years. To choose any one person or persons who have most influenced this faith community would be an injustice. A long line of kind-hearted and worthy priests, parishioners and staff stand as examples of the parish's rich faith tradition, and its continuing response to heed God's call to worship Him through lives of holiness.

ST. Callistus Catholic Church

Garden Grove

"carved out" from the mother parishes of St. Boniface in Anaheim, St. Columban's in Garden Grove, Holy Family in Orange and St. Joseph's in Santa Ana. Parish boundaries stretched from Katella and the Santa Ana Freeway on the north, Bristol Street on the

celebrated there in February of 1963. Growth and expansion moved quickly. In September of 1963, the school opened and was staffed by the Dominican Sisters of Mission San Jose. Bishop Timothy Manning formally dedicated and blessed

Saint Catherine of Siena

Laguna Beach

In 1909, the Joseph Yoch family purchased a one-room school, built in 1888 by members of a Mormon settlement living in Laguna. The building was relocated into the village and became the first Catholic Community in Laguna Beach, St. Joseph's Chapel.

In 1927, the name of the chapel was changed to St. Catherine's. It is speculated that the reason for the name change may be found with the Yoch benefactors. The chapel had been named after Joseph Yoch's patron, St. Joseph. So too, with its status as a new parish church, and the death of Joseph Yoch in 1926, a new name was chosen, St. Catherine of Siena, the patroness of his wife, Catherine Yoch.

Over the years, the community grew and the chapel was too small to accommodate the crowds. The need for a new church building became obvious. In 1930, Father Jeremiah Lehane was appointed as Administrator of St. Catherine of Siena parish and plans for a new church structure began.

The property, on Temple Terrace, was purchased and construction began. Amazingly, church construction was completed in less than two months at a cost of approximately $11,000.

Since its construction in 1931, St. Catherine of Siena has served as a spiritual center for Catholic families living and vacationing in Laguna Beach. Membership has increased over the years and now approaches 1600 families.

Over the next 84 years, only minor repairs were made to the church structure and office building. In 2003, the groundbreaking was begun for a major remodel and renovation. The renovation project required the buildings to be brought up to code and to be made handicap accessible. It was an opportunity for the community to also bring the church furnishings up to current liturgical standards. A Blessed Sacrament Chapel was added, as well as reconciliation rooms designed so that penitents have the option of either face-to-face or behind the screen confessions.

Dating back to 1947, the original artwork in the sanctuary was originally hand-painted on canvas. During the renovation, the murals were cleaned and restored. With the tabernacle now located in the Blessed Sacrament Chapel, there is room for a cross in the sanctuary behind the altar. The corpus of Christ that hangs on the new cross, the statues of Mary, the Mother of Jesus, and John, the beloved disciple, were all hand crafted by artisans in Spain specifically for the parish.

The community also took the opportunity to expand the administration building. For the first time the parish has multiple meeting rooms for use by the many ministries and groups.

The hillside behind the church and administration building previously unusable was recreated as a liturgical garden with a "Rosary Walk" and "Walking Stations of the Cross". The garden was designed in its entirety by one of St. Catherine's parishioners, Robert Mueting.

Saint Cecilia

I n 1956, St. Cecilia's parish was established, the only Catholic Parish still in the city of Tustin. When the Prescott family learned that James Cardinal McIntyre wanted to establish a parish in the area, they donated their homesite on Newport Ave near 17th Street. Although the church structure was never built on that site, the parish was named in honor of the Prescott's mother whose middle name was Cecilia. Ireland-born, Father Michael J. Moran the founding pastor was transferred to Tustin from San Pedro where he had served at Holy Trinity Catholic Church. Masses began in a storefront church/hall at 130 West Main Street. To cover the expense of altar boy cassocks and surplices, pictures of the first Mass were sold at $1 each. Parishioners were asked to purchase chairs and kneelers at $15 each. In January of 1959, the parish opened its first Youth Center and in December of 1959, Father Moran purchased the property on Sycamore Street – St. Cecilia's home today. In 1961, the last bus load of children were taken to Mission Capistrano for Religious Education Classes and classes began at St. Cecilia's.

In 1960, Father Moran was reassigned and Msgr. John Sammon was appointed pastor. The new church structure was built and dedicated in June of 1964 and the first 8th grade class also graduated from St. Cecilia's school. In 1967, Monsignor Sammon began radio broadcasts of the Sunday Mass on KTBY and KYMS. Msgr. Sammon guided the parish as it grew rapidly into a vibrant community active in its outreach to the poor and especially to the Missions. Under his pastorate, many young men entered the seminary and became priests for the Diocese of Orange. It was during this time (1975) that some of the first Vietnamese families were resettled into the Diocese. They became the first seeds of the St. Cecilia's Vietnamese Community.

In 1976, Msgr. Patrick Doherty was named pastor and oversaw construction of the new parish hall and the renovation of the church building.

Over the years and with each new pastor, St. Cecilia's has grown in size and in diversity. Through the loving care of Father Tim MacCarthy, the parish grew into a family that celebrates liturgy in English, Spanish and Vietnamese.

In 2005, Father Alfred S. Baca was appointed pastor, the first Mexican American pastor and native of Orange County. St. Cecilia's is now home to the Filipino Community and the Indonesian Catholics of

Tustin

South County. The parish school, named a Blue Ribbon School in 2006, is at full capacity. There are presently over 4,600 registered families in a city that is still growing and developing. St. Cecilia's continues its commitment to the Missions and is noted by the Bishop's Conference as one of the top churches in the United States in its outreach. This legacy of almost 50 years of Catholic life and presence in the City of Tustin continues to be the foundation for the parish as it nears the celebration of its Golden Jubilee.

Saint Columban

Garden Grove

St. Columban Parish was established by the Columban Fathers who began their work in the area as early as 1941. A group of 35 families bought a parcel of land at the corner of Fourth Street and Stanford Avenue and began construction of the new church structure in June, 1946. Construction was completed in six months at a cost of $15,000. Still considered a mission site, the church building was dedicated on March 16, 1947 by Bishop Timothy Manning, Auxiliary Bishop of Los Angeles.

Within seven years the Catholic population increased from the original 35 to 600 families and the church at Fourth and Stanford was soon overcrowded. Five acres of land were purchased on Stanford Avenue between Euclid and Nelson Streets and the parish of St. Columban was officially established on October 9, 1953. Reverend Michael J. Murphy, a native of Templemore, County Tipperary, Ireland was appointed as the first pastor.

The decision was made to build a multi-purpose hall, a building that would serve as a place for liturgy for a number of years and then could be converted for use as the parish hall. The building was designed to seat 900. The first Mass was offered on August 28, 1955.

The first unit of the school was opened to 150 students in September of 1956 staffed by the Irish Sisters of Charity. The second unit was completed in 1958. The school reached its highest enrollment of over 700 students in the late fifties.

The "new" and present church structure with its landmark 110 feet high bell tower, was not constructed until 1967. Designed to seat 1,400 it is still the largest church building in the Diocese of Orange.

Because of its seating capacity it hosts many diocesan events including ordinations. Cost of the unfurnished building was $559,154. It was dedicated on April 21, 1968.

Reverend Michael Murphy served as pastor until he retired at the age of 75. He was succeeded by Reverend Eamon O'Gorman who served from 1982 to 1993. The third pastor, Reverend Donald Romito, served from 1993 until June of 2003. Reverend Juan Caboboy, the fourth pastor assumed leadership in July of 2003.

In October of 2003, the 50th Anniversary as a parish was celebrated in 2003. They have grown to a faith community of over 5,300 families who enjoy a rich cultural mix of Anglo, Vietnamese, Spanish, and Filipino members.

There are ten liturgies every weekend, five in English, four in Vietnamese, and one in Spanish. Religious Education classes are offered in three languages to 950 elementary school students and there is a vibrant Life Teen program involving over 200 junior-high and high school youth.

Among the significant community events participated in by St. Columban parishioners are the annual Thanksgiving Mass, with the blessing of the peace officers and firefighters in the community. Parishioners participate in feeding the homeless every Saturday morning, and the annual Garden Grove Christian community Walk-of-the-Cross on Good Friday. The local St. Vincent de Paul Society Conference helps the poor and hungry.

Saint Edward the Confessor

Dana Point

In the 1940's, Father Ozias B. Cook was the pastor of Our Lady of Fatima in San Clemente. He began approaching members of the community now known as Dana Point and Capistrano Beach about building a chapel to serve the people of that area. Mrs. Edward Doheny, a close friend of Father Cook, graciously donated the funds for the building. The land was donated by Mr. and Mrs. Aaron Bucheim. St. Edward Chapel (now known as San Felipe de Jesus), was built and dedicated in 1950. At the request of Mrs. Doheny, in memory of her late husband, the chapel was named after St. Edward the Confessor, the pious King of England who founded Westminster Abbey.

Father J. Augustine O'Gorman was the interim priest and was succeeded by Father Michael J. Carlos. In the early 1960's, Cardinal McIntyre placed it under the Mission, at that time pastored by Msgr. Vincent Lloyd–Russell.

In 1969, Father Louis F. Knight from Ascension Parish in Los Angeles was appointed Pastor. He developed a 25 year plan for the 15 acres of land overlooking Dana Point Harbor. The design of the first building was thought to be temporary. The first mass in St. Edward Church (now known as Knight Hall), was on Christmas Eve in 1971, and the dedication was March 5, 1972.

Fr. Knight oversaw the building of a religious education center which opened in 1980. It served the religious education needs of the parish, including the only Catholic preschool in south Orange County, an elementary school K-8 serving approximately 620 students, a religious education program serving 800 and many other adult formation programs.

Father Knight worked tirelessly to create a parish that was truly in line with the Documents of Vatican II, a parish that was built on the principle of collegiality – shared responsibility of leadership by lay people. The Parish Assembly, made up of interested parishioners, acted in an advisory capacity to the pastor.

In January 1981, St. Edward Parish consisted of 1400 parishioners. The Dana Point area grew rapidly and so did the population of the church. Fr. Knight articulated the need for a larger, more permanent church and the response was tremendous. Their aim, in conjunction with Fr. Knight's vision, was to utilize the environment, highlighting the spectacular view of the Pacific Ocean. The ground-breaking ceremony was April 5, 1992; it was dedicated by Bishop Norman McFarland on December 11, 1994. Unfortunately, Fr. Louis Knight's death in November 1994, prevented him from ever seeing its completion. Sadly but fittingly, the first mass celebrated in the new structure was his funeral mass.

In July 1995, St. Edward parish welcomed its new pastor, Fr. John Lenihan. Full of energy and enthusiasm, the parish community began a capital campaign to purchase adjacent property, expand the Religious Education Building, and build a Pastoral Center.

In 2001, Fr. Steve Sallot, rector at Mater Dei High School, was appointed administrator, then pastor in 2004. In addition to serving as pastor at St. Edward, Fr. Steve became the administrator of the neighboring parish, San Felipe de Jesus in Capistrano Beach.

Saint Elizabeth Ann Seton

Irvine

St. Elizabeth Ann Seton (SEAS) parish was founded in 1971 as a community annex of Our Lady Queen of Angels Catholic Parish in Newport Beach. The SEAS community spent its first decade meeting and celebrating Mass in private homes and public facilities. Rev. Thomas Gannon served as founding pastor. In 1976, the mission church was designated a parish within the newly formed Diocese of Orange. The original all-purpose parish hall, which served as a community gathering spot as well as a worship space, was completed in July 1981. At that time the second pastor, Rev. Kenneth O'Keeffe, was named. The new worship space was dedicated by Bishop Norman McFarland in 1994, following the appointment of SEAS current pastor, Rev. Thomas Pado. Since 1994, the parish added a new youth center and remodeled the parish hall to accommodate more fully the needs of the faith community. Also, a Korean language Mass was added as well as various ministries in Korean to serve the approximately 350 Korean families that are now part of the parish community.

The parish of St. Elizabeth Ann Seton is today a vibrant community with a great deal of diversity. In addition to the Korean community that is a formal part of the parish, there are members of this church from every ethnic group that is representative of Orange County.

There is a full complement of young families, senior citizens, youth, and college students from the nearby University of California Irvine campus. The community life reflects the rich gifts of the people, with active ministries in outreach, social justice, faith formation for all ages, social gatherings, and spiritual life. Liturgies are lively and still prayerful with a wonderful ministry. The parishioners look forward to the growth and challenges the future will reveal.

Saint Hedwig

The Roman Catholic Parish in Los Alamitos was founded in 1922 under the patronage of St. Isidore, the patron saint of farmers. Father John Purtill was the first pastor. 17 pastors served St.Isidore's parish.

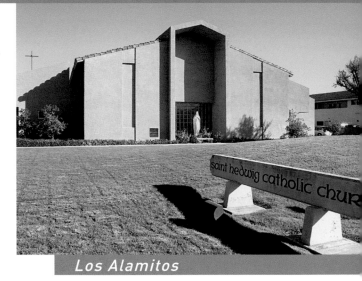

Los Alamitos

As the area expanded, there was a need for a larger church structure as well as a school. Around 1960, Father Dominc Daly, the pastor obtained land for the new church building through Mr. Ross Cortese, the developer of Rossmoor. Plans were drawn for the new church, convent and an eight room school. The first school, staffed by the Irish Sisters of Charity, opened with four classes. Each year another grade was added until all eight classrooms were in use.

The new parish building, St. Hedwig, was named for a polish noble woman who gave her life and goods to the Catholic Church. Her feast day is celebrated October 16.

Father Desmond Quinn was appointed Administrator in 1962 and served in that capacity until 1964 when he was named pastor.

In response to the area's rapid growth, he supervised the development of eight additional classrooms for the school.

As the area grew, so did the parish and its programs. It was also under his direction that the St. Hedwig Athletic Association was formed. This unique addition to the parish has been appreciated by hundreds of families in the surrounding communities.

In 1989, in order to reflect the liturgical and pastoral mandates of Vatican II, plans for the renovation of the original church building were drawn up. The last mass was Easter Sunday, March 26, 1989. The first mass in the new structure was celebrated on Christmas Day, 1989. Dedication of the newly renovated church building took place on Sunday, June 10, 1990.

Presently there are over 3000 families registered in the parish and 480 students enrolled in the school. The School of Religious Education program provides religious training for over 400 students. Many of the young men and women of St. Hedwig Parish have achieved numerous scholastic and professional honors. Four pastors have served the people of St.Hedwig's. Rev. Kenneth Schmit is currently the pastor.

There are numerous parish lay organizations with hundreds of volunteers.

The parish staff strives to provide for the needs of the people through its service programs and ministry support groups.

Numerous parishioners have become involved in the larger community of Los Alamitos through the establishment an development of the ministries, "We Care" (providing assistance to those in need in the area), Casa Youth Shelter (providing safe shelter for run away teens and working to reunite them with their families), and Precious Life Shelter (providing housing and care for unwed pregnant women).

St. Hedwig is proud of its history, its place in the community, and especially, its people.

Saint Irenaeus

Cypress

School auditorium at the corner of Lincoln and Grindlay. The Saint Irenaeus church building was erected in 1963. The first mass in the church structure was celebrated on September 8, 1963 and it was dedicated on April 26, 1964.

The school was constructed simultaneously. The first classes were held in the new schoolrooms on September 9, 1963. There were approximately 275 students in grades 1 through 4.

The parish has grown significantly from the initial 600 families and the first organizations (e.g., the Altar Society, the Choir, the Holy Name Society). Today there are over 5600 registered families and more than 30 organizations and ministries. There are active Hispanic and Filipino communities. Cultural diversity is celebrated in many ways including Pentecost Sunday. Through the blessings that God has given the people and the various ministries, they are able to serve the needs of the parish and the less fortunate of the community.

St. Irenaeus Mission Statement: We come together as a community of many backgrounds to follow Jesus Christ and his teachings; we gather around his altar as baptized people and go forth to carry his message to all, to serve others in their needs and to grow spiritually.

Saint Irenaeus Parish was established on May 3, 1961 under Cardinal Francis McIntyre of the Archdiocese of Los Angeles. Saint Irenaeus continued under the Archdiocese of Los Angeles until the Diocese of Orange was formed in 1976 under Bishop Johnson.

The first pastor was Father Peter Caslin, followed by Fr. John R. Keller, Fr. Mike Heher and Fr. Pat Rudolph. The Presentation Sisters, who came to Saint Irenaeus in August 1963, initially staffed the parish school. Their order is from Ireland; but the first group of sisters came by way of Pakistan.

The first mass was celebrated on June 6, 1961 in the Cypress Elementary

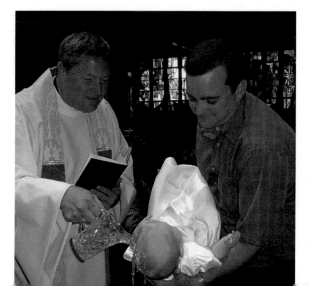

Saint Joachim

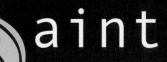

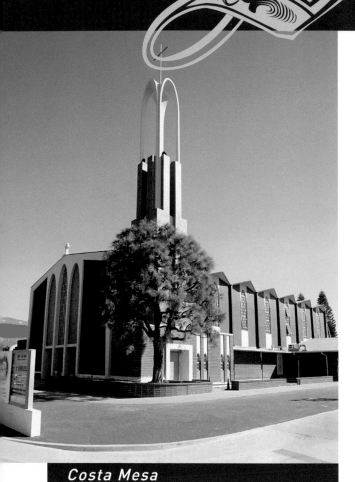

Costa Mesa

Saint Joachim and Saint Anne are venerated as the parents of the Blessed Virgin Mary. Hence, it is fitting that the parish would be named after the husband of the saint whose name was given to the neighboring city, Santa Ana. The founding Pastor, Msgr. Thomas Nevin, had his first priestly assignment in Santa Ana. The new parish was founded on March 16, 1947. At its beginning, the parish territory included all of the city of Costa Mesa and parts of Newport Beach.

Costa Mesa traces its history to a Spanish land grant in 1810 to Jose Antonio Yorba. By 1880, settlers had bought sections of the land grant from the Yorba heirs and had established the town of Fairview. A storm in 1889 destroyed the small town. A new small town, called Harper, named for a nearby rancher, was established and it gradually grew. In 1920, Harper officially changed its name to Costa Mesa, meaning "Coastal Table Land" in Spanish, and continued as an agricultural community. The city survived the Great Depression, in spite of the collapse of many businesses, and during the Second World War, it was the training site for thousands of people at the Santa Ana Army Air base. When Saint Joachim Parish was founded some of the old buildings of this Army base served as temporary quarters for parish activities.

The land for the parish was purchased in the summer of 1947. The old base chapel was moved to the property and remodeled in time to celebrate Christmas Masses that year. On June 13, 1948, Bishop Timothy Manning dedicated the new church building. On September 12, 1949, the new school was opened, under the leadership of the Sisters of St. Joseph of Orange, using barracks also transferred from the base. In 1954, a new addition to the church building was completed, doubling its capacity. In 1965, the current church structure was built and dedicated.

As Southern California expanded over the decades, so has the parish, reaching its current membership of nearly 3,000 families and reflecting the ethnic mix of the changing times.

In 1960, one half of its territory was transferred to its daughter parish, St. John the Baptist.

The parish embarked on a major expansion of its facilities in 2004, building new classrooms, administration offices, a rectory and a parish hall. The parish is led by the current pastor, Father Enrique Sera, two vicars, Fathers David Vuelvas and Michael Nguyen, a professional pastoral staff and school principal, Sister Kathleen Marie Pughe, C.S.J. The community is also blessed with very able volunteers who serve on lay boards and councils. The mission of the parish is to open its doors to all who wish to follow Christ in the Roman Catholic tradition and to reach out in love to all of its neighbors, Catholic and non-Catholic alike.

IN LOVING MEMORY
OF THE
VICTIMS OF ABORTION

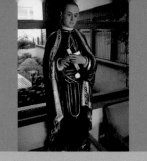

Saint John Neumann

St. John Neumann Catholic Parish in Irvine was formally declared a parish community by the late Bishop William Johnson on December 1, 1978. Father Colm Conlon was appointed the first pastor. The parish was placed under the patronage of St. John Neumann, the first male canonized saint of the United States.

The first masses were celebrated in the gymnasium of Irvine High School and in Good Shepherd Lutheran Church. Ground breaking for the new church building took place on June 15, 1980. The first mass was celebrated in the new structure on November 8, 1981. Since St. John Neumann was the fourth Bishop of Philadelphia, Cardinal John Krol of Philadelphia consecrated the building on June 6, 1982. Ground for the new offices was broken on June 6, 1992. The new parish center was completed in March of 1996. A new parish, St. Thomas More, was established from St. John Neumann in the northern part of Irvine on July 1, 1996. A new youth ministry building was added in 1999 and a new parish rectory completed the building program in 2001.

The beautiful large mosaic in the sanctuary was dedicated in August 1988. It is the work of the noted artist sisters-- the Piczeks who are known worldwide. Isabel Piczek described the mural, "The imaginary six foot priest at the altar is re-created as the twelve foot Christ crucified and the eighteen foot resurrected Christ emerging from a chrysalis. As disciples of Jesus, we are reminded that our growth as Christians and as a community of believers depends on our unity with the suffering Christ. The golden chalice in the middle of the mosaic gathers the blood of Christ. 'We will drink of the chalice of the Lord' it says--the one Jesus drank! The cross' shadow which lies diagonally across the bottom of the mosaic is green to signify the hope of all the world in His resurrection."

The parish carries on the work of Jesus Christ through Worship, Service and Discipleship. As commanded by Jesus Himself, there is an extensive program in training, involving and equipping lay people to minister to others in the community. A strong relationship with St. Paul's Greek Orthodox Church includes monthly spiritual book discussions. A lasting friendship with the Islamic group, Global Cultural Connections, and other interfaith groups were formed. For many years, blessed with numerous bible sharing groups, strong adult formation teams were developed, thus continually renewing commitment to Living, Loving and Learning our Faith.

MISSION STATEMENT

We, the Parish Community of St. John Neumann, proclaim the Message of Jesus Christ and rejoice in His presence and action in our lives. As a parish of the Roman Catholic Diocese of Orange, in California, in union with our Bishop, we live and teach the values of our faith. We gather each Sunday for the sanctification of ourselves and all creation, and to glorify God who is manifested as Father, Son and Holy Spirit.

Saint John the Baptist

The story of St. John the Baptist parish begins with its neighboring parish of St. Joachim in south Costa Mesa. In 1958, due to increasing enrollment at the parochial school, the leaders of the Archdiocese of Los Angeles gave permission to build a new school in north Costa Mesa. Ground was broken on Christmas Eve and the school opened in September 1959. Two months later the church building was completed, and Mass was said there for the first time on November 8, 1959. Msgr. Thomas J. Nevin, pastor of St. Joachim, also administered what was known as "St. Joachim's Annex."

Costa Mesa

Only six months later, in May 1960, the "Annex" was officially named St. John the Baptist. The new pastor, Fr. Anthony McGowan, celebrated his first Mass on May 18 of that year. The Women's Council and the Holy Name Society members helped to improve the parish buildings and grounds. A number of notable priests served St. John the Baptist. Father Joseph K. McEneany, SS.CC. was chaplain to the nearby Fairview Developmental Center for 37 years. In 1978, Father Denis Lyons succeeded Monsignor McGowan as pastor, then in 1997, Father Jerome Henson. In 1977, Msgr. Daniel Brennan began to serve in the parish while working at the newly formed Orange Diocesan offices.

The Sisters of Mercy began their ministry to the parish school in 1959. Six sisters came from Ireland. In 1962, a young Sister Mary Vianney Ennis came to join the faculty. After teaching for a number of years, she became principal of the school, a post she has filled with love and dedication ever since.

In 2002, the parish was entrusted to the Norbertine Fathers of Orange. Father Martin Benzoni was named pastor and three confreres joined him as parochial vicars. The Norbertines are especially devoted to the Holy Eucharist and they initiated adoration of the Blessed Sacrament Monday through Friday.

St. John's developed as a multi-ethnic community in the last few decades. In 1975 Vietnamese Catholics, who found a new home in Orange County, began the nucleus of a community at St. John the Baptist. As their numbers grew, priests were assigned to serve their spiritual needs. In 1977, Fr. Thomas Ha celebrated the first Mass in Vietnamese. The community grew from a small handful of people to 3000 families.

The Latino presence at St. John's also developed. The Spanish Mass on Sunday attracts many. In addition, there is a complete catechetical program for Latin American children and adults.

Even in the 1990's, it became clear that a new church should be built, and plans were drawn for a completely new parish plant. However, the bishop's decision to build a new cathedral just a mile from the parish, caused those plans to be changed. In 2004, permission was granted to begin a major renovation of the church. Talleres de Arte Granda of Spain were commissioned to create the liturgical art, and construction began in May 2005. On February 26, 2006, the church was re-dedicated by Bishop Tod Brown.

ST. JOHN VIANNEY CHAPEL

Saint John Vianney

Balboa Island

The only Parish Church on Balboa Island, the landmark St. John Vianney Chapel, had a significant presence and influence on the Island since its establishment in 1941 as a mission church of Our Lady of Mount Carmel Parish on the Balboa Peninsula of Newport Beach.

Many island residents are Roman Catholic, descendants of those who came from Los Angeles and built summer homes on the Island in the 1930's.

The chapel was dedicated by Archbishop Cantwell of Los Angeles in August 1941 with Father Patrick J. Beary, Mount Carmel's pastor, as its first administrator.

According to "The Catholic Church on Balboa Peninsula," a book published in 2002 which`profiles the parish of Our Lady of Mount Carmel, parishioners from Balboa Island and Corona Del Mar were most appreciative of the convenience of the new "chapel of ease" which enabled them to attend mass without making the arduous journey to the peninsula. Priests from Mount Carmel made the sea voyage across the bay on the ferry each Sunday for 20 years until the Balboa Island Chapel became the canonical mission church of the newly established Our Lady, Queen of Angels Parish in 1961.

Msgr. Harry Trower was the chapels' first resident administrator (1976-78) and was succeeded by Msgr. Joseph Sharpe who served from 1978 until his retirement in 1997.

Msgr. Lawrence J. Baird, the current administrator, was appointed by Bishop Norman F. McFarland in 1997. He describes St. John Vianney chapel as "the church on a remote island on the rim of the Pacific."

With the appointment of Msgr. Baird as the Pastor of Our Lady of Mount Carmel Parish in July 2006 by Bishop Tod D. Brown, St. John Vianney Chapel was returned to the patrimony and pastoral solicitude of the peninsula parish.

The Island Parish is home to 700 households.

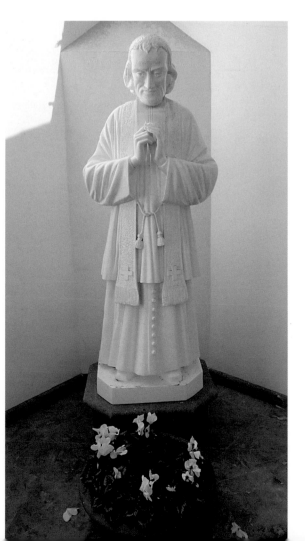

Saint Joseph

Placentia

In its beginnings, St. Joseph Catholic Parish was a mission that grew out of neighboring parishes serving Spanish-speaking people. In 1952, a new parish was established including both St. Joseph and another chapel, Santa Teresita, which today still offers a weekly Spanish Mass.

Rapid growth, from 400 families in 1957 to 2000 families in 1967, created a frenzy of building activity, which included the expansion of the Church structure, a school, and a parish hall. The Holy Name Society and the St. Joseph Guild were major fund raisers for these endeavors. Reflecting the Rancho period of local history, huge fund-raising barbecues attracted all of Placentia and its surrounding communities.

Religious education was first directed by the Sisters of St. Joseph of Orange. The Franciscan Missionary Sisters of the Immaculate Conception came in 1960 to teach in the new school. They withdrew in 1985, and the school presently operates with a credentialed administration and staff. Today, in addition to the parish school, a variety of faith formation opportunities are available for young children, teens, and adults in English and Spanish.

In a continuing effort to promote evangelization and spirituality, the parish has committed to several programs over the years: "Project Understanding" (1967), a narrated Mass and tour of all facilities open to the public; "Renew" (1984-1986), small neighborhood discussion groups; JUBILEE 2000 (1997-2001), small faith sharing groups during Lent and Advent and monthly large group meetings offered in English and Spanish; and the ongoing "Disciples in Mission Program 2000," small prayer discussion groups.

An active St. Vincent de Paul Society meets weekly to assist over 300 families in need. The Knights of Columbus provide spiritual, social and other support services to the parish. Many individual parishioners work with the neighboring Presbyterian Church at H.I.S. House, a half-way living facility helping the homeless.

With the pastor, priests, parish staff, liturgical ministries, parish organizations, and 4000 families their spirit is expressed in the following statement, "We, the Catholic community of St. Joseph, Placentia, with the guidance of the Holy Spirit, live the message of Jesus Christ. As a welcoming, inclusive community, we provide and support strong faith formation through Eucharist, sacraments, education, stewardship and service."

Saint Joseph

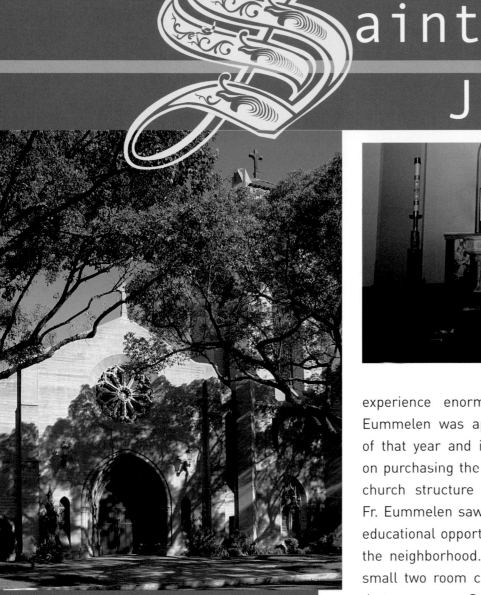

Santa Ana

In 2007, Saint Joseph Parish will celebrate its 120th anniversary! In 1887, the parish began worship in a simple mission chapel located at the corner of Lacy and Stafford (now Civic Center Blvd). Previously known as, Our Lady of the Rosary or "The church by the depot", it served the spiritual needs of the pioneer Catholics. In 1896, the church building was completely destroyed by fire. A new structure was quickly built on the same site and dedicated to Saint Joseph. The faithful continued to be served by the priests of Saint Boniface in Anaheim.

On July of 1903, Fr. Joseph O'Reilly was named the first resident pastor of Saint Joseph. In 1913, the parish began to experience enormous growth. Msgr. H. Eummelen was appointed pastor in April of that year and immediately began work on purchasing the property adjacent to the church structure for a parochial school. Fr. Eummelen saw a great need to provide educational opportunities to the children of the neighborhood. Saint Joseph School, a small two room cottage, opened its doors that same year. Soon after it's opening, the school's enrollment grew beyond its limits. Both pastor and parishioners made an "Investment of Faith." In 1916, the Sisters of Saint Joseph of Eureka, California, now the Sisters of Saint Joseph of Orange, were invited to teach in the school. The school building was enlarged three times due to the growing enrollment. The parishioners of Saint Joseph continued their "Investment of Faith" over the next several years and helped purchase additional land. In the 1930's and 40's, the parishioners fulfilled their dream of constructing a larger church building for the faithful to gather to pray and hear the Gospel of Jesus Christ proclaimed and shared. Over the last 60 years, there has been a tremendous growth at the parish and the registered households now number 3500 with over 14,000 individuals.

Saint Juliana Falconieri

St. Juliana Parish began as an annex to St. Mary's in Fullerton. Its founder, Monsignor John Siebert, pastor of St. Mary's, set the stage for a new parish and school. The church building was originally intended to be a gym with a permanent structure to be built at a future date. Dedication of St. Juliana's took place in August 1965. The first rectory (currently parish offices) was furnished by ladies who collected Blue Chip stamps and donations of new and used articles.

A Men's Club, Women's Club, and "Inquiry Class" for converts (now known as R.C.I.A.), Parent's Club, Music Ministry, and CCD were a few groups founded in the early years, bringing about important growth in the community. With Monsignor Terence O'Brien, the foundation that is the basis for much

of their success was built. The Sisters of St. Joseph of Orange staffed the school until 1987 and they are credited with integrating Catholic Christian values into every aspect of the children's education.

From 1981 to 1993, Father Robert Vidal served as pastor. Two permanent deacons were ordained in May 1990. (Another deacon from the parish was ordained in May 2003). Parish festivals, pictorial directories, a monthly newsletter, California State University Newman Club, and many other organizations were initiated under Father Vidal's leadership.

In 1993, the Order of Servants of Mary (Servite) priests were offered the pastoral care of St. Juliana's by Bishop Norman McFarland. Father Jude Herlihy, OSM, served as pastor until July 1, 2006 when Father Luke Stano, OSM, was appointed. Currently, Father Jude and Father Pat Donovan, OSM, serve as parochial vicars and Father Pat is chaplain of the California State University Fullerton Newman Club which meets at St. Juliana's.

Under Father Herlihy, a parish pastoral council was formed and new opportunities for active involvement in the community were offered such as "Welcoming and Belonging," Stewardship, and Small Faith Communities.

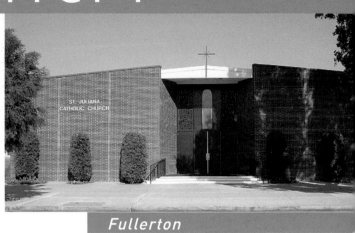

Fullerton

More than 40 ministries now actively exist in the parish of over 1550 families.

A 1999 engineering study revealed that both the school and church building were "high risk" structurally should an earthquake occur in our area. A comprehensive capital fundraising campaign and development of a Master Plan were undertaken for much-needed improvements to the complex.

Given the theme "Honoring our Past, Building our Future", the plan consists of three phases. The first phase, to upgrade and retrofit the school, was completed in 2001. The second phase, now underway, is to build a parish center. Present facilities are inadequate for the increasing number of families and ministries. The third phase will be to seismically retrofit and renovate the church building.

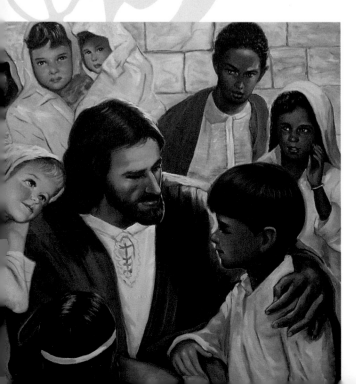

MISSION STATEMENT

St. Juliana Falconieri Catholic Community is a sacramental family called to welcome and encourage all people to accept and celebrate the free gift of eternal salvation, Stewards of the new creation in Christ, we strive to bequeath to future generations a kingdom of love, justice, and peace through liturgy, sacraments, scripture, education, loving service, and fellowship

Saint Justin Martyr

Anaheim

St. Justin Martyr Parish is a thriving, growing, and faith-filled community dedicated to loving and serving God, guided by His love, the teachings of Jesus, and the wisdom of the Holy Spirit.

The parish was established in 1958 to serve west Anaheim and the nearby Sacred Heart Mission (Misión del Sagrado Corazón). Fr. Hugh O'Connor (later given the title of Monsignor) was appointed as pastor of the new parish, a position he held until his retirement in 1990. Liturgies were held in a local warehouse which served as the home of St. Justin's until the newly erected church building was opened in July 1959. The parish school opened two months later, with the rectory, convent, and parish hall opening in the 1960's, and additional offices and meeting rooms in 1970.

Volunteers immediately began arranging for the needs of the new parish, setting up Religious Education classes, holding fund-raisers, and beginning various groups. This established the foundation of parishioner involvement that remains an integral and necessary part of parish life. Currently under the leadership of Fr. Joseph Nettekoven, pastor since 1990, St. Justin's continues to serve the community by offering liturgical, spiritual, educational, outreach, social/well-being, cultural, and youth programs, ministries and services.

Under the jurisdiction of St. Boniface Church until St. Justin's was formed, Sacred Heart Mission was established in 1926 to serve the Hispanic community. This community built a small church structure which was used until 1968 when a larger building was constructed. The original building and portable on-site classrooms are now used for Religious Education and liturgical, spiritual and social gatherings. In order to accommodate the growth of the Hispanic community, all weekend Masses were relocated to the larger St. Justin Church building in 1999. Weekday liturgies are still held at the Mission.

The changing demographics of the surrounding area are reflected in the parish's multicultural population. In addition to the Hispanic community, St. Justin's is the religious center of Chinese culture, a thriving Filipino community and a Tongan community. All which add to the richness of the parish.

St. Justin Martyr Parish was profoundly changed on July 25, 2005 when an arsonist set fire to the church building. Much of the choir loft was destroyed, and the interior and its contents had severe smoke and water damage. A large tent to accomodate liturgies was erected in the parking lot. The building was rededicated in 2006.

Saint Kilian

Mission Viejo

On July 1, 1970, a new parish was founded at one of the farthest reaches of the Los Angeles Archdiocese. This parish authorized by Cardinal Timothy Manning was named in honor of the Irish bishop and martyr, St. Kilian and was an off-shoot of St. Nicholas parish in El Toro. Msgr. Michael Hughes began a 20 year commitment as pastor of this new parish. Initially, the parish was centered in a rented house on Veracruz Lane which served as the first rectory. Daily Mass was held in the residence with weekend liturgies being held on Saturday night at the local grammar school and Sundays at Mission Viejo High School where its first communicants had their official photograph taken on the front steps. The first parish get together was a picnic off Ortega Highway. This event, the next year, was held on parish property and for many years after it would be the annual fiesta.

On October 22, 1972, the new church structure was dedicated. Between 1972 and 1976 St. Kilian Church continued to expand, adding a rectory and a hall which completed the plant of "Kilian's Isle." The primary purpose has always been to provide a place for worship and to shepherd the spiritual needs and education of the people of the St. Kilian family. Support of Catholic Schools, a decade of Vietnamese resettlement projects, Catholic Charities and "Christian Action Now" were a few of the many outreach efforts that were set in place during the first 20 years.

On July 1, 1990, Fr. James Dunning became the new pastor of a church already rich in tradition as well as debt free. In addition to helping continue all of the good works already established, Fr. Jim added a Lenten Fish Fry and Backyard Theology - a summer program, the annual Oktoberfest, annual drama presentations by the Drama Ministry, and a food outreach program, and numerous adult faith formation programs, to name a few. The number of lay ministries has flourished and numbers more than 50. He has helped to further the participation of parishioners in these ministries, allowing for more service to others.

Today, St. Kilian Parish has more than 5,300 registered families; 1032 are in religious education from Pre-K through Confirmation. It is one of four parishes supporting and providing governance to Serra Catholic Elementary School.

Since Fr. Jim's arrival, the parish has continued to thrive and grow. A building/renovation project is underway with plans for a new, larger church building, parish administration and meeting rooms with a re-model to Hughes' Hall to include a new and improved childcare center and a new Youth Center.

Saint Martin de Porres

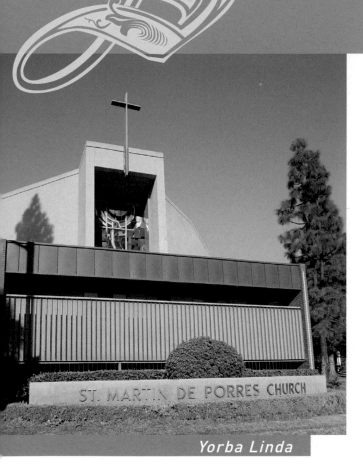

Yorba Linda

In 1970, Cardinal Timothy Manning launched the parish with a nucleus of 200 families who had been attending St. Joseph Parish in Placentia. The city's population was just over 10,000. In 1971, through the generosity of the original parishioners, construction was begun on the multi-purpose building; the first Mass was celebrated at St. Martin's on Easter Sunday, 1971. Father Robert Gara was the first pastor.

St. Martin's second pastor, Father Daniel Johnson, was appointed in 1974. Two years later, on June 18, Orange County was split from the Archdiocese of Los Angeles. Marriage Encounter flourished in the parish during these years and helped to develop leadership for parish ministry in the succeeding years.

In 1978, Father Daniel Hopcus took over as St. Martin's third pastor. As the parish grew to over 2,000 families and the population of Yorba Linda swelled to 29,000, the dream of a new parish church became a reality with the first Mass being offered in a beautiful, modern structure on the Feast of the Assumption, August 15, 1982. With a growing parish population of 2,400 families, a neighboring medical building was purchased in late 1986. The structure was remodeled to accommodate parish, youth ministry, and adult education offices.

Father Richard Delahunty became St. Martin's fourth pastor in June of 1990. After several years of visioning, planning and fund raising, St. Francis of Assisi Catholic School opened in 1998, serving the families of St. Martin de Porres and San Antonio de Padua parishes. The school now also serves the families of Santa Clara de Asis. A house was purchased just above the church property and renovations were completed to convert the home into a new rectory for the priests.

In June, 2003, Father Joseph Knerr became St. Martin's fifth pastor. The current parish membership is 3,210 families. Construction of new homes to the north and west of the parish is anticipated to bring many new members into the St. Martin Catholic Faith Community. A master plan was developed that will include renovations to the church building and new office and meeting spaces, creating a welcoming plaza for fellowship, hospitality and ministry.

It is only because of the generosity of its members that St. Martin's has grown and continues to grow. Always remaining true to its mission that states, "To build God's Kingdom by calling forth one another's unique gifts through openness to the Holy Spirit, we use our gifts for the common good."

Saint Mary

Saint Mary's Parish was created by Bishop Conaty on June 29, 1912 with Father John Gallagher as its first pastor. Services were held in the Odd Fellows Hall which at the time was located at the Northwest corner of Commonwealth and Harbor. Daily masses were said in the home of Mr. and Mrs. Frank Dauser where Father Gallagher lived for the first six months of his stay in Fullerton. Father Gallagher immediately started work toward the building of a church structure. Mrs. Maria O. Bastanchury donated a plot of land on the corner of Malden and Commonwealth Avenues and there a mission type structure accommodating 350 persons was built. Mrs. Bastanchury also donated the altar. The first mass was said on Easter Sunday, 1913.

In 1923, Father Pendeville moved the church building to the present site at 400 W. Commonwealth Avenue. A parish house for the priests was also built at that location.

Tragedy struck St. Mary's at 5:00 AM on Sunday, September 16, 1968 when a disastrous fire completely destroyed Saint Mary's church building. Only the tabernacle was recovered intact. The Blessed Sacrament and the sacred vessel were also saved. The badly damaged outer walls were left standing but the roof had caved in and the interior was ravaged.

The fire apparently started in the furnace area under the building and spread through the walls to the attic. No masses

were held that day but by the following Sunday arrangements had made with the Boy's Club next door to hold Sunday services in their gymnasium. Daily masses were held in Saint Mary's convent and in the school building. Work was started immediately to rebuild Saint Mary's. Within months, work was under way and on Christmas day, 1970 masses were celebrated for the first time in the new building. Its capacity was also increased form 700 to 900. This is where the parish stands today in expectation of celebrating its 100th anniversary in 2012.

Fullerton

nder Father Michael Galvin's pastorate (1918 to 1923) a two acre plot of ground was purchased on West Commonwealth, the site of the present complex, to be used for a school building. The school construction was started in 1922 and completed in 1923. It opened to 40 pupils in September of that year.

Saint Mary's By the Sea

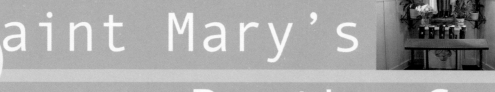

Huntington Beach

In 1905, St. Mary's was established as a mission of St. Joseph's Parish in Santa Ana. A former church building and property were purchased at Tenth & Orange Streets in Huntington Beach. Later the name was changed to Sts. Simon & Jude to avoid confusion with St. Mary's Parish in Fullerton. A new church building and rectory were built in 1923 at a total cost of $21,000.

In 1976, the Diocese of Orange was established, and the parish officially became St. Mary's by the Sea. Rev. Daniel Johnson was assigned in 1978. Father Johnson celebrated his 50th Jubilee in 2004. During his tenure, he saw the parish grow from about 400 people to over 1500 families. Father Johnson walked through the whole parish community almost five times during his 25 years and invited lapsed Catholics and other interested people to come to Mass.

Father Sy Nguyen was Administrator from 2004-2005, and Father Martin Tran is now the current Administrator.

One of the unique characteristics of the parish is its small size, which means that there is a special closeness among the parish families. Also, the beautiful church structure built so many years ago provides a most inspiring and spiritual environment for liturgies.

Organizations and activities include the Legion of Mary (two adult groups and one junior group), Ladies' Altar Guild, St. Vincent de Paul Society, Faith Formation Classes and R.C.I.A., a Pro-Life Committee and two choirs. Social Activities include pancake breakfasts and Octoberfest and Mardi Gras dinners. Adoration of the Blessed Sacrament, Eucharistic Devotion, and 24-hour Adoration are integral.

St. Mary's by the Sea is a Christian community of faith, hope, and love, journeying together in the spirit of hospitality, stewardship, respect, unity and charity, welcoming and serving all brothers and sisters in Christ, under the mantle of Our Lady.

Saint Nicholas

Laguna Hills

to oversee the spiritual care of the sick, homebound and elderly of the parish. In 1987, they welcomed the first nine Associates of the Little Company of Mary. Today there are 92 men and women Associates who work closely with the Sisters in ministering to shut-ins.

On the eve of St. Nicholas Day, December 5, 1965, groundbreaking took place for the newly-formed St. Nicholas Parish in Laguna Woods. The construction of the church building (capacity for 750), a small meeting hall and rectory began shorty thereafter. Fr. Otto E. Sporrer, a recently-retired Navy Chaplain was appointed Administrator of the new parish.

The first Mass was celebrated on August 28, 1966 at 9:30 a.m. Father Sporrer wrote, "May God be praised with joyous hearts as we raise our voices with happy thanks to Him for His goodness." The first baptism took place following the 11:00AM Mass that same day and on September 10, the entire parish was invited to the first wedding. Ten months later, on July 9, 1967, his Eminence James Francis Cardinal McIntyre, Archbishop of Los Angeles, officiated at the dedication of St. Nicholas.

Father arranged for a parish-owned bus to take students to San Juan Capistrano Mission School and St. Catherine's School in Laguna Beach. In 1968, permission was given to build a new hall/auditorium that would accommodate religious education classes, an administration office, storage space and a kitchen. On January 25, 1970, the hall was ready and the first religious education classes moved into the rooms.

The parish continued to grow during the 70's – living up to its namesake, St. Nicholas, by the generosity and kindness of its parishioners. One bold undertaking was the resettlement of Vietnamese refugees. They had fled their homeland after the fall of Saigon in 1975, and the parish took on the mission of resettling as many refugees as possible. Today, there is a large Vietnamese Community who celebrates Mass on Sunday and have religious education, language and culture classes.

In 1983, the parish welcomed two Sisters from the Little Company of Mary

Upon Fr. Sporrer's retirement in 1987, Fr. Ted Olson was appointed pastor and during his tenure, oversaw the building of a new parish office and meeting rooms. Fr. Juan Caboboy was installed as the third pastor in 1993 and during this time, a Eucharistic Chapel was added to the church building. Now in their 41st year, St. Nicholas, under the direction of their fourth pastor, Fr. Richard Delahunty, is planning the construction of a new SRE/Parish Center. St. Nicholas continues to truly embody the spirit of St. Nicholas.

MISSION STATEMENT
St. Nicholas is a Catholic community celebrating our faith through the Sacraments, Liturgy and Prayer. We strive to nurture family life and to create one body out of many in the Lord. We share the Good News with people of all ages, cultures and faith backgrounds.

Saint Norbert

In April 1963, St. Norbert Parish was spun off from Holy Family Parish, now Holy Family Cathedral, with 928 families. Presently there are 3300 registered families. Father George Kass was the founding pastor. During 1965 and 1966 the church building and school were constructed with the school opening in 1966.

While the church structure was under construction, parishioners first met at Abrams Dance Studio for the celebration of Sunday Mass but were asked to leave because the chairs scratched the wood flooring. The second location for Mass was a warehouse next door to a pub, "Father's Tavern." The Los Angeles Archdiocese owned property in Villa Park. Building a parish there was not possible, however, because a city ordinance prohibited any religious denomination from building a place of worship in Villa Park.

San Antonio Parish in Anaheim Hills was spun off from St. Norbert in 1987, taking 425 families. Currently the school has nine classrooms, K-8. There is a library, computer center, learning center and a science classroom/lab. The Monsignor Falvey

Orange

Building, named after a former pastor, has a faculty lounge and lunchroom, an after school day-care center and a kindergarten classroom. A beautiful Ramada was added adjacent to the church building during Father John Janze's tenure as pastor.

In 1997-1998, under the leadership of Father John Joyce, the church building was earthquake retrofitted and the interior was remodeled. During that time, daily Mass was held in the Parish Hall and Sunday Mass was celebrated in the midst of the construction. Shortly after the remodel was completed, the parish embarked on a fundraising program to build a new Ministry Center. The center was completed in 2002 and houses offices for Christian Service Ministry, Hispanic Ministry, Adult Faith Formation, and Liturgical Ministry, as well as the pastor and parochial vicars.

In 2003, Monsignor John Urell was named the fifth pastor. Looking to the future and the needs of an active, growing parish, the community plans to begin work this fall on the conversion and expansion of the "Old Parish Hall" into a "Family & Youth Center." The completed project will house a much needed gymnasium/multi-purpose facility, and will include a Youth Ministry Center, Christian Service Center and a new kitchen.

Saint Philip Benizi

Fullerton

In January of 1958 a new parish, St. Philip Benizi, was carved from three neighboring parishes: St. Mary's, St. Boniface, and St. Pius V. Fr. Manettus L. Ortmann, O.S.M. was named pastor. While there was an existing school, St. Mary's Annex, there was no sanctuary. Sunday liturgies were held in the nearby Merilark Roller Rink.

On August of 1958, construction of a new 740 seat church building began. In December, masses on Sundays and Holy Days were moved from the Roller Rink to Servite High School. The first masses in the new building were held on July 19 and the dedication held on August 23, 1959, the feast of St. Philip Benizi.

On August 17, 2000, tragedy struck St. Philip Benizi when an arsonist set a fire which gutted the building and left a brick hulk. In response to a generous offer of help, Sunday masses were moved to Orangethorpe United Methodist Church and Servite High School until a temporary tent could be raised on the parish parking lot.

In March of 2001, life began in the "circus tent." It was difficult, but the united theme remained, "We will rise from the ashes." It was decided that a new building would be erected and on March 12, 2005, the new structure was dedicated by Bishop Tod Brown.

Catholic education has been a priority since the beginning of our parish. In 1958, St. Philip Benizi Catholic School opened. Due to decreasing enrollment in 2002, St. Philip Benizi School and St. Mary's School merged. The combined school was established on St. Philip Benizi Campus and in 2005 named Annunciation Catholic School and is now serving students from both parishes.

The community is ethnically diverse with trilingual liturgies on Sundays and Holy Days. The scriptures and music are proclaimed in Spanish, Indonesian, and English. During the annual Fiesta and other events throughout the year, the food and music of the Philippines, Indonesia, and Mexico is represented. Inclusion is a priority in liturgies, parish committees, and parish activities.

Since that first day in 1958, the community of St. Philip Benizi has grown to over 2,800 families.

Jesus said: "Love the Lord your God with all your heart, with all your soul, and with all your mind...and love your neighbor as yourself." Our mission is to live Jesus' command in community.

- We grow through prayer, especially Sunday Eucharist and reception of the Sacraments.
- We teach our youth and fellow adults.
- We visit the sick and homebound.
- We welcome visitors and strangers.
- We help the poor.
- We bear with one another in peace and civility.
- We seek economic and civil justice for all.
- We are a Catholic Christian Faith Community.

Saint Pius V

Buena Park

The city of Buena Park had a population of about 5,000 and, while still largely agricultural, was becoming home to a number of industries when St. Pius V Parish was established in 1948. Fr. Frederick J. Kass was the founding pastor and served until his death in 1969. He oversaw the construction of the original church building that was later expanded to accommodate the growing parish. Members of the Altar Society, the Holy Name Society and the Legion of Mary served the community as it grew. Fr. Paul Konoske was pastor for a year and Fr. James Pierse shepherded the parish from 1970 to 1977. It was during this time that the Christian Service Program was founded to help the aged and the sick. Today, the *Happy Hearts* ministry continues this service by providing a monthly luncheon preceded by a Mass.

The Irish Augustinian Fathers served the parish from 1977 to 2005 bringing a close connection with their missionary work in Africa and South America. Bishop Norman McFarland dedicated the new parish structure that seats 1,250 on November 6, 1994. The church building, new offices and meeting rooms were constructed to serve the growing parish community which now numbers over 5,000 families.

The parish school was constructed in 1959 and staffed by the Sisters of St. Joseph of Orange and lay faculty. Today, the school staff consists of 18 lay faculty plus instructional aides to accommodate the 557 students in K through 8th grade. 1,015 children are served through the parish Faith Formation Program.

Fr. Theodore Olson became pastor in July 2005 when the Augustinians left the parish.

The faith community of St. Pius V welcomes all in fellowship by sharing the many gifts of multi-cultural traditions through liturgy, prayer and service.

Saint Polycarp

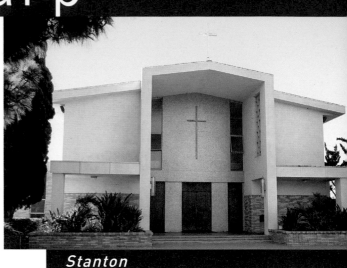

In the 1920's, the first mission, annex of Blessed Sacrament Parish was located on Flower Street. Within the walls of this small wooden building, the faithful came by horse, car and foot to sit on hay bales and hard benches. The families were mostly of Mexican heritage, along with Japanese-Americans and those who came from the Midwest after World War II.

Surrounded by strawberry and bean farms to the south, and a working farm to the east, Saint Polycarp School was built of brick by parishioners, and opened grades 1-4 in 1959. Later a second wing for upper grades was added. Navy housing was built for service men and women, but by the late 1950's, huge stucco housing tracts and apartments were built to serve the growing population. In 1956, Stanton incorporated as a city. In 1962, James Cardinal McIntyre, Archbishop of Los Angeles, placed the cornerstone for the large new building dedicated to Saint Polycarp, a disciple of Saint John, a Father of the Church, first bishop of Smyrna, defender of the Faith and martyr.

Saint Polycarp's was purposely built to hold 999 people since it was planned that it would become the cathedral of the diocese when a new one was created. The structure was decorated with inlaid terrazzo floors, museum quality mosaics, custom brass work, marble statues and Italian rose marble altars and railings. Father Daniel McLaughlin, a Rhodes Scholar, Irish missionary and personal friend of the Cardinal's, was installed as the first pastor. In the early 1960's, Father McLaughlin brought five Apostolic Oblates, a religious community of consecrated lay people from Italy, to staff the school which grew to over 600 students. To assist the pastor, a Women's and Men's Council were formed as well as the Saint Vincent de Paul Society and Knights of Columbus.

The 1970's saw many changes: Msgr. McLaughlin retired and was followed by Father Frank Buckman; the first Permanent Deacon, Rev. Mr. Jim Larkin was ordained. In 1976, Pope Paul VI carved the Diocese of Orange from Los Angeles. To the surprise of local parishioners, Holy Family in Orange became the Cathedral.

In the '90's, Jaime Soto, Saint Polycarp School Alumnus ('70), was ordained a priest for the Orange Diocese. His first Mass was held at St. Polycarp. The Vietnamese Community formed separate ministries and a formal Spanish Council began. From a grant from the Monsignor Harvey estate and Catholic Charities, the Family Support Center opened in McLaughlin Hall to serve the poor. To the delight of the parishioners, Msgr. Jaime Soto,

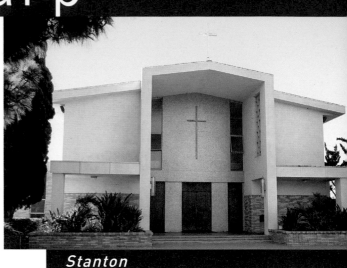

Stanton

Vicar to the Hispanic Community, was named Auxiliary Bishop of the Diocese of Orange.

Father Frank Buckman, Lawrence Baird, Thomas Pado and Ed Poettgen all served as pastor. Under the leadership of the current pastor, Fr. Quang Vinh Chu, a Pastoral Council was formed to assist in serving the needs of a large, diverse community. Deacon Ramiro Lopez and Fathers Kiem Tran and Leonel Vargas, parochial vicars, celebrate over 25 weekly liturgies. St Polycarp is the home parish of over 5,000 registered families.

Saints Simon and Jude

Huntington Beach

The parish now known as Sts. Simon & Jude was established in 1905 as a mission church of St. Joseph's parish in Santa Ana. The parish was established in 1912, and was called St. Mary's. The parish purchased a protestant church (with a house) at Tenth and Orange Sts. in Huntington Beach. In 1921, the parish name was changed to Sts. Simon & Jude.

In 1964, the Franciscan Friars of St. Barbara Province were invited to staff the parish, and Fr. Colman Colloty, OFM, was appointed pastor. The kindness of the Friars and their vivacious spiritual influence are still felt today. In 1966, land was purchased at the corner of Indianapolis and Magnolia for a new church building. Education has always been a vital ministry of the Parish, so in 1967, St. Francis School opened its doors to the children of the parish. It was later re-named Sts. Simon & Jude School in 1973.

At the present time, Sts. Simon & Jude parish is a vital community of more than 4,700 registered households. It is a community where people come together often—in worship, in service, in learning and in love. It has been their experience throughout the years that people always find comfort and unity in the Eucharist, especially during difficult times. The liturgies are filled with energy and prayer, and everyone feels welcome.

Guided by faith and sense of mission, the many ministries of Sts. Simon & Jude are dedicated to supporting the community. Pastoral leadership actively encourages lay leadership through the establishment of a Pastoral Council, Finance Council and School Council, as well as the following boards: Liturgy, Stewardship, Catechetical, Youth and Young Adult, Communications and Festival. Assisting these councils and boards are the following commissions: Prayer and Devotion, Hospitality, and Justice, Peace and the Integrity of Creation. A Building Project Task Force is presently working on the renovation of the church structure.

The councils, boards and commissions are based on a consensus model of governance. The Parish Plan, written by the Pastoral Council, is prepared in consultation with the boards and commissions, and takes into consideration the on-going work of these groups. Twice each year, the Pastoral Council hosts a town hall meeting to report to the parish at-large on the progress of the Parish Plan.

In September 2006, the parish established a relationship with St. Paul the Apostle parish in New Orleans. This relationship is not merely to assist the victims of Hurricane Katrina with monetary support, but also to share faith and community experiences together. In January 2007, the leaders of the two parishes came together to share a day of retreat in Huntington Beach.

A history, by its nature, can never capture the totality of the experience. Guided by faith and strengthened by tradition, the community continues to provide fulfilling sacred experiences that will forever be part of their history.

MISSION STATEMENT
We are Catholic disciples of Jesus Christ, celebrating Eucharist and welcoming all God's people in the spirit of our brother, Francis of Assisi.
Parish Values: Gospel, Eucharist, Stewardship and Hospitality.

Saint Thomas More

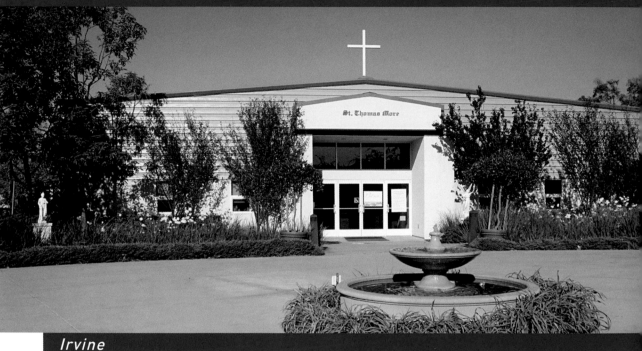

Irvine

St. Thomas More Parish was formed on July 1, 1996, by Bishop Norman McFarland to serve the growing Catholic population in the northern part of Irvine. Rev. John E. Janze is the founding pastor. Most of 1200 families came from St. John Neumann Parish as a result of the changing boundaries. In 1997, the parish welcomed Father Bill Krekelberg as parochial vicar and Sister Frances O'Leary as pastoral assistant. Father Krekelberg is also the archivist for the diocese and the author of this book. Monsignor Timothy Doyle, the retired pastor of Holy Spirit Parish, joined the staff as senior priest (and resident leprechaun).

From the beginning, the parish has experienced the concept of pilgrim church in the literal sense. Sunday liturgies were celebrated in the multipurpose room of a local middle school for the first four years. Daily Mass and parish business were conducted from the rectory. On July 4, 1998, ground was broken at the parish site on Remington St. Monsignor John Sammon, Vicar for Pastoral and Community Affairs for the Diocese of Orange, presided with Father Janze. Civic Leaders and many parishioners attended.

In April, 2000, the community joyfully moved into a new multipurpose building. Parishioners of all ages participated in a planting party to landscape the site. The new building accommodates liturgies, organization meetings, social events and parish offices. Many gatherings, including religious education classes, continue to meet in homes.

In 2004, Bishop Tod D. Brown offered the parish a larger site on Irvine Blvd. to better serve the growing population. The congregation is currently making plans and raising funds to construct a permanent parish center at this new location.

The first "Christ Renews His Parish" retreats on the west coast were presented by and for St. Thomas More parishioners in 2002. The program continues to offer four adult retreats each year. Inspired by their personal experience, some parishioners have adapted the retreat format so it can be used in prison ministry.

Don Jensen, a founding parishioner and long time Irvine resident, was ordained to the permanent deaconate on May 3, 2003. Deacon Don continues to serve the parish as well as the nearby parish of Santiago de Compostela and the needy and marginalized members of the diocese.

More than 40 different groups actively minister at the parish. Some serve at liturgies and conduct prayer services to parishioners of different ages and nationalities. They raise funds for parish needs and for social service agencies outside the parish. These same groups sponsor a variety of social events to strengthen the community spirit within the parish. Throughout its young history, St. Thomas More Parish continues to be a vibrant community of faith, compassion and hospitality.

Saint Timothy

Laguna Niguel

In 1964, property for a new parish site in Laguna Niguel was purchased by the Archbishop of Los Angeles. Sunday Mass was celebrated for the new parishioners of the area at a variety of locations, including the Monarch Bay Plaza movie theater, Shepherd of the Hills Church and the Crown Valley Elementary School, by priests from Saint Catherine of Siena Parish in Laguna Beach and Saint Edward Parish in Dana Point.

Bishop William R. Johnson, the first Bishop of the Diocese of Orange established Saint Timothy Parish at a Sunday Mass in Crown Valley School on July 13, 1980. Formal building plans were announced, and a house on Via San Sebastian was purchased as a rectory. Father Harold Fumo, administrator, oversaw the construction of the first multi-purpose building, with groundbreaking on February 22, 1981. In December 1981, Christmas Mass was celebrated inside the yet unfurnished building. The first Mass in the completed structure was held on March 20, 1982. In November, 1984, Father Bruce Lavery was appointed first pastor of Saint Timothy's.

Within eight years the multi-purpose building in which Sunday Mass was celebrated, became too small. Bishop Norman F. McFarland, who succeeded Bishop Johnson, originally thought another site would be better but in 1989 he reconsidered and a major building fund drive began in 1991.

The crib wall, which enlarged the property, was completed in June 1994 and the two-level parking garage in April 1996. At the same time, the new Church structure was under construction, additions to the original multi-purpose building were made which included new parish offices, a remodeled parish hall and a kitchen.

The first Mass in the new structure was celebrated on Palm/Passion Sunday 1998. Dedication was presided over by retired Bishop McFarland on May 8, 1998. During construction of the Church building, Fr. Bruce, whose background was landscaping, added considerable effort to the present grounds. This is evident when looking out the window, inside the Church building, at the "Four Seasons Garden."

In early 2004, the final building phase was begun. By the end of the year, the "Upper Room" building and the Faith Formation offices were completed. The Faith Formation offices are located partly over the parking lot and the existing kitchen. These offices are bridged to the other new building where the "Upper Room" is located. The "Upper Room" is an affectionate name for the upstairs large meeting room which is used for parish gatherings. Adjacent to this room is a well equipped kitchen. The administration/business office is downstairs, next to the nursery.

Today, St. Timothy's, "The Friendly Parish," ministers to over 2400 families. Their Family Faith Formation begins at age three, with Tiny Tims, and continues through High School. Adult Education is also a high priority especially with Scripture studies and women's activities. Knights of Columbus keep the men involved. Spiritual Direction, and contemplative prayer groups are offered. Deacon Eddie Salgado oversees parishioners and young people involved with house-building projects in Mexico, Corazon.

Saint Vincent de Paul

Huntington Beach

Saint Vincent de Paul Parish was established by the Diocese of Orange on September 27, 1977 with four acres of undeveloped cemetery property from Good Shepherd Cemetery. It was formed with families from Saints Simon and Jude, Saint Bonaventure, and Holy Spirit Parishes. The Vincentian Fathers faithfully served until July 1995. The priests of the Diocese of Orange began serving the parish after that time.

The members of Saint Vincent de Paul have been gathering together in various places for prayer and other community activities since its beginning. It started with the first Mass on October 2, 1977

celebrated by 150 families at Dilday Mortuary which became known by parishioners as "Saint Dilday's." The parish has grown to over 2,700 registered parish households.

The parish hall was built in 1981 and served the parishioners for almost every purpose. Masses were celebrated in the hall for 20 years. The construction of the meeting rooms which was completed in 1994 allowed for more space for the growing number of parishioners to gather. The parish office which

was enlarged in February 1996 also provided a larger area to serve the growing parish.

In January 1997, the parish began the challenge of planning to build a church structure to better serve the liturgical needs and increasing number of parishioners. The CHURCH CAMPAIGN 2000 was begun to provide funding to construct a permanent worship space for the parish.

The church building was solemnly dedicated by Bishop Tod David Brown in the Mass of Dedication on February 2, 2002. The first parish Masses were then celebrated on the First Sunday of Lent, February 16 and 17, 2002.

The tabernacle, which was created especially for the Blessed Sacrament Chapel by the German artist Egino Weinert was blessed by Father Jerome T. Karcher and installed in the chapel on March 25, 2006 on the Solemnity of the Annunciation of the Lord.

Since 1977, many individuals and families have contributed to the fabric of the parish history through lives of faith, hope, and charity. Some parishioners have been involved for many years while others are recently registered. Over the years, many whom have been loved and with whom lives were shared have died and gone before us with the hope of everlasting life in Christ. Others have moved away. Yet each one holds a place in the heart, in the Body of Christ. As many more people join the parish community, they will share faith in Jesus Christ according to the teachings of the Roman Catholic Church.

San Antonio de Padua del Cañon

MISSION STATEMENT

We the people of San Antonio parish strive to be a community of faith, hope and love. We find our identity and mission in Jesus Christ and His Gospel. We celebrate our life as Catholic Christians in word, worship and service. By recognizing our baptism, we accept our call to personal renewal and reach out with the gospel message to families and individuals, extending an invitation to fellowship with us.

Anaheim Hills

The parish of San Antonio de Padua del Cañon was established on September 23, 1977 with Reverend Seamus A. Glynn as its founding and current Pastor. The name of the parish dates back to a family chapel built by Bernardo Yorba in the 1830's. He dedicated his chapel to St. Anthony of Padua.

San Antonio is and has always been a vibrant active parish based in its service to the community. At the heart of the parish are many Catholic education programs, serving the spiritual needs of the people. The children of the parish are served in the pre-school through 8th grade Religious Education Program and the high school Youth Ministry and Confirmation Program. An extension of

the high school Youth Ministry is the Young Adult Ministry. The educational needs of the adults are served through Adult Confirmation Instruction, Parent Preparation for Infant Baptism, Faith Formation Programs, Small Faith Sharing Communities and Bible Study Groups.

Evangelization is a priority through the Rite of Christian Initiation (R.C.I.A.), New Parishioner contact and Re-Membering Church. Outreach services include the Family Assistance Ministry, Family Life Ministry, which provides counseling for individuals, married couples and those preparing for the Sacrament of Matrimony, and many other ministries which focus on Christian service and fellowship.

In 1998, St. Francis of Assisi Catholic School was established by San Antonio and St. Martin de Porres parishes. St. Francis School

has since become a tri-parish regional school with the added support of the new Santa Clara de Asís parish.

Approaching the celebration of its 30th Anniversary, the parish of San Antonio has experienced tremendous growth. Through the inspiration of the Holy Spirit, continuous leadership of its Pastor and the dedication of countless numbers of parishioners, San Antonio has grown from 853 registered families to over 3900 registered families.

The community of San Antonio de Padua del Cañon continues to strive to live out its mission to be a community of faith, hope and love through Jesus Christ and His Gospel.

San Felipe de Jesus

Capistrano Beach

San Felipe de Jesús parish community began in 1950 as a "chapel of convenience" for workers in the area. The chapel itself was first named St. Edward since it was financed by the Doheny Family of Los Angeles and named after the patron Saint of Edward Doheny. The small parcel of land was donated by the Bucheim Family of San Juan Capistrano.

The people who attended Mass in the early years were served by a number of priests coming from San Clemente and the Old Mission San Juan Capistrano. The population grew in South County and a larger site was needed. The larger St. Edward parish of Dana Point was established in 1969 and dedicated on March 5, 1972. The St. Edward Chapel and St. Edward Parish shared a name. But in 1981, Bishop William Johnson established the boundaries of a new parish in an area known as Capistrano Village and renamed the new parish, the former chapel, San Felipe de Jesús in honor of Mexico's first Mexican citizen to have been canonized a saint. San Felipe was a hero-martyr Franciscan Missionary who died in 1957 in Japan. Bishop Johnson's intent was to serve the Spanish speaking Catholics of South Orange County.

Msgr. John V. Coffield was appointed Administrator in 1981. In 1982, Father Colman Nolan, S.T. was named as the first pastor and installed on September 12, 1982 by Bishop Johnson. He was assisted by Msgr. Coffield who retired but volunteered to share the sacramental work of the parish.

Funds were raised from the community to remodel the church structure and build meeting rooms and a parish hall. Although there were a few large "outside" donations, much of the money was raised through the weekly sale of Mexican foods and other parish sponsored events. The renovated church building and the new catechetical center were completely paid for by the time of their dedication by Bishop Norman McFarland on Feb. 8, 1992.

On July 1, 1995, Fr. John Bradley was appointed pastor and remained in service until July 1, 2004. During that time the 60th anniversary of the priesthood was celebrated by Msgr. John Coffield who remained active in the community.

In July 2004, the parish was placed under the administration of Fr. Steve Sallot, pastor of St. Edward in Dana Point. The three priests from St. Edward serve the Sacramental needs of the community. The religious education program is run by Deacon Victor Samano and his wife Martha. Today the parish has 567 registered households and 231 children attend religious education in Spanish.

San Francisco Solano

San Francisco Solano Catholic Church

Rancho Santa Margarita

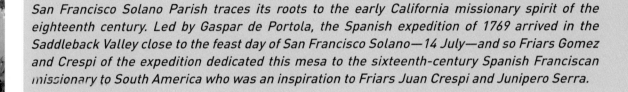

San Francisco Solano Parish traces its roots to the early California missionary spirit of the eighteenth century. Led by Gaspar de Portola, the Spanish expedition of 1769 arrived in the Saddleback Valley close to the feast day of San Francisco Solano—14 July—and so Friars Gomez and Crespi of the expedition dedicated this mesa to the sixteenth-century Spanish Franciscan missionary to South America who was an inspiration to Friars Juan Crespi and Junipero Serra.

Some 220 years later, on 3 July 1989, when Bishop Norman F. McFarland established a parish to serve the newly-established communities surrounding this mesa, he wisely placed the land and its people under the protection and patronage of San Francisco Solano. 17 years later, they are a parish of 4,200 families.

The "Parish Mission Statement" expresses succinctly the life and identity as San Francisco Solano Parish.

MISSION STATEMENT
San Francisco Solano Parish continues the early California missionary spirit to spread the Good News of Jesus Christ. We are committed to Word, Sacrament, and Service.

The liturgical and sacramental life of the parish stands at the heart of their life and identity as Catholics. As a community of faith, they are the sacrament of the encounter with the Risen Christ. It follows that they value and strive for strong and faithful proclamation of God's Word, especially through homilies, and celebration of the Eucharist marked by a prayerful spirit, reverence, transcendence, and beauty, leading all to deeper conversion of life and charity and service to neighbor.

At San Francisco Solano Parish, a large number of parishioners engage in some aspect of pastoral service, such as religious education, RCIA, youth ministry, outreach to the poor and needy, the SFS Food Bank, visitation of the sick and homebound, bereavement ministry, and various liturgical ministries. Serra Catholic School, a multi-parish school, has a current enrollment of over 1,000 students, Pre-K through Junior High. Over 1,300 children and youth are enrolled in Religious Education, Confirmation Preparation, and Youth Ministry. Each year, the RICA assists persons in their discernment and movement toward the sacraments of initiation. A 55 & Better Group serves the senior members of the parish. Outreach to the poor and those in need is provided locally, nationally, and internationally. Each year in July, the founding of the parish is celebrated through a weekend Fiesta de Solano. San Francisco Solano Parish demonstrates that its gifts are blessed when placed at the service of one another.

Throughout life, holy places are discovered, where seeking leads to finding, where spiritual longings find refreshment, where love of God and neighbor meet, where Christ is encountered, where faith is enlivened, and where a deep identity is confirmed. San Francisco Solano Parish exists to be one such place.

Santa Clara de Asis

Yorba Linda

Santa Clara de Asís was founded July 1, 2001. Father Michael Hanifin, chosen by Bishop Brown, has been the pastor since the founding of the parish. The Diocese first identified the need for a parish in East Yorba Linda and acquired the property for the parish and the adjacent School, St. Francis of Assisi, in 1983. The school opened in 1999. Santa Clara opened July 2001 with it first Masses held in the multi-purpose room of St. Francis School. Approximately 150 families registered in the parish during the first month. The Mass attendance immediately mushroomed necessitating a much larger space for Masses than St. Francis could provide. Santa Clara soon held Masses in the much larger multipurpose room of Bryant Ranch School. The parish was blessed by the generosity and kindness displayed by Bryant Ranch during the first critical years of the parish's existence.

With the help of the Diocese and a successful capital campaign, Santa Clara broke ground for its first building on October 3, 2004, the 779th anniversary of the death of Saint Francis of Assisi, the friend and mentor of the parish patroness, Saint Clare, and the 17th anniversary of the ordination of Fr. Mike. The first Masses were celebrated on March 4-5, 2006, in their new home, The San Damiano Center, which is a 16,000 square foot multi-purpose facility has a large gathering area, sacristy, classrooms, offices, and kitchen.

The parish now has 40 ministries and nearly 600 registered families who worship in a parish marked by its contemporary music and a strong commitment to stewardship inspired by St. Clare's example of service, prayer, and community.

Santiago de Compostela

Lake Forest

of Santiago de Compostela in Spain. It was blessed by Bishop Michael Driscoll on the feast of St. James, July 25, 1993. The three foot carved statue of St. James was placed in its shrine niche in the church on August 1, 1993.

The Parish Center/Hall was completed in October of 1997. Fr. David Gruver was named the fourth pastor of Santiago de Compostela in July of 2001.

Santiago de Compostela was established as a parish of the Diocese of Orange on September 1, 1979 by Bishop William Johnson, the first Bishop of Orange. It was named after the Shrine of St. James of Compostela in Spain. The first pastor was Fr. John Shetler. Originally, Sunday Mass was celebrated at the nearby Los Alisos School while the church building was being constructed. The parish's founding predates the incorporation of the city of Lake Forest by 12 years. The church building and rectory were completed in 1984. The second pastor was Fr. William Krekelberg who served until 1991 when Fr. Ken Schmit became pastor.

The first Galician Granite Pilgrimage Cross in the United States is now located in the parish fountain. The cross was a gift to the parishioners from the mother church

Korean Martyrs Catholic Center

Westminster

Korean Martyrs Catholic Center was founded on September 22, 1977 as a Korean faith community. Through the generous donations and determination of many church members, the facilities were constructed, and on March 18, 1984 the first Mass was held. Due to rapid and significant growth, on June 7, 1987 a group of members left the community to begin St. Thomas Korean Center in Anaheim. Furthermore, on September 18, 1994 another group of members started the Korean faith community of St. Elizabeth Ann Seton parish in Irvine. Despite establishing these two communities, the original community continued to grow and as a result facilities were expanded and remodeled in 1995. The first Mass following this last reconstruction took place on September 24, 1995.

The Korean faith community facilitates fellowship and growth through the enrichment of Korean culture and identity. As a united body, they strive to not only maintain their identity as Korean-Americans, but also to satisfy their thirst for the Word of God and nourishment of their spirit. An important focus for the community is to remain as one body in Christ and encourage prayer and closeness within the family and fellowship among its members. This is accomplished through the generous support of many members who encourage and support the activities.

An essential aspect of the center is the ministry provided for the youth through activities such as summer camps, winter retreats, Sunday school, Korean language school, youth council, praise nights, and youth nights. All of these events and activities are supported not only monetarily by the community, but also through the sacrifice and dedication provided to the youth by many volunteers. The youth of the community will shape the future and become eventual spiritual leaders. Therefore, focusing on their spiritual enrichment and well-being is critical to the community.

In addition to focusing on the youth, another facet of the mission is maintaining a close family unit as a church community as well as in their own individual families. Small groups are established in the community by separating members by the city or zip code they live in. These groups then meet regularly to pray, eat, and laugh together at a member's house. Gatherings rotate every month. This facilitates fellowship and a sense of community. The focus on prayer is especially evident when it comes to praying as a family. It is strongly suggested and encouraged that families take the time to pray together as often as possible. This not only sets a good example of prayer and communication with God, but also with each other.

Pope John Paul II Polish Center

Yorba Linda

In 1974, Orange County belonged to the Los Angeles Archdiocese. At the request of Rev. Zbigniew Olbrys, pastor of Our Lady of Bright Mount Church in Los Angeles (a Polish Church), Alexander Romanski notified a small group of friends and acquaintances that lived in Orange County that Mass in Polish would be celebrated monthly in Orange County. Rev. Olbrys celebrated Mass at St. Anthony Claret in Anahiem. Later, the community moved to the Sister's Chapel at Rosary High School, then to Daly and Bartel Funeral Home and finally, St. Justin Martyr parish. From the very beginning, the small community of Polish Americans had a dream--to have their own place of worship where weekly masses would be celebrated.

In 1976, Bishop William Johnson appointed Rev. Joseph Karp as a Spiritual Director of the Polish Community; shortly thereafter permission was given to have Mass celebrated in Polish every Sunday.

In 1982, representatives of the community, Stanley Pawlowski, Martin Krawiec, Regina Kobzi, Robert Kraszewski and Maria Romanski met with Bishop William

Johnson and obtained permission to purchase the present site of the John Paul II Polish Center. It consisted of a small hall and a small office building. Bishop Johnson loaned the Polish community $450,000 with a stipulation that $100,000 be paid back in one year. The loan was totally repaid in 1984. First Masses were celebrated on Christmas Eve on December 24, 1982 and December 25, 1982.

The Polish Community grew rapidly as Polish refugees arrived in Orange County. The need for a larger space was evident since many people had to stand outside during Mass. Classes for preparation for driver's license tests and English classes were held to help the refugees in their transition to the United States. Religion classes and a children's choir were started. Several organizations were formed such as Ladies Guild, Knights of Columbus, Seniors Club, and a Dance Group that still exist today.

February 13, 1984, members of the community met with Bishop Johnson to

seek permission to build a church structure and parish hall. Alex Kuryllo, a contractor and parishioner, agreed to undertake the construction project at no profit. The Bishop agreed to another loan and on January 20, 1985, Bishop John T. Steinbeck broke ground. Dedication of the new buildings took place on December 24, 1985. The stained glass windows were created by a parishioner, Krystyna Durian and paid for by individuals.

October 19, 1986, a commemorative plaque to Father Jerzy Popieluszko was placed on the outside wall. This plaque was installed to honor a Polish Priest, a Martyr who died for the cause of Christianity.

In 1987, as a symbol of Polish unity, three bells were imported from Poland and donated by parishioners Anthony and Izabela Pedzich. On November 26, 1989, on the feast of Christ our King, the bells and bell tower were blessed.

John Paul II Polish center has had three directors: Father Joseph Karp 1982 – 2000, Father Douglas Cook, 2000 – 2006, Father George Blais 2006 – present.

Saint Thomas Korean Catholic Center

Anaheim

In 1987, Bishop Norman F. McFarland established the St. Thomas Korean Catholic Center (STKCC) in Anaheim to care for the growing
Korean American Catholic population in north
Orange County. Father Gabriel B. Chang of the
Diocese of Cheong-Ju, Korea, who later became
the bishop of his diocese, was appointed as the
first Director of the STKCC.

On a humble storefront rental space in
Anaheim, the center instantly became
a vibrant Catholic community providing
the Korean American Catholic community
with much needed spiritual nourishment,
social activities, and language and culture
classes.

In 1988, STKCC purchased a
protestant church in Fullerton, which
provided a place for weekday Masses, various
ministries, meetings and the rectory. Under
Fr. Gabriel's leadership, the community
witnessed a phenomenal growth from 300
families to 900 in a mere four years.

STKCC has come a long way since, but
it would not have been possible without the
dedication of the priests from the Cheong-
Ju Diocese: Frs. Paul Y. Park, Benedict B.
Kim and Anthony C. Jeong.

From 1991, under the pastoral care
of Fr. Paul, the community continued to
flourish and by 1995 STKCC was able to
purchase the current five-acre facility in
Anaheim. By October 1996, Fr. Benedict,
the new director, completed the relocation.
In 1998, Fr. Anthony succeeded Fr. Benedict,
and Fr. Roy Kim of the Diocese of Orange
was appointed to the assistant directorship.

In July of 2001, Bishop Tod D. Brown
appointed Fr. Alex K. Kim, the first Korean
American priest ordained in the Diocese
of Orange, to be the director of the center.
Fr. Alex introduced a new wave of fresh
ideas and changes, which enabled the
community to work in better harmony with
organizational efficiency commensurate
with the population growth.

In 2004, Bishop Tod D. Brown granted
STKCC permission to start its ambitious new
project, "Building the Future." The new
church structure with its 1,200 seats, will
no doubt become another milestone in the
annals of STKCC, is slated to open by 2008.

Currently STKCC consists of
approximately 1,500 households, including
a significant number of Tongan Catholics in
addition to Koreans. STKCC boasts various
dynamic and diversified ministries and
apostolic movements, including the Legion
of Mary, Cursillo, Marriage Encounter, and
the Charismatic Renewal. The recently
implemented Small Faith Communities
became a stock-in-trade in pastoral and
ecclesial channels.

STKCC's vision is to create a bilingual
and bicultural community that proclaims the
Gospel in unity. Through regular celebration
of Masses in different languages, active
community involvement, and best of all, the
prayers of its community, STKCC is confident
that its goal is at hand.

Vietnamese Catholic Center

Santa Ana

After the fall of Saigon (April 1975) to the Communist regime in Vietnam, most of the Vietnamese refugees settled in Orange County, California. There were about 3,000 Vietnamese Catholics living in the county toward the end of 1975, but the number rapidly grew to 7,000 by the year 1982. Liturgy was celebrated in Vietnamese weekly at nine different parishes in the Diocese of Orange but the people longed to have a place of their own for faith sharing and other cultural activities. Thus the idea of a Vietnamese Catholic Center in the Diocese of Orange gradually took shape.

On November 25 1983, Bishop William Johnson, the first bishop of the Diocese of Orange responded to the request of the Vietnamese Catholic community; an office complex together with three acres of land in the city of Santa Ana was acquired to serve as the temporary Vietnamese Catholic Center. Rev. Ha Thanh Do was appointed the director.

In 1990, Msgr. Peter Tien Duc Nguyen, the new director, presented a building and fund raising plan to Bishop Norman F. McFarland. After his approval, a building committee was set up to carry out the project.

On September 26, 1992, Bishop McFarland and Bishop Michael Driscoll presided at the official ground breaking of the new Vietnamese Center.

June 24, 1994 marked the completion of one building, which included a large hall (seats 600 people), a kitchen, the parking lot and the surrounding fence. In May 1995, the second half of the project was completed, a two-story building. The upper level includes the living quarters for priests, a library, and a recording studio. The lower level includes offices, four classrooms, and two garages. In addition, a front gate and a bell tower were erected at that time.

Construction was begun in July 1995 on the chapel, a shrine in honor of the Vietnamese Martyrs. It was completed in May, 1996 and officially dedicated on September 14, 1996. This chapel holds 200 people for daily mass, retreats and prayer services.

From 1983 to 1993, the Vietnamese Catholic population grew to 30,000 in Orange County. They contributed more than $5,000,000 to pay for the land and to build the center.

In 2001, Bishop Tod David Brown appointed Father Michael Khai Hoan Mai as the third Director of the Center. Under his leadership, the Vietnamese Catholic Community took a greater role in providing financial support to the Center. Many more services for seniors and youth are provided to Vietnamese Catholics as well as non-Catholics. The Center is regarded as the pastoral, cultural and social center serving more than 45,000 Vietnamese Catholics and thousands more non - Catholics in the Diocese as well as various Vietnamese groups and associations in the U.S. and abroad.

The Vietnamese Catholic Center continues be the symbol of the Vietnamese Catholic faith and their deep devotion to the traditional and cultural values. Above all, it will remain a living legacy for future Vietnamese generations in the United States.

Eastern Rite Churches

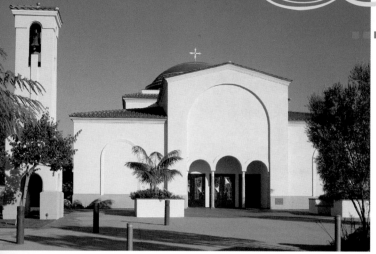

Annunciation Byzantine Catholic Church, *Anaheim*

Established **1969**

135 Registered Families
Rev. Msgr. George N. Vida
Byzantine Eparchy of Van Nuys
Most Rev. William C. Skurla

St. John Maron Church (Antiochene Syriac Maronite), *Anaheim*

Established **1988**

350 Families • Rev. Antoine Bakh
Eparchy of Our Lady of Lebenon of L.A
Most Rev. Robert J. Shaheen

Holy Cross Melkite Greek Catholic Church, *Placentia*

Established **1973**

345 Registered Families
Rt. Rev. Archimandrite James Babcock
Diocese of Newton (Melkite Greek)
Most Rev. Cyril Salim Bustros, S.M.S.P.
Eparch of Newton

St. Thomas the Apostle Syro – Malabar Church, *Santa Ana*

Established **2001**

100 Registered Families • Rev. Dr. Jacob Kattack
St. Thomas Syro – Malabar Catholic
Diocese of Chicago
Most Rev. Jacob Angadiath

St. George Chaldean Catholic Church, *Santa Ana*

Established **2001**

130 Registered Families
Rev. Zuhair G. Toma
Eparchy of St. Peter the Apostle, Chaldean
Most Rev. Sarhad Y. Jammo
Eparch of St. Peter the Apostle (Chaldean)